# WHAT YOUR
# DREAMS
# CAN TEACH YOU

*Also by Alex Lukeman:*

*Nightmares*
*Sleep Well, Sleep Deep*

# WHAT YOUR
# DREAMS
# CAN TEACH YOU

## ALEX LUKEMAN, Ph.D.

*M. Evans and Company, Inc.*
*New York*

M. Evans and Company, Inc.
216 East 49th Street
New York, New York 10017

SECOND EDITION, REVISED


Library of Congress Cataloging-in-Publication Data

Lukeman, Alex, 1941–
    What your Dreams can teach you / Alex Lukeman — 2nd ed.
      p.  cm.
    Includes index.
    1. Dreams. 2. Self-actualization (Psychology) I. Title
    BF1091-L83    1997
    154.6'3—dc21                                              97-23110


Book design by Evan Johnston

9   8   7   6   5   4   3   2   1

*All of the dreams presented in this book are real dreams told to me by real people. As you will see, when someone tells a dream they make themselves vulnerable. Dreams reveal our most intimate selves. To protect their privacy, all of the names of the dreamers have been changed. I gratefully acknowledge their trust and help, without which this book would have been impossible to write.*

*I am grateful to two people in particular, Brugh Joy and my wife, Gayle. Brugh, because he inducted me into the experience of the mystical heart and into a conscious experience of transpersonal energies that hastened my understanding. Gayle, because she has unfailingly supported me when I needed it, in this as in so many other things.*

# Contents

# Preface to the New Edition

Dreams are a window through which we see the glory of Spirit and the potential of our souls, a path for personal spiritual and psychological discovery. It requires practice and guidance to understand what we see in dreams. Not everyone has the benefit of an experienced and capable teacher to help them with dreams, or can find the leisure and funds to pursue private work with a good therapist or counselor. That is why I wrote this book: it can be your teacher and can open the door to the meaning of your dreams.

A personal relationship with a good teacher takes time to develop. Just relax with the book and allow yourself to follow along when an exercise or suggestion is given. The book contains many examples and interpretations of real dreams, accompanied by in-depth explanations of how the meaning was revealed. By looking at the dreams of others and seeing how it is done, you can learn how to do it for yourself. Practical tools and techniques are scattered throughout the text, with clear instructions on how to look at your personal dreams.

This revised edition contains new material on several dream subjects, including prophecy, the new millennium, UFOs, and lucid dreaming. I reworked the book to smooth over the rough edges from previous versions. Corrections of grammar and style make the book easier to read. You will find a helpful glossary of terms, an index, a bibliography, and an online reference page that lists interesting resources on the Internet. The index is a quick reference for finding examples of many dream symbols. If you have a dream that includes one or more of these symbols, you can refer to the text and see what the symbol meant for that particular dreamer. What a dream image symbolizes for one person is often very different in meaning for someone else, so don't assume it will be the same for you. However, by looking at what an image meant for someone else, you may get an intuitive sense about what it means for you.

Dreams fall into two distinct categories, often overlapping one another. The first category consists of what I call psychological dreams, dreams that arise from and concern the personal self. The second category consists of transpersonal dreams, dreams that come from a dimension of consciousness independent of our personal selves. In these kinds of dreams we find the breath and touch of spirit, and experience our connection to a much larger consciousness than our own.

Dreams are a vehicle for spiritual discovery, if we choose to use them in this way. The path of spiritual discovery leads through the mystical inner landscape and forests of the self. Our dreams reveal the landscape and illuminate the way. They are a resource of magical energy worthy of Merlin himself. All you need do is let your dreams take flight and follow the path of spirit they will reveal.

May love fill your inner vision and guide you safely through.

ALEX LUKEMAN

# Introduction

The world of dreams has fascinated me since I was a small child. I have always had vivid and complex dreams and began to look for information to help understand them. Like most of us, I did not know what my dreams meant or what they were trying to show me. In those days there were few books about dreams and the ones I found were not very helpful. Some talked about intriguing but impractical metaphysical belief systems, while others consisted of leaden and lifeless lists, predefined interpretations of symbols and events. At that time I was not familiar with the works of Carl Jung and other seminal thinkers who had seen that dreams were a key to unlocking some of the mysteries of the human psyche.

The book you hold in your hand is the expression of over twenty-five years of work focused on exploring human consciousness and seeking self-understanding. All of it has been relevant to understanding dreams. *What Your Dreams Can Teach You* reflects many influences, experiences and exposure to different viewpoints and cultures that have formed my life experience.

Years before I understood much about dreams, I kept a dream journal. I was remembering as many as six or seven complex dreams almost every night. I could see that certain themes repeated themselves, and that similarities existed between characters and events in my dreams. Sometimes I would wake with an electric sense of certainty about the meaning of the dream, later borne out in waking life. I learned there were distinct variations in dreams that served to emphasize the importance of the content.

However, more often than not I had no real understanding.

In 1979, I was handed a copy of *Joy's Way,* by W. Brugh Joy, M.D. The book affected me deeply. In those pages, I found needed validation for the energetic phenomena and experiences happening in my own life. I wanted to explore the ideas talked about in the book and signed up for a two-week residential retreat in the high desert of California. During that conference, a series of unusual and powerful experiences profoundly altered my perception of life. The ability to understand dreams truly opened to me, although it took me three years to trust the accuracy of what I discovered. Dr. Joy talked about something he calls the "Dream Interpreter." I call it the "Dreamer Within." Once we learn how to evoke this aspect of our consciousness, it leads us to an accurate and true understanding of our dreams and can easily read the dreams of others.

The basic requirement for connecting to the Dreamer Within is a conscious "shift" of awareness. We can learn to move from our familiar modes of perception to something experienced in a much different way. The Dreamer Within is a piece of our psyche that truly does know how to interpret dreams. It requires practice to tap into this source, a willingness to explore and a developing sense of self-trust and self-love. It requires honest and open receptivity to what dreams reveal when seen from this perspective.

Speaking of honesty, it has become clear to me over the years that dreams are indeed honest and do not lie to us. This is a very controversial idea, not usually accepted in the conventional, psychoanalytical sense. It is crucial to the understanding of dreams to approach them with this assumption. Dreams do not come from the part of our psyche concerned about falsifying something in order to obtain some advantage. If you work consistently with dreams, you will discover the truth of this statement.

If it is true dreams are truthful, it becomes even more necessary to understand them. It also follows that confusion about the message of a dream arises from the interpretive levels brought to bear by the conscious mind. This is important to remember when doing dream work.

We all have unconscious, observable and consistent patterns of perception and response that influence and shape our lives and experiences.

These unconscious (and therefore unappreciated) patterns affect the way we see and relate to life, but we are unaware of them without training and guidance in identifying them for what they are. Dreams show us the patterns, if we know how to look. This concept is fundamental for using dreams as a focus of self-growth and spiritual discovery.

The recognition of unconscious patterns is basic to psychoanalytic approaches, found in the pioneering works of Freud, Jung and others seeking understanding of human behavior and consciousness. Dreams are a way we can identify and understand these patterns. Recognition opens options for change unavailable to us until the determining patterns emerge into conscious awareness.

My challenge in this book was to present the power of dreams as a tool for personal and spiritual discovery. I wanted to write something people could use systematically, with practical benefits and applications.

Most of us do not have the benefit of an extensive background in the fields of psychology or dream research. We do not have the cultural traditions of dreaming found in living mythology, or in the few remaining tribal societies where dreams are still seen as important. What we do have is years of experience of dreaming without understanding. I have tried to bridge the gap between experience and understanding. This is a practical manual for dreamers, a workbook for referral and use as needed. It is a course in self-discovery through the exploration of our inner selves as seen in dreams.

The text contains a systematic and proven approach to understanding dreams. It does not contain lists of dream symbols, accompanied by interpretations for each symbol: only you can discover what the images in your dreams mean for you. In these pages you will find step-by-step information that can lead to success in discovering the meaning of your dreams, success that will bear fruit in your waking, outer life in the real world.

*What Your Dreams Can Teach You* is divided into two sections. Section One covers all the fundamentals you need to know to begin interpreting dreams. With the information contained in this section, you can immediately begin getting useful information from your dreams. Section Two develops these fundamentals and brings in additional ideas and tools for interpretation. The examples of dreams illustrate interpretation through step-by-step analysis.

Throughout the text you will find sections or ideas emphasized by the phrase "KEY POINT." These are set aside from the main text and highlighted. Pay attention to these essential ideas and you will quickly master the tools for interpreting dreams with increasing accuracy and understanding. This book contains a great deal of information about dreams. It is compact and specific. Expect to refer to it often, as you would any resource manual.

Everything in these pages is based on extensive practice and experience. In dream groups and workshops, I often see people who use this approach break into excited understanding, as the meaning of their dreams becomes clear. They use the information they discover to improve their lives and gain new understanding.

In our modern world, information is power. Your dreams offer you information and the power of understanding self. Through that power, you can discover an avenue to understanding others. Dreams contain practical information for you and about you. As your knowledge grows, your ability to shape life as you choose will increase. You will use the knowledge you gain to break down barriers to success and health, love and relationship.

You are about to embark upon an exploration of the rich and mysterious world of dreams. It is my hope this book will help you understand and discover the fascinating secrets your dreams can bring to you.

I wish you good fortune on your journey.

ALEX LUKEMAN

Section One

# CHAPTER 1

# AN INTRODUCTION
# TO DREAMS

Why do we dream? Since the dawn of history, myths and spiritual teachings from every culture relate stories of dreams and the power of dreams as messages from the gods or some other mysterious source beyond human understanding. In tribal societies surviving today, dreams are still seen as important messages from supernatural realms. In these cultures, dreams are either sought for guidance or viewed with deep suspicion, according to the tradition of the tribe.

Dreams have decisively influenced the course of history at certain critical moments. A famous example concerns the Roman emperor Constantine. On the eve of the battle for Rome, in 312 A.D., Constantine is said to have had a vision of a fiery cross in the sky. That night Christ appeared to Constantine in a dream, telling him to place the sign of the cross on the armor and shields of his army. He was told, "In this sign shall you conquer." When he woke, Constantine followed the commands of the dream and pledged that with victory on the coming day he would establish Christianity as the official religion of the Roman Empire. Constantine did conquer, defeating Maxentius at the battle of the Milvian Bridge. He kept his vow and Christianity gained protection and support as the official religion of the Empire. Because of a dream, the course of Christianity's evolution as a world religion was set firm and steadied.

In ancient Greece, dreaming was big business because many wished to receive guidance from the gods. The biggest, and most famous temple of dreaming was located at Delphi. Kings, senators, merchants and generals petitioned the Oracle of Delphi to have their dreams interpreted and the messages of the gods made clear to them. In the temple at Delphi, special rooms and benches were set aside where the supplicant could lie down to sleep and dream. The next day the Oracle interpreted the dream, accompanied by suitable ritual and offerings. The Oracle was trained by priests and priestesses from an early age for her mysterious role. She knew something we can rediscover:

---

## KEY POINT
**Dreams are a direct link to a source of wisdom and knowledge not usually available to us in our waking consciousness.**

---

Dreams are an open highway into the mystery of spirit and expanded consciousness. In some dreams, we tap into prophecy and other kinds of information that cannot be known in the ordinary sense. Not every dream connects directly to the divine, but even the ones that do not still access the knowledge and experience of our unconscious mind.

The unconscious is like a vast library, a repository of our life experience and wisdom. In dreams we can go to the library and look up something we need to know. Confusion arises in our waking mind only because the language of the unconscious is symbolic rather than linear. By learning the language of dreams, we open up entirely new possibilities for self-understanding. Most of this book is about learning the language.

Dreams are crucial to everyday health and well being. Studies by sleep researchers show that bizarre things start to happen when people are prevented from dreaming. Exhaustion, confusion, hallucinations, irritability and physical illnesses begin to manifest. It is not just interrupted sleep that leads to these unpleasant results. People who sleep for brief periods and who do not have their dreams interrupted may be tired, but they do not display the other symptoms of distress in the psyche. This indicates that dreams provide an essential, balancing force for our well being, independent of the body's need for sleep. True understanding of this balancing aspect can lead to a deeper appreciation of ourselves on many levels.

## The Language of Dreams

The language of dreams is symbolic. A symbol, by definition, stands in the place of (or represents) something else. It is not merely a substitution for something else. To be a symbol, the image or representation must contain many shadings and nuances of depth and meaning. A symbol conveys essential meaning that goes far beyond the outer appearance. We have all heard the phrase "a picture is worth a thousand words." We recognize that a picture conveys more information to us than even the best description. The same principle applies to all symbols and to all dream images.

As with any unknown language, we must take the time to study and reflect upon it if we wish to make sense of it. Would you expect to pick up a book written in an unfamiliar language and immediately understand what you were reading? You would not know if you held a novel, a textbook, a poem or a grocery list! You might recognize a word here and there that seemed familiar. You might then think you knew what you were reading; but after learning the language, you might discover you were completely mistaken. So it is with dreams. The images in the dream may seem familiar, but we often make the mistake of thinking the appearance of the dream image is literal in its meaning. This is a very common error of interpretation, and in most cases, it is a mistake.

---

### KEY POINT
**The images of our dreams always contain hidden layers of meaning beneath the outer appearance of the dream symbol.**

---

This can be confusing! For example, if your mother appears in a dream, you will have a tendency to think the dream is about your real, physical mother. But if you pause for only a moment and think of all the things mother means to you, you quickly realize that the image of "Mother" is far more than a simple picture of a person. "Mother" is a powerful and immensely complex range of possibility of meaning, a symbol.

---

## KEY POINT
**The symbols appearing as images in your dreams are most often personal in nature. Therefore, only you can ultimately interpret the correct meaning each image holds for you.**

---

This means it is not possible to pick up a convenient list of interpretations of dream symbols and get an accurate meaning for your dream.

Although this kind of list can stimulate thinking, successful interpretation requires discovering the feeling and meaning each dream image/symbol holds for you alone. Later we will explore ways to understand your personal dream language. For now, simply remember that there is a language of dreams, that it is written in symbols, and that you can learn to understand it.

# The Conscious and Unconscious Mind

To help us understand dreams I am going to simplify psychology and divide our consciousness, our awareness, into two parts. I will call these the *conscious* and the *unconscious* mind. This is a very broad oversimplification of a very intricate process called consciousness, but we have to start somewhere! If we take this approach, we can define the conscious mind as the part of our awareness functioning when we are awake and going about our lives. It is an observable and observing part of us, expressing our outer personality and ego structure, or "I." It is the part that acts out the end results of our decision-making processes. It is our perceptual interface with life and the world.

The unconscious mind is not so easily defined. In essence, it can only be defined in contrast with the conscious: in other words, what is not conscious is unconscious. By definition, if something is unconscious we are not conscious of it and therefore do not even know it exists! Right away, you can see how difficult it is to try to understand anything to do with the unconscious mind. Since dreams arise from the unconscious, they are a principle way to observe and discover what is actually happening there.

The unconscious mind is by far the greater part of our total awareness. Think about this for a moment: without knowing anything about psychology, you can easily see that we are performing many different kinds of unconscious functions at any given instant. Take the complex process of regulating our body and life forces, for example, or think about accomplishing "simple" actions like driving to work or watching television. These are miracles of sophisticated, unconscious synthesis and oversight, not normally possible from a fully conscious level of supervision.

The unconscious mind is usually not available to us without training that allows it to be seen and appreciated by the conscious part. Since the unconscious speaks to us in dreams, dreams are one of the most direct ways to see the unconscious and discover more of who we are.

It is not a new idea to suggest or say that the unconscious part of our mind is by far the greater part. It is also not a new idea to say that the unconscious never forgets anything we have ever experienced in our lives. All of the information and experience of our lives is stored in the unconscious. It is probably just as well that most of it seems unavailable, or we might be overwhelmed by the sheer amount of our psychic material.

---

## KEY POINT
**Dreams are a way for the unconscious mind to give us information as needed. From the wealth of information in our lives that has been stored and never forgotten, dreams access our personal library of wisdom and present that wisdom symbolically to our conscious awareness.**

---

If we can understand the messages dreams contain, we can bridge the gap between conscious and unconscious. Dreams are the easiest and fastest way to access the unconscious wisdom we all possess.

Later in the book we will look more carefully at the unconscious and see if we can understand why it presents material to us in dreams. In addition, we will try to understand why some of the dream material can be unsettling or frightening to us. The unconscious is a mystery we can explore with some success, as long as we do not make the mistake of placing our conscious judgments and belief structures upon it.

---

### KEY POINT
**We cannot understand dreams from our usual points of conscious reference, because the viewpoints of the conscious and the unconscious mind are often very different. It is a mistake to impose outer beliefs and values upon the images seen in dreams, although the contrast between the two can give us valuable information.**

---

# Expanded Awareness and Wisdom

So far, we have been looking at the idea of the conscious and unconscious mind as a personal expression of who we are. This is sufficient for a good understanding of dreams, because there is plenty of material for our minds to consider based only on our life experiences. We contain a huge personal reference library of everything ever presented to our awareness; every book, every film, every sight and sound, every feeling and sensed perception. All of this life material can be used by the unconscious to create scenarios in our dreams. This would be more than enough for a rich dreaming experience.

But what if another, transpersonal dimension is added? For example, there are many recorded instances of prophetic dreams foreshadowing real events in the world before they actually happened. Accurate dreams have been reported of events occurring at places far distant from the dreamers, dreams that could not possibly be based on personal experience.

From the viewpoint of hard science, these kinds of phenomena are anecdotal. This means they cannot be proven to have happened, since the report is based on a personal event and cannot be duplicated by scientific experiment. Each of us must make our own choice as to whether we feel this kind of dream has validity or not. The idea is easier to accept if we have personal experience of prophetic or clairvoyant dreams.

There are also dreams that reveal new discoveries and ideas. The discovery of Benzene is a well-known example. The structure of this then-unknown substance was presented in a dream. The molecular model that appeared in Freidrich von Kekule's dream revolutionized the science of organic chemistry. Similarly, the formula for insulin (Frederick Banting) was written down in the middle of the night after waking from a dream. There are many examples throughout history.

---

## KEY POINT
**Dreams are a way we can connect to a greater awareness. This awareness is not based on, or dependent upon, our personal experience. This awareness may contain all wisdom and knowledge.**

---

If this is true, then our unconscious mind is a complex transceiver, capable of linking to a greater, transpersonal awareness that exceeds our normal human experience. Information is communicated to us through the process of dreaming. Dreams potentially bring the information to the attention of our waking and conscious mind.

## KEY POINT

**Our unconscious mind is connected to powerful intuitive/wisdom areas existing independently of our "normal" awareness and experience. Dreams are a way for this larger source of awareness and information to make itself known to us.**

Sometimes people say dreams are nothing more than meaningless garbage of the mind, a kind of random firing of neural electrical patterns. At best, the people with this point of view consider dreams to be a sort of "street sweeping" process, a periodic removal of psychic clutter and debris. This kind of thinking is a natural result of living in a society that has learned, over many centuries, to suppress and deny intuitive and non-logical dimensions of thought and existence, except in very specific situations and circumstances. The truth is that dreams are far more than a psychic cleansing process. They are a highway to expanded dimensions of understanding and consciousness, a gateway to the soul.

# CHAPTER 2

# HOW TO BEGIN WORKING WITH DREAMS

## Recording Your Dreams

Before you can do anything with dreams, you must first become skilled at recording and remembering them. Most of us remember occasional fragments of our dreams or longer stretches and scenes. Often the dreams we remember best are those which shock or horrify us—the "nightmare." Nightmares are certainly a way to get our attention because the terrifying material imprints itself on our waking mind, although we may not understand the meaning or simply shrug it off as a "bad dream." If you want to look at nightmares in detail, I have covered them in depth in one of my other books, *Nightmares: How to Make Sense of Your Darkest Dreams*. For more information about nightmares, please see Chapter 16.

There is no such thing as a "bad dream." All dreams are useful to us. A particularly shocking dream usually means the underlying psychic material is important to understand. It is the unconscious mind's way of trying to get through to the waking mind. It is possible to understand the message of a nightmare. Once understood, the feeling of horror transforms.

Fortunately for our peace of mind, most dreams are not like this. As we begin making the effort to remember our dreams, a rich and intriguing world opens to us. Every night can turn into an adventure, better than going to the movies, and cheaper, too!

Sometimes people believe they never dream, or if they know they have dreams, never remember them. If you are one of these people, be assured you do dream and you can learn to remember. When your unconscious gets the message you are genuinely interested in what it has to say, you will be surprised at the number and depth of the dreams you start to remember.

## How to Begin

The first thing you must do is prepare yourself to record your dreams in some manner. There are three basic ways to do this.

○ **Place a pad, paper, pen and small light by your bed when you prepare for sleep.** With this technique you teach yourself to wake up when you have a dream. You write down on the pad everything you can remember, or at least key events and scenes from the dream. Get a small flashlight to see what you are doing, or one of those neat pens with a light built into it. The light is a good idea, as any of you know who have tried to write in the dark and read your writing in the morning! In the morning, rewrite the dream legibly with any extra details or events you remember and may not have put down during the night.

○ **Get a small tape recorder that plays and records, such as a Sony Walkman or similar small machine.** A voice-activated recorder may be a good choice for you. Turn on the power at night and make sure there is a blank tape or space on the tape for the dream. When you have a dream and wake up, simply turn on the recorder and speak the dream as you remember it into the built-in microphone. This technique has the advantage of not needing a light or of having to wake up enough to write something down. In the morning, or at your convenience, listen to the dream you have recorded and write it down.

○ **When you wake in the morning, write down any dreams or fragments of dreams you remember.** Although this may seem the easiest method, it has the disadvantage of losing whole sections of the dreams, which may vanish with waking consciousness. Dreams are stored in very short-term memory. Particularly if you wake with an alarm, you may find the images are driven right out of your conscious mind and will be lost to you.

I have used all three of these methods and they all work. The tape recorder provides the most complete detail for me, although writing the dream down during the night can also be very complete.

---

### KEY POINT
**The first step for working with dreams is recording everything you can remember, no matter how fragmentary or unimportant the dream may seem to you at the time. Without recording the dream, memory fades and the information in that particular dream is lost to you.**

---

# Remembering Your Dreams

Of course, recording dreams is not much use if you cannot remember what you dreamed. Then you would have nothing to record! Preparing to record the dreams is the first step because this alone may stimulate the memory. You must be ready to record any dream you might have. Usually we need to do something to stimulate our ability to remember. Further along in the book is a meditation you can use to help you. The important thing is to prepare the mind for the memory of dreams.

The best time to touch the bridge between the conscious and unconscious mind is in the "twilight zone" between sleep and wakefulness. During this temporary period, many of the filters imposed by the outer mind are removed. The lines of communication are more open. Material can flow more freely between conscious and unconscious. This is a good time to tell yourself that you want to remember your dreams. Try this simple technique.

## Preparing to Remember Dreams

1. Lie comfortably on your back as you quietly prepare for sleep.

2. Be sure you will not be interrupted or disturbed—not a bad idea for simply going to sleep!

3. Place your hand over the center of your chest, letting it rest lightly and comfortably. Feel the warmth of your hand and your chest.

4. Say to yourself, "Tonight I am going to remember my dreams. Tonight I will remember my dreams. I want to remember my dreams." Each time you say the words, press a finger into your chest, until you have repeated the words ten times.

5. Continue to repeat this to yourself for a few minutes. You may or may not say the words out loud. Be aware of your hand resting lightly on your chest. The hand signals that you are ready to remember your dreams.

You may vary the wording or phrase you choose to repeat to yourself. For example, you might add your name to the phrase, telling yourself that you will remember your dreams. After you have done this for a few minutes, simply relax and drift off to sleep. Make sure you have prepared to record your dreams.

This simple approach is very effective for stimulating memory. I have had people who did this report to me that they began dreaming again after many months or years with no memory of dreams. They were excited by the detail and richness of what they remembered. You can do it also.

Remembering and recording your dreams will become easier with practice. Don't be discouraged if at first not much seems to happen. Stick with it and the results will come. Don't be a taskmaster to yourself about remembering and recording. Set up a context of discovery and co-operation with the part of you that dreams. You will be pleased when the results do come.

---

### KEY POINT
**The state of consciousness between wakefulness and sleep is a unique and effective time for helping you remember your dreams. By telling yourself you wish to remember your dreams while drifting off to sleep, you let the unconscious know you are serious about listening to the messages of your dreams.**

---

## Keeping a Dream Journal

A dream journal is one of the best ways to work with dreams. When you write down the final copy of the dream, keep it in a special book set aside for just that purpose. Blank books nicely bound in various sizes can be purchased at any good bookstore.

The advantages to keeping a journal are several. First, it gives you a convenient place to keep a record of all your dreams. When you record the dream, leave a blank page beside it. Later you may have new thoughts and ideas about the dream you will want to write down. It is much easier to read all your dreams in one place than to shuffle through various sheets of paper and little notes to yourself. Take my word for it, a dream journal is one of your best tools for understanding.

Over time, a series of dreams will often present a pattern of events and images. A message will be contained in the pattern of the separate dreams and their similarities. This may not be immediately apparent. The dreams could extend over months or even years, and you will probably have forgotten them. When you go back through the dream journal something may leap out at you as you find similarities between the dreams. This can lead to practical results, because as you learn to see the pattern revealed by a sequence of dreams relating to an issue or problem you may be able to resolve it.

A pattern is always predictable in its result. When a tailor uses a pattern to manufacture a shirt, the result is always a shirt. One never gets a pair of pants from a shirt pattern! If you can see a pattern, you can then predict the result. If you do not like the result, you can change the pattern. This is one way your dreams can become a practical tool for change. Understanding the pattern in a dream means understanding how the pattern works in waking life, and how you relate in real life to whatever the subject is that was presented in the dream. This gives you information you need to make any necessary changes.

---

## KEY POINT
**Over time, a series of dreams may present you with similar images—pieces of information about the same issue in your psyche. If you can see a pattern in the dreams, you may be able to resolve the issue by taking action based on the dream advice.**

---

# Psyche

The word "psyche," mentioned above, needs clarification. The traditional Webster's dictionary definition describes psyche as "soul, spirit, mind; the principle of mental and emotional life." The word is Greek in origin; from this root come related words like psychology, psychiatry, etc. I think of the word psyche as our personal totality of mind, body and spirit—the whole ball of wax.

I am interested in discovering more of who I am in my totality. It seems to me that the more I understand about myself, the more options will be available to me and the more I will be able to enrich my experience of life. Dreams are an immediate and accessible tool for this inner exploration. Dreams reveal the depths and heights of our psyche, opening windows to a source of infinite wisdom.

# CHAPTER 3

# HOW TO BEGIN INTERPRETING DREAMS

## The First Interpretation

Now that you have remembered and recorded your dream, it is time to see if you can understand it. It's important to tell yourself you can do it! The part of your mind that is sure you cannot do something is never able to accomplish the task at hand. You have within you a part that knows very well how to interpret dreams. After all, you had the dream, didn't you? That dream came from somewhere in your unconscious. Something in your unconscious decided the images of the dream had clear meaning and importance for you. It created images to communicate with you. It knows the meaning of the images, even if your conscious mind is not at all sure what those images mean. Therefore, something in you knows the meaning of the dream. Something in you knows how to make the meanings of the dream images clear to your conscious mind.

## KEY POINT
**Something within you brought you the dream. Something within you knows the meaning of the images of the dream. Something within you knows how to interpret the dream to your conscious mind.**

I call the piece that knows how to interpret the dream "The Dreamer Within." We might think of this as an aspect of ourselves willing to help us understand the meaning of our dreams. The first thing I do when I want to interpret a dream is *ask* for this part of me to come forward and help. Sound silly?

Remember that we are dealing here with areas of our psyche not clearly understood. It is a great help to take time to ask for assistance from our own unconscious. This sets the stage for an inner feeling of co-operation, rather than struggling to figure something out with a part of our mind that has no real ability for the task of dream interpretation. Trying to make sense of a dream from our usual sense of consciousness is mostly a waste of time. It's like trying to start your car by kicking the tires! This is one of the reasons people have so much trouble understanding dreams. It is as if we were trying to mow the lawn with a snow shovel, or find our apartment in the wrong building. It won't work.

## KEY POINT
**ASK your unconscious to help you understand the dream. The Dreamer Within knows how to interpret the dream, and will help you if you learn to work with it.**

Developing a sense of the Dreamer Within is essential for understanding a dream. To get to this piece it is necessary to shift away from your ordinary state of consciousness.

The first interpretation of a dream is usually not very accurate, but will sometimes provide you with good information nonetheless. There are three levels to look for when interpreting a dream. This idea will develop further as we move along in the book. For now, think of the first interpretation as being on the "first level." On this level, dream images are interpreted by association with something readily familiar to you in your conscious mind. For example, suppose that a friend you know in real life appears in your dream. On the first level, you think the dream has something to do with this real person; this will be true, but not in the way you think!

When you begin working with dreams, it is helpful to write down your first impression of what the dream might mean, especially your feeling about it. You may have a sense that the dream is more or less important, or that you feel happy, sad, thoughtful, angry, frightened, aroused, confused, or something else. Write this down.

As you know, when you are dreaming it seems just as real to you as your waking life. You have feelings during the dream, just as you do in waking life. How you feel about something in the dream and how you feel in waking life may be significantly different. The difference provides important information. Make a note of everything you can remember about the dream. You may have forgotten something when you first wrote it down. If so, write it down when you return to begin the interpretation. No detail of the dream is unimportant.

---

# KEY POINT
**All the images and details of a dream are important, no matter how insignificant they may seem at first.**

---

# Getting Ready for the Interpretation

Let's review what we have covered so far about beginning the interpretation:

**1. ASK for help from your unconscious in interpreting the dream.**

**2. Remember that something in you knows how to interpret dreams.**

**3. Write down your first impression of what the dream means.**

**4. Write down how you felt during the dream.**

**5. Write down how you feel about the dream now.**

**6. Write down any further details that you may remember.**

**7. Write down what you think the dream means.**

Remember: your dreaming consciousness is not the same as your waking consciousness. You as the dreamer in the dream may feel differently about something than you do when you are awake. How you feel in the dream is valuable information, especially when compared with how you feel about the same thing when you are awake. The difference, if any, provides a clue for the interpretation. As you start interpreting dreams, this will become clearer to you.

---

## KEY POINT
The differences and similarities between how you feel in dreaming awareness and how you feel in waking awareness provide you with valuable clues and information about the real content of the dream. This becomes clearer with practice and observation.

---

# The Deeper Interpretation

In some ways, interpreting a dream is like reviewing a movie. A movie presents an array of images that establish setting, mood, and feeling tones. There are characters in the movie, and you have feelings and judgments about them. Each character has a role to play to fill out the story line. The actions of the characters, combined with the setting and the story line, establish the theme of the movie. The story line then develops to elaborate on the theme and create a whole that is the film.

One approach has proven very helpful to me in interpreting dreams. Simply put, the idea is that each dream, if it is longer than a brief scene, will begin with a section that establishes the overall theme. This is just like the opening sequence of a movie. It will contain the core elements of the entire composition. Sometimes you sense something was forgotten in the dream before the section you remember, but generally the first part you *do* remember will state the theme or central message of the dream. The rest of the dream will develop this theme and give you more information about the subject.

---

### KEY POINT
**The first part of a dream establishes the theme and symbolic "message" of the entire dream. If you can understand this initial presentation, you can understand the rest of the dream more easily. The remainder of the dream will generally develop the theme stated in the opening sequence.**

---

How do we begin getting to a deeper understanding of the dream? You have already made a *first* level interpretation by looking at how you felt during the dream, what it first seems to mean to you, and writing down whatever comes to mind about it. For the moment, set this first interpretation aside. It is important to let go of what you think the dream means at this point. Even if your first interpretation turns out to be correct, it is still necessary to set this aside and take a fresh approach.

---

## KEY POINT
**Even if your first interpretation of the dream turns out to be accurate, you must always seek a fresh perspective that views the dream anew. This can provide the insight and intuitive understanding necessary for successful interpretation.**

---

Now we have to go to the *second* level of interpretation. The second level makes logical associations and deductions about the symbolic images and events seen in the dream, beyond the surface meaning of the images. It is detective work, and can be a lot of fun. There are always distinct sections in a dream. Each section will contain new elements to identify and consider for symbolic content.

From now on, I am going to give examples of actual dreams to illustrate the points I will be making. At this stage in our journey, I will also give detailed interpretations with the examples, to give you a feel for how it is done. This is the way I do it in dream groups to teach people the needed skills, and it has proven effective. Later you will use worksheets presented in the book to make your own interpretations.

# Carl's Dream

*Something is missing or incomplete. I am in a large church, very dim, looking for something. I can't find it. As I turn to go out, I realize that what I have been looking for is a paper hidden behind the altar. I have been "listening" to find it and realize there was a flaw in what I heard, an extraneous noise. Now that I know this, I can find the paper. I am saying, almost shouting, "I can use it! I know what to do! I won't abuse it!" I go back in and am even willing to interrupt the service to get to the paper, but David stops me.*

*Later, I am relating this dream to John, who appears interested. I tell John*

*that all my dreams lately deal with something missing or incomplete. True—*
*he agrees.*

You do not need to know anything about the dreamer to understand a dream reasonably well, but any extra information is helpful. If you are the one who had the dream, then the information is available. If someone you know has a dream, you can ask questions to help find out what certain people or images may mean for them. In this case, I will give you some background about Carl that will help us get to the meaning of the images.

Carl is a person who has spent many years on what might be termed a "spiritual quest." He has taken on the role of teacher for others who also are searching for meaning and understanding in their lives. When he related this dream, he was uncomfortable. He sensed that his dream might indicate some primary flaw in his work and perception. This was born out by interpretation.

---

## KEY POINT
**The interpretations that follow throughout the rest of this book come from the Dreamer Within. The Dreamer Within speaks with certainty about the meaning of the symbols in any given dream. This does not mean these symbols always represent the same thing. A symbol appearing in one dream may mean something entirely different in another. Since each dream is unique, and since each of us has a personal symbolic language, it is a mistake to assume a symbolic dream image always stands for the same thing.**

---

You can begin right now to practice shifting levels of awareness and getting in touch with the Dreamer Within. Close your eyes, take a few, deep breaths and sit quietly for a moment. When you feel calm, simply ask something to come forward within you that knows how to interpret dreams. You may or may not get a sense of a different feeling. Just take what you get. It does require practice, so now is a good time for you to start.

The opening sequence of Carl's dream indicates the theme that will be developed. "Something is missing." This is a straightforward statement that essential information, material, or connection is not present. The nature of whatever is "missing" is indicated by the setting of the dim, large church. The setting of a dream sequence always tells us something. This setting tells us that the theme of the dream will have to do with the spiritual area of this man's consciousness.

The lighting is another clue. The dimness emphasizes the hidden nature of the material. This is something not clearly seen. After all, Carl's mind could have presented a church brightly lit, but this would not be consistent with the theme of something hidden expressed in the dream. The lighting is an important detail.

How did I arrive at this interpretation? This is where the second level kicks in. I think about the image of a church. What is a church? A church is a place of religious worship where people go to honor God and spirit. A church is a building, a place people recognize as focused on spiritual ideas and practices. A church is also a community center, where weddings and funerals, baptisms and other ceremonies take place. It is a place for personal and community functions. The common element in all activities occurring in a church is spiritual, even if the event is a picnic or a garage sale! In other words, the church is a spiritual context. Anything that happens there is under the umbrella of spiritual connection. We could just as easily substitute a synagogue or mosque for a church and come up with the same associations.

What else do you think a church represents? A church is not merely a place where one goes to practice one's religion, or participate in activities of a spiritual or religious nature. A church is also a building, a structure.

What is a church/structure? We must learn to ask this kind of question if we want to reach the heart of the dream. In this dream, the church represents part of the dreamer's consciousness concerned with spiritual pursuits. A second level reading emphasizes church as structure: church—structure—spiritual beliefs, held in form. Okay so far?

---

**KEY POINT**
Dreams can be understood on several different "levels," each level providing more information than the one before. To interpret a dream, you must take time to search out each level for the expanded meanings that can always be found.

---

It is a large church. We might be looking at a symbol of a well-developed and established belief system regarding spirit and God. This is a logical, second level deduction. Formal religious structure is a way of containing, understanding, and setting boundaries on the spiritual. It is, in essence, a masculine approach (more about the difference between masculine and feminine later). It is an attempt to define through structure something not understandable in normal, linear terms. It is a way humans try to understand, contain and experience the mystery of divine spirit and universal consciousness.

Based on this way of looking at the church symbol in the dream, what can we discover? Remember that Carl is searching for something hidden from him in the church. The theme developing in this dream concerns the dreamer's search for something he feels he needs and does not possess. This search takes place inside the boundaries of Carl's well-developed belief system, the context of his perception of spirit and the spiritual.

How are you doing so far? Do you get a feel for how even the simplest beginning contains a wealth of symbolic information for the dreamer? Does the interpretation feel "right" to you? We need to look at each detail of the dream, and attempt to come to an understanding of the meaning of each symbol. When we think of "church," we might be tempted to rush on by, dismissing the symbol as mere setting and skipping over the meaning, so we can get on to the rest of the dream. We might also be satisfied with an initial interpretation as "spiritual area," and thus miss a few more clues.

---

**KEY POINT**
To interpret a dream, you must be patient and
carefully examine every detail. It is always
worthwhile to think again about familiar items
and situations, to see if you are really feeling
into the depth of what the images hold. The
church in the above dream section is an
example of this point.

---

As the dream continues, Carl turns to leave the church, unable to find
what he was seeking. This action symbolizes a part of his consciousness
discouraged with the approach he has been taking. In his waking life,
Carl at this time was at something of a dead end in his work. He was seeking new spiritual stimulus and was disillusioned with what he had
accomplished so far.

Suddenly Carl realizes (in the dream) that what he has been looking for
is a paper hidden behind the altar. He also realizes he has been "listening"
in order to find it, but that there is a flaw in what he has heard.

At this point, the dream is beginning to elaborate on the basic theme.
A paper contains information of some sort. There was a sense by Carl
when he related the dream of something written on the paper. This is the
information he has been seeking. "Paper" and "information," like
"church," are words/images/thoughts that need to be examined. Paper—
information—knowing. The paper symbolizes knowledge the dreamer is
not yet in touch with consciously.

Do you see how we arrive at this interpretation?

The flawed "listening" is dream talk, a message that Carl has been
incorrectly interpreting what he has "heard." It is a reference to the information, knowing, and experience he has been building up (structure
again) about the spiritual for many years. The dream then tells Carl that
since he now knows this, he can find the missing paper hidden behind
the altar.

The altar represents the essential mystery of Spirit. The altar is the heart of every church or temple. Carl has to approach this mystery anew in order to find the knowledge he seeks. He now knows something is flawed in his perception.

The deepest interpretation of the dream comes from understanding the implication of the dream message. In this case, the message is that recognizing the flaw in perception, and by implication correcting it, will lead to what is hidden from him in his spiritual quest—the symbolic paper behind the altar. This is practical advice for the real world; *Find the flaw in your perception of spirit that you now know exists, and the knowledge will be revealed to you.*

We have now arrived at the third level of interpretation. The third level appears through intuitive deduction and a leap of understanding. This is where we discover the true message of the dream. Here is where we find practical advice for conscious action in our waking life. Usually it is not stated directly, but is implied by the images the dream offers.

---

## KEY POINT
**The message of a dream is usually understood by implication, rather than by direct advice. A dream will present the current state of affairs and sometimes indicate a course of action to follow, if action is necessary. Just as often, what is not shown or stated is as important as what is shown. This is one reason dreams are difficult to understand.**

---

I want to make another "Key Point" here, that I will explain more thoroughly in the chapter about the Unconscious Mind. For now, please consider it a working context for looking at dreams.

---

**KEY POINT**

Dreams always tell the truth about what is really going on in your unconscious mind. This concept is essential for successful dream interpretation. Dreams never lie to you. Confusion comes not from the dream, but from the outer mind's attempts to understand.

---

Now comes a very interesting part of the dream, because it reveals parts of Carl's psyche he might like to ignore. These are the statements, almost shouted, "I can use it! I know what to do! I won't abuse it!" Abuse what? When I asked Carl about this, his response was the "power" this information might give him. He was uncomfortable, because he recognized the less enlightened side of his "spiritual quest." Part of Carl is motivated by desire to gain spiritual power for its own sake, not for service or to be useful as an instrument of spirit. Carl thinks he might be unable to use power without abusing it. He is caught between desire for spiritual knowledge and uncertainty he could use it wisely. This is a self-judgment that emerges when talking with him about the dream.

When statements are shouted out, or images in some way appear to stand out from the rest of the dream, it is for emphasis. This helps us remember it; the psyche has gotten our attention.

---

**KEY POINT**

When you want to understand a dream, you must be completely honest with yourself and tell the truth to yourself about how you feel.

---

---

**KEY POINT**
Emphasis in a dream through sound, color, or
repetition it is important. Emphasis is a signal
to pay extra attention.

---

Are you still with me? If this were your dream, could you feel into the symbols and situations presented? It was uncomfortable for Carl to discover self-serving motivations for his spiritual work. The dream comments upon this theme and develops it further in the next sequence.

Carl is even willing in the dream to go back into the church and interrupt the service in order to get what he wants! David prevents him from doing this. In order to discover David's symbolic meaning I asked Carl what he thought about David in real life. Anyone we know in real life, who appears in a dream, must generally be treated as representing something in our own nature, a composite of qualities and perspectives to consider symbolically. There are exceptions, but this dream is not one of them. It turns out that David is a very complex symbol. In conversation with Carl, this is what emerged.

David was once a friend of Carl's, a charismatic leader who had become successful by conducting a series of popular trainings in self-discovery featuring an elaborate belief system about spirit and God. The community that developed around the beliefs and the leadership dynamics met all the psychological requirements for a true cult. At one time Carl participated in this training and was deeply committed to its belief system.

By following the rules, Carl gained a position of personal power in the training community. However, the power was dependent on maintaining the belief system the training presented. As Carl matured in understanding his inner motivations, a conflict developed. It became increasingly difficult to reconcile his growing understanding of self with the belief system that he taught in order to preserve his power and position in the community. Eventually he broke completely with the teachings, an emotionally difficult decision.

In Carl's dream, the figure of David represents this emotional conflict and community history, a belief about life and spirit not consistent with Carl's current understanding and spiritual realizations. In the dream, it is David who stops him from going to the altar where the information is hidden.

What does this mean? Can you take a moment, now, and feel into what the message of this symbol means to Carl?

If you thought David represents a part of Carl's own consciousness, psychically supporting the old beliefs and dogma, you are right. Inside Carl a piece is alive and well that holds to the old viewpoints. On the negative side of things, this aspect wants authority and power over others. It is concerned with beliefs about spirit and being dogmatically right about those beliefs.

The message for Carl is this: he needs to recognize how these false beliefs block access to the symbolic dream altar and what is hidden there. The hidden object represents an essential truth and deeper connection to God. This is what is missing in his current state of awareness.

---

## KEY POINT
**People you know in real life who appear in your dreams symbolize not only past or present associations, but also ways of perceiving life and reality. Because they are in your dream, they represent parts of your psyche that may also perceive life in that way.**

---

As the dream continues, the next sequence emphasizes and restates the same information. Carl dreams he is relating the dream to John. John is a teacher and friend of Carl's, a person who also symbolizes many things. One of these is wisdom in the spiritual sense. John is interested in the story about the hidden paper, emphasizing its importance to Carl. Carl again repeats the theme (in the dream) of "something missing or incomplete in all my dreams lately." John, the symbol of spiritual knowledge, puts a symbolic capper on the importance of the dream by agreeing that this is true.

We have now completed a complex analysis of the dream. The message can be decoded and summed up. If Carl received a telegram from his psyche with the dream message, it might read as follows:

```
Dear Carl: You need to pay attention to the
following. STOP. You are not seeing clearly
what needs to be done. STOP. You have not cor-
rectly understood the information you have
received. STOP. The information you seek is
contained in the structure of spirit you have
created but is still hidden from you. STOP. You
must pay attention to self-serving areas still
seeking power from the position of spiritual
authority. STOP. You should review past ideas
and perceptions of what constitutes spiritual
truth and discover if you are still holding on
to ideas that serve self primarily. STOP. The
information you seek is not available to you
until you have done this work. STOP. You feel
```

No wonder Carl feels uncomfortable about this dream! Wouldn't you feel uneasy, getting a message like that?

This next dream was told to me by a woman in her early forties. She has been attempting to understand herself and make sense of an unhappy life. We will look at the dream in sections and see how the theme and information develops.

Use the previously given key points to discover what the dream means as you go along. Long dreams, like this next one, are best thought about in bite-sized sections. By breaking a dream down into sections, we can discover many interesting things often overlooked when viewing the dream as a whole. This is an effective way to work with interpreting any dream.

## Mary's Dream: Section One

*I was standing at a corner. A sidewalk ran in from the corner toward a magnificent old oak tree. The tree trunk was very thick and the canopy was a rich, summer green with no dead leaves or branches. I spent some time with this tree, placing myself on different branches. The sidewalk circled the tree and led on to the corner of a building.*

This is a good example of how the opening sequence of a dream states the theme. Take a moment, now, to feel into the images presented, especially the large, magnificent oak tree.

The central image in this section is classic, seen in many myths and stories of humankind's search for conscious interaction with God. It appears as the tree of life and knowledge in these stories, symbolizing an essential and primal life force. The Tree represents something divine and central to all life in the universe. It is a transpersonal symbol, found in almost every culture and time. It is a collective image, common to all humans.

Transpersonal means "beyond the personal." A transpersonal force, by definition, is not concerned with personal agendas and individual egos. A transpersonal force surpasses the individual—but when it appears in a dream, we are completely involved with it personally. When a collective image appears in a dream, we know the dreamer is looking at something fundamental about self in relationship to life and spirit. One of the great challenges we face in a vast and impersonal universe is to discover our own personal and unique relationship to these larger forces.

Mary is first standing at a corner, a place where she has a choice of direction. From here a sidewalk leads to the tree. This is significant, because it could just as easily have been a path or a thicket! Remember, the dreaming mind can choose any symbol it wants. A sidewalk is neat, orderly and man-made. It is a clear path, but it also has the qualities of the logical mind inherent in its nature. Mary is able to walk to the tree on this sidewalk. The image suggests she has built up a mental area of logic and order that she uses as a path through life. We can say this is a more masculine side of her psyche, if we generalize and assume the masculine is more focused on order and logic.

By contrast, her feminine areas are less concerned with control and order and more involved with feeling and natural expressions. The tree symbolizes primal energies of life, made accessible through the symbolic sidewalk.

Mary explores the tree, placing herself on different branches. This is an excellent omen for her outer life, and her participation with life. As we shall see, though, there is more to come. The sidewalk circles the tree and leads on to the corner of a building.

# Mary's Dream: Section Two

*The building was quite large and was of heavily carved stone. It reminded me of old court houses that were built by communities more as a statement about themselves than for the function of the building. It was four complete stories with a smaller fifth floor situated on the roof of the fourth floor. The fifth floor had a domed roof supported by a series of columns. There were large columns at each corner of the building that ran the full height of the four floors and smaller columns supporting the curved archway over the entrance.*

Why do you think Mary has the thought in the dream about "communities?" What does the symbol of the large building mean? Her psyche is giving her information about her inner community, composed of all the things that make up who she is, known and unknown. It is a statement telling her she has built a solid, strong structure internally.

It reminds her of a courthouse. A courthouse is a place where records are kept, administration is focused, where "court" is held, where law is administered, where judgment is pronounced. What a powerful symbol for the mind and its view of the world! Judgment is implicit in the symbol of "courthouse," along with an ordered, logical approach to life. This is what Mary has created in her life, perhaps at the expense of something else. If that is so, a later section of the dream may reveal what is lacking or in need of correction.

Numbers appear here, and numbers can be confusing in dreams. The study of numbers as symbols is called *numerology*. In numerology, all numbers have meaning, since they are symbols. All multiple numbers can be reduced to a single number, by adding all the digits together. For example, 27—2 + 7—9. 3582—3 + 5 + 8 + 2—18—9.

The building has four main stories supporting a fifth, domed structure. The columns suggest strength and the domed structure, if you can see it in your mind's eye, might resemble a temple. You do actually see such temple-like top stories on older official buildings, reflecting a neo-classical style based on the architectural influence of Greece and Rome and the Italian Renaissance. Symbolically these architectural designs are intended to suggest authority. They speak of the influence of gods, temples of power and mystery, graced and authorized by the divine presence. So it is in Mary's dream.

Four is a number associated with foundational energies. The square or rectangle, with four sides, is a core element in design. There are four winds, four seasons, four directions, four corners of the Earth in the old mythologies. In a metaphysical context, the heart energy of divine and unconditional love is associated with the number four.

The fifth and domed or rounded top represents a different area of this internal structure. It is clearly part of but different from the rest of the building. Five has been called the number of man, and can be taken to represent the human condition.

It is not necessary to know anything about traditional interpretations of numbers to understand that the fifth floor in this dream symbolizes something different from the rest of the building.

---

## KEY POINT

**It is not necessary to be familiar with symbols or their meanings in order to get a full understanding of a dream. Each symbol in a dream carries its own inherent message. If you take the time to feel into the image presented, the essential meaning of the image will become clear to you.**

---

The fifth level is resting on all the levels below it. The entrance, a curved archway in a square structure, suggests contrast between feminine (curved archway) and masculine (square structure). This is an important detail. It says access to this strong and spacious building is through feminine modes, not masculine. Mary will have to think about what that actually means to her.

## Mary's Dream: Section Three

*The entrance was located in the corner and seemed small when compared with the scale of the building. Over the entrance was an inscription and the building's address, "12345."*

The path from the tree leads to the corner of the building (a corner again) and to the entrance. It's not a grand entrance, as one might expect in such a building. This dream comment suggests humility is called for to gain access. The orderly sequence of numbers implies possibility of movement from one level or floor to the next. What do you think the numbers mean?

"12345" adds up to fifteen. 15—1 + 5—6. Remember that when looking at numbers you can always reduce the total to a single digit. What does six sound like? To the unconscious "six" and "sex" could be the same! You can see dream numbers are tricky! The only reason I know that six and sex are equivalent here is because I have seen that symbolic meaning appear before, in many different dreams. This is not a dream about physical sex, which does not occur: sex is about relationship, the relationship of energies. Six is a number of relationship. The relationship in Mary's dream is the internal relationship of masculine and feminine forces. This shows up clearly later on in the dream. For now, we are working with the "feeling" of curved, square, natural and man-made.

## Mary's Dream: Section Four

*I found myself on the second floor sitting in an overstuffed chair of rich purple velvet. The chair was placed in the center of the room with its back against a small yellow supporting wall. There were square support columns at each end of the wall. The chair was very comfortable and I sat there simply enjoying the room.*

This section marks a transition in the dream to images elaborating on what has already come before. The theme is being filled out and developed.

By implication, the second floor is reached through the entrance on the first floor. This is a step in the progression, and the rest of the dream will take place in this room. Further progress through the building and what it symbolizes will depend on using information presented in this setting. That is a third level observation, an unstated implication derived from what is shown in the dream.

Close your eyes, and see if you can picture the setting. See the colors and try to feel into the images of the dream.

The chair is set exactly in the center of the room. This is the seat of experience for Mary in her dream and is central to her understanding. It is backed by a supporting wall of yellow; the square (masculine) columns emphasize strength. The yellow color is traditionally a color of mental and emotional involvement. It is also a color of life and radiance, the color of the sun. These associations with yellow suggest a strong support system in Mary's psyche that "backs her up". The purple velvet is a royal color, like a throne, a place of security and strength. These symbols tell her she has the support and comfort she needs to deal with whatever the dream is about.

# Mary's Dream: Section Five

*There was brilliant sunlight streaming in from floor to ceiling windows, but the room felt cool and pleasant. The floor was a golden oak covered by a rose carpet with green ivy vined around the edge. The walls were pink, and when struck by the sunlight turned a golden peach. The high, arched ceiling was deeply carved to present a pattern of leaves and branches. The furniture seemed antique but wasn't worn or faded. The furnishings had been well cared for and the wood was oiled to a soft luster. Small conversational group-ings conveyed a sense of coziness despite the size of the room. There were flowers in vases placed throughout the room.*

This is quite a room! The emphasis is on quality, comfort, spaciousness and beauty. The colors are pleasing, feminine, a setting for discovery and conversation, arranged for pleasant usage. The flowers in vases emphasize a feminine touch, adding color and life. The room is brilliantly lit, indicating willingness to see and understand the unconscious content of the dream. Overhead, the ceiling picks up the theme of the tree outside and the emphasis on nature and natural expression. So does the rug with its twining vines of green. Rose is a color of life energy, a soft and comforting but vital color. The room is very spacious, indicating a lot of potential for expansion and discovery.

She is on the second floor. In metaphysical approaches, the second chakra, or energy center, is associated with life forces—sexuality, reproduction, creation, the energy that drives and births new possibilities, and the balancing of masculine and feminine. The theme of the dream is this material, an area not well resolved in Mary's outer consciousness.

## Mary's Dream: Section Six

*I was reading a newspaper supplement that contained the history of the building and acted as a tour guide. I noticed a small piece of furniture beside me. It had gears, a wooden wheel, and a piece that was flat, possibly a seat.*

Have you remembered to ask something within you to come forward, something that knows how to interpret dreams? It really is necessary to ask for this, if you wish to understand. You will know it is present because you will get "hits" of understanding and distinct feelings about the dream.

A newspaper presents news. This is a supplement, therefore, this "news" is in addition to what she already knows. Although she does not consciously remember what the supplement said, somewhere in Mary's psyche is the information she needs about the entire image of the building and all it represents. There is even a tour guide for the exploration.

The piece of furniture is interesting. It is mechanical in nature; perhaps one can sit on it. The chair suggests some kind of mechanical involvement with the psychic material of the dream. Perhaps Mary looks at issues of femininity and sexuality, life and vitality, from a mechanistic standpoint.

## Mary's Dream: Section Seven

*A man approached me and began to address me in a familiar manner; but I didn't feel I knew him. I thought this was odd; however, he was quite pleasant, and we began a conversation. He brought over the one piece of furniture that had been neglected. It was a small, delicate chair with three legs. One of the legs had dried out and drawn in under the chair. He showed me it was unsteady and wobbled.*

This is a crucial section of the dream. There have been three chair images; the chair in which Mary sits, the mechanical piece of furniture on which she might sit, and now a third, neglected, delicate chair. Remember that in the beginning of the dream she sits in different places in the tree. All of these images are related to each other. Do you think these separate and different images of "a place to sit" might be important?

---

### KEY POINT
### Important symbolic images in a dream may appear with variations for emphasis.

---

In Mary's dream, the chair is one example. Another is the motif of nature and natural forces presented first in the tree, then in the rug and on the ceiling. The place where one "sits" is the place from which one acts and has one's being. Her dream shows Mary some of her resources, current options and possibilities of self-expression.

The man who approaches symbolizes some aspect of Mary's psyche. As a general rule (there are exceptions) it is always wise when interpreting a dream to assume that all characters and activities in the dream represent some aspect of the self.

This man is friendly but not recognized. He represents a supportive, masculine area not consciously appreciated. A masculine psychic area acts in ways different from its feminine counterparts. This is something each of us needs to find out for ourselves, one of the rich discoveries awaiting us as we start to feel and appreciate the differences between these energies.

The man shows her the one neglected chair. Three legs might suggest many things. How about Mind, Body and Spirit? It might also represent the physical, the emotional and the mental. One thing is clear; something is off-balance.

One leg of the triad is not functioning correctly. The implication of the image is to pay attention to something that has been neglected. The triad, or trinity, is a metaphor for the wholeness of Spirit.

## Mary's Dream: Section Eight

*The man and I were standing by a large, thick, curved table of dark wood. I was trying to find something in the newspaper supplement that was of interest to him. The corners of the paper were covered with fabric shields and as I turned the pages, I caught whiffs of my perfume. I hoped he could smell it and would find it as pleasant as I. He said, "Do you get the sense of what is meant?"*

This is the final section of the dream. She wants to please this man and find something contained in the history of the building (the news supplement) that interests him. The feminine is emphasized by the fabric shields and by the perfume. "Shield" is an interesting word here, as Mary has spent a lot of time protecting (shielding) herself from men and avoiding the issues men bring up for her.

Perfume appeals to the senses and is usually associated with feminine expression. Perfume is literally the essence of something. A woman's perfume is a statement she makes about herself, an essential statement. Mary wants this man to find the perfume as pleasant as she does. She wants him to approve of who she is. The dream is making a statement about the essence of self.

The man's question, "Do you get the sense of what is meant?" is a powerful summation of the dream. Something in Mary wishes her to understand. Something is telling her she needs to appreciate self. The dream's images of nature, the feminine, and the places from which Mary views the various actions of the dream all indicate a significant internal shift.

The question at the end is a humorous emphasis by Mary's psyche. The "sense of what is meant" is like "scents" (perfume) and "essence" (perfume). Sense, senses, essence, scents—all related to the images and the message of self. The dreaming consciousness is sometimes very fond of puns and plays on words. Do you get the sense of what I mean?

This woman holds a wonderful, inner potential for appreciation of life, something difficult for her to connect with in her past. She has a combination of feminine and masculine energies that can support and enhance each other. The dream asks her to pay more attention to the feminine side of herself, while recognizing and appreciating the strong masculine structure she has already established.

Please take time to review the systematic process used to work through the dream. The best way to learn how to interpret dreams is through observation of seeing someone else do it. We learn to use the mind's ability to associate images and actions with thoughts and ideas, calling upon the help of an inner aspect that really knows what dreams mean. There will be many dream examples in the following chapters and you will have plenty of opportunities to practice.

# CHAPTER 4

# HEALING DREAMS AND DREAMS OF HEALTH

Dreams are particularly valuable when they give us information about health. If we pay attention, our dreaming consciousness will forewarn and advise us about the health of our bodies and the course of any disease process. It may be something simple, like advice about what we eat, or an allergy we might have. When there is serious illness, such as cancer, the dreams will keep us informed of the progress of the disease and will tell us if we are on the road to recovery or moving towards death.

Healing does not always mean curing. If we look at Native American cultures, for example, we find that the primary emphasis is on the restoration or establishment of inner harmony. A physical cure may take place or it may not. Healing from this point of view is to make whole, to bring about a sense of connection and harmony with the forces of life. These forces include disease.

The Navajo culture has several beautiful ceremonies meant to restore an ill person to this sense of harmony. The Navajo phrase that sums this idea up succinctly is "to walk in beauty." The idea of the healing ceremony is to renew the patient's sense of connection to spirit, community and harmony with life. Harmony is thought of as our natural and correct state of being, very much a function of how we relate to the beauty of life that everywhere surrounds us. When harmony is restored, the patient is considered cured.

Dreams tell us when our inner harmony is disturbed. If we can restore that harmony, healing is accomplished. In our modern culture, we see this ancient idea gaining strength in the example of hospice work done with the terminally ill. In a hospice, it is not expected that the patient will be cured of the disease. Rather this important work focuses on restoring or establishing a sense of harmony for the patient. If this is accomplished, the process of moving towards death changes dramatically, and all benefit. Dream work can be an important tool in this difficult situation.

Here is a short dream I had that provides a good example of simple and helpful advice for personal health and spiritual well being.

## Coffee Grounds

*I am standing in front of the kitchen sink. The sink seems to be blocked up, and water cannot go out through the drain. I see that the drain is blocked by a coffee filter, full of old grounds. I clear away the debris of the old coffee and the water rushes in a spiral down the drain.*

What advice is this dream giving me? If you had this dream, assuming you drink coffee, or if someone related the dream to you, how would you interpret it?

At the time I had this dream I was addicted to coffee, always drinking at least one pot of strong coffee each day, often more. I had always liked coffee, and liked the "wake-up" effect. I awoke from this dream with a strong feeling that I ought to pay attention.

Everyone has a different tolerance for substances such as caffeine and the other elements found in coffee. I took this dream to mean that the toxic residue of the coffee I had been drinking (the filter full of grounds) was blocking effective elimination of these substances and by-products. It was also affecting the clear flow of energy through my body, symbolized by the water.

Coffee is processed by several different organs of the body. It can affect the adrenals, intestinal system, kidneys and liver, among others. In fact, I had been experiencing symptoms of letdown and tiredness after the initial caffeine rush, and vague feelings something was not right.

Much as I regretted giving up coffee, I decided this was what the dream was calling for. To my surprise I found it was rather easy to stop, and I began to feel much better in just a few days. The dream clearly told me something my conscious mind wanted to ignore, and gave me the incentive to shift. This was especially interesting to me because I am not someone who believes everything we are told about substances such as coffee (and all of the other things we are told are "not good for us)." I do believe, however, in honoring what the body tells us is not good for us, even if it is not easy for the outer mind to accept.

Remember the KEY POINT given earlier about different levels in dreams? All dreams have levels that contain progressively deeper meaning and new information. The initial interpretation given above is a first level interpretation. There is a "second level" to this dream as well. Do you have a sense of what that might be?

What we have so far is useful. It brought advice that resulted in feeling better physically, the result of not drinking coffee. The second level addresses more than physical health. It is about spirit and the healthy, free, flow of spiritual energy. We are a configuration of energies. It can be said we are nothing more nor less than energy. Taking this viewpoint, the dream suggests spiritual health is also involved.

Every substance carries its own energetic patterning. This dream says coffee is a substance that has become counter-productive for me. The old coffee grounds and filter block the flow. When I remove this in the dream, the sink drains quickly with a strong, spiral flow. Spirals are a basic pattern of energetic structure, found on every physical level humans are able to scientifically perceive.

The kitchen sink is a symbol we can look at on the second level. A kitchen is the place where food is prepared. Food is washed at the kitchen sink, cleansed. Food—nourishment—nurturing. Therefore, removing the coffee grounds and the "old filter" will provide nourishment. Filter—something through which something else is strained so that part of the original thing is left out. Filters block light, for example. We "filter" information selectively and unconsciously. The dream says free energy flow is blocked by residue left in the psyche from an older way of seeing things or responding to things. What exactly the older viewpoint entails is not directly stated.

We could go deeper, a third level. On this level, we have to reach for an understanding not merely deductive or associative. The most important image is old coffee blocking the flow. What does coffee represent, aside from the actual substance? Coffee in the dream becomes a symbol for something else. The first level sees that coffee as a substance needs to be eliminated. The second level associates removal of the actual physical substance with restoration of energy flow and health, physical and spiritual. Coffee is an addictive substance. The third level sees coffee as a symbol of addictive patterns of behavior. What patterns of behavior am I addicted to that hinder the free flow of energy and, perhaps, spirit? How do these patterns affect me? The dream indicates I have the ability to remove such restrictions and restore the flow.

Here is another example of a health dream, from someone with serious illness. He received information in a dream about his disease. Diagnosed with a massive and inoperable brain tumor, doctors gave George six weeks to live.

## George's Dream

*I am walking through a large house with many rooms. Some of the rooms are disused and empty, and there is an air of neglect. Some of them seem familiar. I enter the living room and I see a large television set standing in the center of the room. The set is not working and smoke and sparks are coming out of it. The repairman is there. Other people are present also, looking at the smoking TV.*

This is an example of a dream indicating the real possibility of physical death. The TV set in the "living room" is dangerously disordered and not working properly. We already know there is a tumor, but even if we did not, the symbol of the TV would suggest a problem with the brain. A television set processes input to create pictures, sound and information. It is a good symbol for the brain, which processes information from life and the outer world.

The repairman is good news, though—he represents something that might be able to "fix" the set. The presence of the repairman is a sign physical healing is possible. The dream shows there is a serious problem (which George already knows) and that psychic energies of "repair" or healing are present and could be activated.

What is harder to see is why the disease took hold in the first place. What disharmony brought about this fatal process? One clue is the large house with neglected rooms. The house is a metaphor for the totality of George's self, his inner "living space." I have seen this image before, with variation, in the dreams of people who are terminally ill or threatened with death.

The neglected rooms suggest a large area of life activity not realized. It is an image of abandonment and neglect, implying that the dreamer is narrowly focused and not making use of the many different possibilities available to him. In waking life, George was a workaholic who took little time away from his work for himself or his family. His lifestyle was becoming more and more of a problem, as he was newly married and his wife was expecting a child.

George was caught in a classic conflict between what his feelings demanded and his mind decided. He had not been able to resolve this dilemma. He was no longer able to control his situation, as the workaholic pattern demanded. The conflict of inner feelings and overriding mental demands was literally killing him.

This particular story has a happy ending. George came to a friend of mine, a well-known healer, for consultation about his illness. My friend invited me to assist with the psychological work and with focusing transformational, healing energetics. During the course of the session, George told us his dream. We did what we could to assist him and activate his healing energies. This included helping him get in touch with some of the observations I have shared with you above. About a month later George had the following dream:

# Monster

*I am walking in an underground cavern, with many winding tunnels. I come to a heavy door. I know there is a monster locked behind the door and that it can not get out. I know it can't get me. There is water on the floor of the tunnel, perhaps six or eight inches deep. I am digging for treasure, which I sense is buried beneath the water.*

This is a dream that unequivocally states the problem has been handled, at least for the time being. The monster locked away behind the door is the death/disease process that had manifested as the brain tumor. Something new has been initiated in George's psyche, because he is now seeking the "treasure" hidden inside himself and covered by the water on the floor of the tunnel. The water represents unconscious issues. The dream says George has started to look more intensely inside himself for the treasures of life and consciousness almost lost to him. There is, however, a potentially disturbing aspect to this dream. Can you see what it is?

If you zeroed in on the monster locked away, you have accurately put your finger on the problem. The monster is not dead, or permanently gone. Although George feels it is now safely locked up and cannot "get him," the monster still resides somewhere in his psyche. It represents not just his physical death, but all of the inner and hidden psychological components that led to the disease process in the first place. These patterns of behavior and perception are still present. George will have to be careful in the future not to slip back into his workaholic patterns, or he may see the "monster" return.

The only way to know for certain that this second dream was actually stating what I have indicated would be through medical confirmation. We would need to see that healing had actually taken place. It follows that if the "monster" is locked away and that this is symbolic of a healing process, we should see results in the real world to confirm the interpretation. That is what actually happened.

After this second dream, George had a new C.A.T. scan which showed no signs of the tumor. That tumor was so blatantly obvious and large that it was apparent even to my untrained eye when I viewed the films he brought to his consultation. All of his symptoms, including pain and the beginnings of paralysis, had disappeared. Years later, as of this writing, the tumor has not returned.

## KEY POINT
If you learn to interpret your dreams with reasonable accuracy, you may recognize potential health problems and take steps to avoid them. If you are ill, you can monitor the real course of your illness and the effect of whatever treatment you are receiving.

It is also true, in my experience, that simply recognizing the inner material involved with the illness is usually not enough. Action is required. Information received is useless if not integrated and applied. Sometimes the unconscious material is so overwhelming that the ill person can not muster the strength and resources necessary to make the change required for a cure to come forward. In cases of terminal illness, the change usually has to be as psychologically great as if the person had actually died. It is easy to see why it might be difficult to make that kind of change.

You can see from the above that I consider the inner psyche to be intimately involved with any illness or problem of health. That has been my observation and personal experience. It has also been my observation that dreams can be helpful in working with illness of any kind, although one must go slowly, carefully and with respect for the viewpoints of the sick person. This is particularly true in instances of terminal disease.

In all dream work, we must remember that people who share a dream with us are vulnerable. When people are very ill, their vulnerability to a careless word or action is greatly amplified. We must lovingly respect that vulnerability.

# CHAPTER 5

# WORKING WITH
# SOMEONE ELSE'S DREAM

The guidelines for working with someone else's dream are basically the same as those you would use for your own dream. There are several important differences, however, that you need to bear in mind. Because it is not your dream, the meaning of the dream images the dreamer tells you often will not be the same as they would be for you.

---

## KEY POINT
**When you work with another to interpret their dreams, assume that dream images familiar to you do not necessarily have the same meaning for them. You must try not to impose your own meanings on their images. Ask them to tell you the dream without any interpretation on their part.**

---

For example, suppose you had a dream about a mountain lake. When you analyze the dream you arrive at a feeling about what the lake means to you, based on your unique experience and perception. If someone else dreams of a mountain lake it can mean something entirely different for them. Suppose they almost drowned in one as a child? That would affect their feelings about the image. Your mission, should you choose to accept, is to find out what the lake means for the person with whom you are working. You and they will both know when you have gotten it right because it will feel right in your bodies.

As the person relates the dream to you, resist the temptation to jump directly into interpretation. The most important step when working with another is to listen carefully. Allow the images of the dream to flow through you, as if you were dreaming the dream with them. Try to feel and see the images they are telling you.

It is challenging to take on the interpretation of another's dream: don't take the task lightly. There is an almost telepathic experience when tuning in to a dream. I came across this idea of telepathic rapport when reading Carl Jung, as he described his thoughts about the correct way for a therapist to work with a patient during dream analysis. Jung recognized the possibility of a telepathic component. If you are interested in Jung's ideas about the relationship between dreamer and interpreter, please see his excellent book, *Dreams*, listed in the bibliography at the back of the book. There are many relevant sections, particularly the chapter on the practical use of dream analysis.

We all have a lot of unconscious material that quickly gets in the way of successful dream interpretation. Chapter 7 talks more about the conscious and unconscious and how they interact. For now, make an assumption you do actually have unconscious ideas or perceptions that may interfere with clear understanding. Don't take my word for it! Rather, use the idea as a working framework for exploration. Pay attention to how you feel, and over time the truth or untruth of what I am saying will become clear to you.

It is important to try and hear the dream as it was dreamed, without ideas about what it means. After you have listened to the dream, the next step is to ask for an interpretation. Let the dreamer make the first attempt, even if there is confusion. This is good therapeutic practice, as it encourages the dreamer's own ability to understand dreams and empowers them. You will be encouraging responsibility for growth and understanding.

At this point, you begin a dialogue with the dreamer to see what the images might mean. You may already have a good sense of what the dream is about, especially if you have learned how to access the Dreamer Within. This is something you develop with practice and will learn to trust over time.

I find it helpful to ask how the dreamer feels about any interpretation I am offering. If you are close or accurate, there will usually be a corresponding feeling of "rightness" in the person telling you the dream. Sometimes you may be quite accurate, but the dream material is too loaded with emotional content for the dreamer to accept the interpretation. Then they may deny the interpretation is valid. You will need to practice and relax, and let go of any investment you might have in being right. You can only do the best you can. If you have a good heart and a good intention, that is good enough.

Your intention when working with someone else's dream makes a big difference in the result of your work. When I take on the task of interpretation, my intention is to discover what the dream means for the dreamer, not what I think the dream means to me: this is a crucial distinction. I set my intention to get out of the way and let the Dreamer Within interpret the dream. This is my best opportunity for arriving at an interpretation not skewed by my own unconscious material. My good ideas about the dream are not important, what is important is attuning to the images the dreamer is sharing and allowing something to tell me what those images mean for the dreamer.

When working with dreams, either your own or another's, set your intention to support the truth of the dreamer revealed through the dream images. Be willing to stand aside and let the images speak to you. Be willing to be wrong. The outer mind, no matter how brilliant or developed, how experienced or practiced, does not have the ability to perceive accurately the full truth of a dream. You can learn to shift to another state of awareness that does have the ability. To me it is wonderful and mysterious that we are capable of doing this.

## KEY POINT
When you take on another's dream for
interpretation, set your intention to discover
the true meaning of that dream for the other.
By coupling your desire for this result with your
will to have the truth of the dream revealed, you
set the stage for accurate interpretation. You must
try to hold your intention in a context of heartfelt appreciation for the mystery of dreams,
life and consciousness.

I have already mentioned the vulnerability of people who share a dream with you. Because the unconscious does not lie when it presents dream images, truth is revealed. If you become adept at interpreting dreams, you will become adept at sensing the dreamer's innermost thoughts and feelings. You must be careful to respect the privacy and confidentiality of dream material. If you are not willing to do this, you should not work with other people's dreams.

# CHAPTER 6

# TOOLBOX

A toolbox contains the tools you need for the job. The purpose of this chapter is to place in one convenient place the main tools you need for the job of dream interpretation. The same tools apply whether it is your dream or another's.

Any complex task requires preparation before you tackle the work. First, you may want to organize your workspace. A lot of dream workspace is internal, and some of us are pretty disorganized! Fortunately, there are things you can do to make the work easier.

Your dream work environment is important. It is helpful to create a pleasant place where you can contemplate your dreams. Light, space and privacy are good to have, if possible. Have some green and flowering plants around you and create a space to look at dreams that radiates a feeling of calm and restfulness, a place for meditation, relaxation and focused attention.

It is quite possible to create such a space in your home. It may be only a corner with a comfortable cushion or chair. You can separate this space from the rest of the room with a few plants and add a small, colorful rug to define the area. If you are fortunate enough to have a separate room dedicated to inner work, so much the better.

You probably have some of the tools, in the physical sense. These would include a tape recorder, paper, pens, perhaps a blank book for dreams, and anything else you can think of that might help you work with dreams. Other tools discussed in this section are tools for the mind, which grow familiar with practice. They include meditation, a worksheet that has proven itself useful and a nine-step guide for interpretation.

We have already covered a simple approach to help you remember dreams and we have discussed keeping a dream journal. You could say we have already taken these two tools out of the box and laid them on our workbench. In addition, you will find pointers on working with the dreams throughout the entire book. Add these to your mental "Tool Box" as seems appropriate to you.

## A Meditation for Understanding Your Dreams

Here is a meditation to help set your intention for interpreting your dreams or the dreams of another. When you practice this meditation, please be sure you will not be interrupted. It is always best to set aside a quiet time and place whenever you wish to meditate.

It does not matter if you are experienced in meditation or not. You can easily learn to quiet yourself and still the inner chatter that is always present when you begin. If you achieve nothing else, at least you will feel refreshed and calmer after doing this meditation.

Begin by making yourself comfortable. Unless you are physically unable to sit up, it is best to meditate in an upright position, comfortably supported. A chair is fine, or you may prefer a pillow on the floor or a small bench.

Begin to breathe easily and fully. I use a long count of seven and a pause of one. Inhale through your nose for the count of seven. Then hold your breath for a beat of one count. When you exhale, place the tip of your tongue gently against the roof of your mouth, just behind the front teeth. Breathe out through the mouth with a soft sound. Repeat this pattern for some minutes: in through the nose for a count of seven, pause one count, out through the mouth for a count of seven, pause one count, and repeat. Do this for as long as it feels comfortable to you.

This is an ancient breathing technique, very effective for calming the mind and body. It is also energizing at the same time. I often use it to begin a meditation, as it helps me calm my busy mind.

When you feel calm and centered, ask for the part of you that knows how to interpret dreams to come forward into consciousness. Focus on these statements at the beginning of your meditation:

1. *I ask for the co-operation of all those beings on the inner and outer planes that guide me for my highest good.*
(This statement energizes unconscious forces within and without your psyche.)

2. *I open to the energy of Unconditional Love.*
(Allow yourself to relax and feel as if something was melting in the center of your chest.)

3. *I ask for co-operation from the part of me that knows how to understand dreams. I ask that this part now come forward to help me.*
(This sets up an inner context of co-operation and mutual exploration. You may actually feel a sense of presence within you.)

These are actual statements you make to yourself as you deepen into the meditation. You can say them out loud, if you wish. After making these statements, simply sit quietly and see if you can feel a response. If you are centered and relaxed, you may feel a physical response to these statements. Take what you get and honor your experience. Feel free to make up your own statements emphasizing the idea of inner co-operation and an opening to the heartfelt energy of unconditional love.

After you have made these statements and noticed whatever there is to notice, shift your attention to the dream you are attempting to understand. Let the images of the dream play through your mind's eye. In your mind's eye, see the dream unfold before you. As you do so, you may have thoughts about what the images mean, or clear intuitive flashes that carry a sense of certainty about the meaning of a particular image or sequence. These flashes are often accompanied by a physical sensation in the body, a feeling you are on the right track. Learn to trust these feelings and act upon them.

This part of the meditation takes as long as it takes. You will know when it is time to end the meditation because your attention will be pulled back to the place where you are sitting. At this time, end the meditation. A good way to end is with a simple statement of gratitude. "Thank You" is enough. It doesn't really matter who you or what you thank. What matters is the feeling of gratitude.

Don't be discouraged if you have some difficulty with this at first. Remember, it takes time and practice to develop the skills that reveal the meaning of dreams. If you work consistently, you will achieve results.

If you are working with another, you can meditate with them on the dream, using the suggestions above. This can be an effective way to arrive at a good interpretation. Not everyone will want to do this, so it is really up to you to take time to prepare yourself when you know you will be doing an interpretation.

## Nine Steps

Let's review how to begin getting the interpretation, step by step. There are nine steps to follow.

STEP ONE:
**Remember and record the dream.**

STEP TWO:
**Quiet yourself and ask for help from the part of you that knows how to interpret dreams.**

STEP THREE:
**Feel into the images presented. Write down any thoughts you have about them.**

STEP FOUR:
**Write down your first interpretation of the dream, whatever it is.**

STEP FIVE:
Pretend you are watching a movie: what does the setting tell you? What is the theme you feel from the images?

STEP SIX:
Let your mind free associate with the images.

STEP SEVEN:
See if you can find a new perspective or point of view about the dream.

STEP EIGHT:
Write down your interpretation and whatever new ideas you have discovered.

STEP NINE:
Review your interpretation and ask yourself if it feels right to you. If it does not, go through the nine steps again.

Remember, honesty is required. You may be uncomfortable with what you see about the dream. Be careful not to avoid this feeling. Sometimes people fool around with an interpretation until they get what they think they want to hear. This is useless.

# A Dream Worksheet

Here is a sample worksheet you can copy and use to help you understand your dream. Write the sentences and questions below on a piece of paper, leaving plenty of space between them for answers. You can use this format to give yourself a consistent framework for the exploration of dreams. It will work equally well with your dream or someone else's. Consistency in approach is especially valuable in the beginning, when you are learning how to do it. I have found this worksheet well worth the time it takes. It will be used throughout the book.

# DREAM WORKSHEET

**1. Write down and review the dream.**

**2. The images or events in the dream that I feel are most powerful are:**

**3. I feel that the most important event or image is:**

**4. The way I feel about this image is:**

**5. This image reminds me of: (put down anything, no matter how unrelated it seems to be, that comes to mind)**

**6. The next image or event I feel is important in the dream is:**

**7. The way I feel about this image is:**

**8. This image reminds me of:**

(Continue to do this with all the images and events in the dream, down to the least important detail)

9. Any other details I now remember are:

10. I feel that the dream is about:

11. Another thing that the dream is about is:

12. The way I feel about this dream is:

13. Some other thoughts that occur when I review the images of the dream are:

14. Review what you have written in response to all the statements and questions above. You may already have a strong feeling about what the dream means.

15. When I ask for help from within about this dream, I sense that the dream is about:

16. My interpretation of the dream is:

You can use this format to help you understand the dream. When working with another person, use this as a guideline for determining how the person feels about his or her dream. When you also work with the meditation, you will quickly develop the capacity to understand. If you try out the Nine Steps as well, you will soon determine the best approach for you when you look at a dream. Remember, ASK for help from your unconscious in understanding the dream.

The key to interpretation is to use what works for you. As you explore these ideas you may develop another approach that works better for you, or modify what I have presented to suit yourself. The most important thing is to remember and trust that something in you knows how to interpret dreams. Anything that helps you get in touch with that part of yourself is valuable.

# CHAPTER 7

# THE UNCONSCIOUS MIND

Earlier in the book, I suggested we simplify psychology and divide the mind into two parts, conscious and unconscious. That could get me into a lot of trouble with some people, because the mind is not that simple! Trying to understand the unconscious is a lot like trying to read a book in a dark closet. It presents problems of perception. When we move into the world of dreams, whether we are dreaming or remembering a dream, we enter a world where the unconscious is King.

Our so-called "conscious" mind is constantly influenced and directed by the unconscious. By definition, if something is unconscious we are not aware of it. This means we often have no idea what we are doing, as you may have noticed from time to time in your own life. However, all is not hopeless. We can learn to recognize how the unconscious mind influences or controls our outer behavior and experience. This is one of the critical challenges for spiritual growth. Dreams are a readily available source of information we can use to take up the challenge.

The unconscious has its own rules. The rules are: There are no Rules! If you don't think this is true, just recall a dream where you acted in ways you would never think of doing in your waking life. In the dreaming interface with the unconscious, anything goes. Please pay attention to what I am about to say, as it is crucial to understanding dreams and to understanding self.

---

## KEY POINT
**The unconscious mind is not concerned with morality, ethical issues or cultural taboos. Because the unconscious does not concern itself with these things, it does not need to present itself as anything other than what it actually is. This means that the unconscious NEVER needs to lie to you. The unconscious is what it is and it will present accurately, in dreams, what it contains.**

---

What it contains is in you. Although the contents of the unconscious may sometimes shock and horrify you, denial of the material will not make it go away. This does not mean we have to act out our darker side. Working consciously with what we see in dreams can lead to acceptance of self and to an integrated experience of life that makes some unpleasant kinds of acting out unnecessary. The secret of self-acceptance is to appreciate the richness and mystery of our life experience in its totality.

A difficult problem arises immediately when we start working with dreams, intimately connected with our unconscious material. This is a phenomenon called *projection*. Projection means just what it sounds like. We "project" our unconscious material onto events, people and things outside of our selves. Life becomes a screen for the movie our unconscious is showing.

What does this mean, practically? What does it have to do with dreams? It means we do not see events, people or things (including dreams) clearly, because our unconscious movie is super-imposed over whatever it is we are looking at. When we look at a dream, we immediately impose an unconscious layer of judgment and ideas about the images of the dream over the actual dream content. This clouds and confuses the meaning.

For example, suppose you have a dream of violence and doing harm to others. This may not present a problem for you if you live a violent life and frequently harm others, but if you are a "peaceful" person and have such a dream it can be very upsetting. Your natural inclination will be to rationalize the images or even dismiss them as "just a dream," a form of denial. Your judgments and ideas about violence will immediately be activated upon waking, and may even be present in the dream. If you view the dream from the perspective of these judgments (violence is wrong, I don't like hurting people, that's sick, etc., etc.) you will never arrive at an accurate interpretation of what the dream actually means. In order to understand the dream, any judgmental state based on your personal beliefs and ideas about life must be set aside.

It is at first difficult to experience the concept of projection as a reality. This is one of the most important challenges for doing successful dream work. Once we get an experience of how we overlay reality with our own material, it becomes easier to see.

It is an ongoing, lifetime work to separate what we think is real from what is actually real. Dream work is one way to practice noticing the overlay and identifying what is you and what is not. Practically speaking, this in turn can lead to a new perspective of life. Wouldn't you like to base your life on what is really going on, instead of an illusion?

One area of our life immediately benefits from taking time to notice how we project our unconscious material, the area of personal relationships. We do not usually see the person we are with. We see instead an illusion of our unconscious projected upon the person, like a movie on a screen. This frequently leads to trouble and disappointment. After all, the other person is not just a screen; they are a unique and independent being. If we are relating to them based on an illusion of unconscious perception, there is bound to be upheaval in the relationship when the illusion finally breaks down. Their reality as a being will eventually emerge. If we are caught in the illusion of an unconscious projection, it will be a shock to see what we did not know was there.

---

### KEY POINT
**Whatever your personal value system and ethical standard of life, you must set this aside when viewing a dream. Because the unconscious is not concerned with issues of right and wrong, it is a fundamental mistake to impose moral or ethical judgments upon the unconscious images presented in a dream. This point cannot be emphasized too strongly.**

---

Please notice that I am not advocating setting aside your personal value judgments and beliefs permanently. I am saying these must be set aside for accurate dream interpretation. Only then will the true meaning of the images become clear to you. Dreams can only be understood from an appreciative and non-judgmental perspective. This is why the phrase "Unconditional Love" appears in the meditation given earlier for understanding dreams. A context of unconditional non-judgment must be cultivated for good dream work.

Why take the trouble to set aside our value systems in order to understand a dream? Because once we understand what the unconscious is trying to communicate, we discover more options for harmonious behavior in life. If we can recognize what our unconscious is "working with" we have a much better chance of seeing how that spills over into our waking life. By paying attention to our dreams, we discover what we really think and feel about things. The unconscious is reflected in all of our activities, whether we know it or not. There are only two ways I know of to see the unconscious in action. One is in dreams, the other in the events and context of our daily lives.

Sometimes we discover that things we think and feel unconsciously result in activities that do not serve us. We may discover patterns of behavior we were unaware of, based on the unconscious material. If we don't like the results we are getting in our life, we can take steps to activate a different pattern of behavior more satisfactory to us. We will look at patterns later, after we have studied some more dreams and kinds of dreams.

When we take time to look into our unconscious through the window of dreaming, we discover more of who we are. What is certain is that sooner or later we are going to come across material we want to deny. Denial is one of the most insidious forces in our psyche. Life often presents us with uncomfortable or difficult situations. We have all developed ways to avoid, deny or ignore things that do not fit with our concepts of how we want life to be. Yet these things don't cease to exist because we ignore them.

I never thought much about denial until 1975. That was a difficult year for me. Things were not going well, I was in a dead-end job, my relationships were lousy and my primary relationship was awful. My health was shaky, and I was drinking heavily. I was at a turning point, without joy of life and feeling at the end of my rope. In desperation and with an attitude of nothing left to lose, I took Werner Erhard's est training, then building to a peak of popularity.

I have many reservations about popular psychological seminars and the belief systems they teach, but there is much value contained in them. One of the principle themes these seminars have in common is the need for telling the truth about how one really feels. Although genuine understanding and resolution of painful feelings and self-destructive behavior may not occur, there can still be recognition of unconsciously held patterns of denial.

Once acknowledged, acceptance and integration of disowned psychic material becomes possible. We can begin consciously reclaiming what we previously pushed away. During that training in 1975, I saw that I was caught in a powerful web of denial of my own creation. By suppressing the truth of my feelings, I was seriously compromising my life and well-being. The recognition was revelatory and led to immediate changes. It initiated an internal process of reclamation that continues to this day: I began to learn inclusiveness and acceptance, of self and others.

Inclusivity is practiced and acknowledged in many tribal societies and eastern religious traditions. The balance of negative and positive aspects is recognized and appreciated. For example, in Bali there are statues and carvings of adult figures whose feet rest on symbolic representations of dark and light. To the Balinese, this indicates the maturity of the adult. Experience has taught adults to recognize that life is more than just the "good" things. It is assumed only an adult can appreciate this balance, and it is thus seen that denial is inappropriate to the adult. Denial is a function of a less mature stage of development.

This concept of inclusivity is fundamental to understanding dreams and the unconscious psyche.

One of the marvelous things about the unconscious is that it is an infinitely rich resource. We can all learn to tap into it, with conscious intention. It is mysterious and infinite in depth. When we embark upon an exploration of the unconscious, we begin an adventure into unknown territory. Like all adventures worth the name, there are trials and difficulties, thrills and spills, exciting and new possibilities, and times when we wish we had never left home. If we take on the challenge, we will map out new territory and discover something about ourselves that would not be possible without undertaking the journey. Dreams are our passport to the adventure.

# CHAPTER 8

# FEAR ABOUT DREAMS

Sometimes people are reluctant to look closely at their dreams. You are probably not like this, since you are reading this book. If you have been following the material about the unconscious in the last chapter, you can see how it might be unnerving or even frightening to look at your dreams. If you have ever had an unpleasant dream, you probably wanted to quickly forget it.

Many people have reported dreams to me that seemed to foreshadow some unpleasant or tragic event, such as an accident or illness involving a friend or loved one. Naturally, we tend to avoid things we don't like.

I feel that the main reason people fear some of what appears in dreams is not because of the kinds of examples cited above, but because we all fear the unknown. When we are dealing with the unconscious, we are dealing with the unknown. Remember that by definition we do not know what the unconscious contains. Most of us would prefer to stick with what we know, and only occasionally cross the boundaries into unfamiliar territory. Even then, we try to control the unknown factors as much as possible, through planning and preparation. Something usually happens, though, that could not have been anticipated.

Have you ever traveled in a foreign country? Did everything go exactly as you planned? Were you comfortable with the strange language, the different food, the hot water handle being in a different place if it was there at all? You may have found the experience stimulating or fun, but was it comfortable? Did you ever experience a little twinge of fear during your journeys? That could be a big twinge of fear in some situations!

I could go on, but you probably get my point. That which is unknown to us is fearful, simply because we do not know what it is.

---

## KEY POINT
**Since dreams are unpredictable by normal awareness and because they present unknown material from the unconscious, we may experience fear when we set out to explore our dreams. An unpleasant or terrifying dream could activate the fear response and cause us to retreat. That is when it is important to re-affirm our intention for self-discovery. We can re-center and remember to move our awareness to a place of unconditional love and acceptance of self. From this point of center and unconditionality, we can safely and accurately explore any difficult dream material.**

---

Dreams provide us with the raw material of personal change and growth. It is only human to fear the change growth might bring. We intuitively know when the unknown is making its presence felt, and our human reaction is usually denial and avoidance, accompanied by differing degrees of fear. Acknowledge the fear and move on: we learn through experience and often through difficult experience. This is a constant path of initiation into the mystery of life. Life would be terribly boring if everything were always easy and perfect; then there would be no need for us to stretch our awareness and learn anything.

Dreams give us information that can lead to new discoveries about ourselves. Part of the fear we may sometimes experience working with dreams is the fear of what such a discovery might bring. Often discovery brings change, which is uncomfortable. We are afraid of how others might react to us if we institute change. Fear of change can stimulate all sorts of unconscious avoidance symptoms. Typical responses include boredom, depression, listlessness, nervousness, anxiety attacks and sleepiness. We might take up compensatory behaviors, like binging on food or excessive drinking. Perhaps you have had an experience like that.

One good way to overcome any fear about dreams is to start trying to understand them and observe how other people have done it. Through years of working with individuals and groups, I have discovered that the best teaching comes through example. This is why so many different dreams are presented in this book. You will see how a dream reveals its secrets when approached systematically, and you will have as many opportunities as you like to make your own interpretation before you come to mine.

Have you ever noticed that it is often easier to see what is going on with someone else? Of course you have! This does not mean you would reach the same conclusion for yourself if you were in a similar situation, or that you would act on it if you did; humans are like that. Nonetheless, looking at someone else's material often gives us insight into our own, and sometimes provides recognition. It is like that when we are learning to work with dreams. The more we see how it works for others, the more we can see about how it might work for us.

This chapter concludes the first section of *What Your Dreams Can Teach You*. The following chapters examine different themes and specific kinds of dreams. In these dreams you may recognize yourself or some piece of yourself. At this point, you now have enough information to begin working successfully with dreams. It's time to put the information to use.

From time to time, I will suggest that you do a worksheet for a dream before you have looked at the interpretation. Of course you may choose not to do this and that will be OK. On the other hand, if you practice as we go along, you will be that much further ahead when you start to look at your own dreams. It's up to you.

Section Two

# CHAPTER 9

# THE MASCULINE AND FEMININE IN DREAMS

This is a very ambitious heading for a chapter. An entire book could be written about either the masculine or the feminine in dreams, and probably will be. It would be impossible to present an in-depth analysis on this subject in a chapter, and I am not going to try. My purpose is to introduce you to some basic concepts and to a helpful framework of exploration. Understanding the symbolism of masculine and feminine is one of the most confusing challenges of dream work. That feels appropriate to me, since it is one of the most confusing areas in our human experience for self-understanding

I want to remind you that a good, general approach to dream figures is personal. By personal, I mean it is generally safe to assume all of the figures in a dream represent aspects of yourself. They are the characters of your play, acted out on the stage of your dreaming consciousness.

However, it is also true that some of these characters may display attributes not entirely personal. In this case, we are tapping into symbols more universal in nature. We have some relationship with them because they appear in our dreams, but they represent something not created by us that exists outside of our personal sphere. This can be especially apparent when we look at some of the masculine and feminine figures appearing in our dreams.

This is not really so difficult to understand, if you stop and think for a moment. What could be more personal and impersonal at the same time than gender? Differentiation by sex is an impersonal process, yet our personal experience of life is irrevocably intertwined with our gender. There are qualities of masculine and feminine that have nothing to do with our personal thoughts about these things. There are also extremely personal qualities of expression we bring to our experience as man or woman.

In our dreams, this personal/impersonal reality is faithfully mirrored. An example is the figure of "mother" or "father." These are individuals in the personal sense and we have a personal, individual history with each figure. This is true even if the parents are not present or are unknown. We have a personal relationship with the physical parents. On the other hand, there is the impersonal energy of masculine and feminine that for humans becomes personified in dream and myth as Father and Mother. These are separate, primal processes that combine to initiate and gestate life and move it from potential to manifestation.

In other words, masculine and feminine are energies of the life process that have different functions regarding the development, evolution, continuation and expansion of life. Life is the important word here. Life is an impersonal process that we humans take very personally!

Once we get past the biological process of conception and reproduction, we can start to explore how we express feminine and masculine. This expression is for all practical purposes infinite in variety. Certain expressions such as mother and father take on collective and cultural values. The roles, over time, become well defined.

Any one definition cannot possibly take in all possible variations of role expression. This is unsettling to the part of our psyche that constantly strives for order, control and understanding through categorization. In our effort to understand what is going on, we make judgments and create categories that further define the mask of the feminine or masculine we are seeing. We say, "She is a good mother" or, "He is a bad father." Immediately a list of criteria for judgment flashes before our mind's eye, based on the belief systems held by our culture and society.

In our unconscious is contained, perhaps, all of the possible energetic variations on the theme of masculine and feminine. It is like the representation of God as gods and goddesses in Eastern religion. We see these powerful dualistic forces presented as demonic or angelic, nurturing or destroying, sincere or full of falsehood and trickery. They appear as ugly or handsome, young and old, beautiful or deformed, and in every conceivable stage and timing of life, personal and impersonal.

So, too, with our dreams. The figures of men and women, boys and girls, young and old, demonic and angelic, nurturing and destroying, wise and foolish appear again and again. Each figure represents some aspect in us that carries a particular quality. The message of the dream figure comes through when we understand our inner relationship with that quality.

---

## KEY POINT

**Our expression as a man or a woman reflects both personal and impersonal qualities of consciousness. It is important to learn to distinguish the difference between the two. The male and female figures appearing in our dreams usually represent facets of self, symbolically presented by the dream image. Some are based on personal experience and some are not. Since we contain these qualities within ourselves, it is possible to see them in our outward expression as man or woman.**

---

I want to spend a little time with this, because it is a very important part of our self-understanding. I am saying we express both personal and impersonal areas of consciousness. It is not beginner's work to discover the difference. By presenting this idea to you in a chapter about masculine and feminine, I am hoping to plant a seed that may bear fruit for you now or in the future.

If what I am saying is true, it follows that we often confuse personal and impersonal energies in our lives. We do not see impersonal energies for what they are because of our personal involvement. In the case of unconscious masculine and feminine dynamics, this leads to mistakes in relationships with other men and women. This has to follow logically if we are unable to see the difference between the personal and impersonal. Something happens in a relationship and we react unconsciously from our personal perception. But what if the triggering event was not a personal expression by the other? Hurt, blame, arguments, anger and violence may easily follow, all a result of taking the impersonal personally.

Working with dreams can teach us something about this personal and impersonal dichotomy. We contain both masculine and feminine forces. As we identify the many faces of the feminine and masculine in ourselves, we identify those faces in others. More importantly, we start to see our projection of inner material upon others and pull it back to ourselves. We begin to see more of who the other person really is rather than the illusion we have unconsciously created about them.

This is not an easy process, and it's not for everyone to do. If we do take on the challenge, we are rewarded with richer relationships that reach beyond our usual ideas of self and other.

Many dreams show us the progress (or lack of it) we are making regarding the task of integration of masculine and feminine expressions. The dreams show us their different qualities and our inner relationship to those qualities. One of the most important lessons for developing heightened awareness is acknowledgment and acceptance of these opposite polarities that exist inside ourselves. The more we are able to accept and appreciate these very different energies, the fuller life becomes.

Here is a dream that illustrates some of what I am talking about.

# Faye's Dream

*I dreamed of understanding, grokking, that birds, plants, animals and humans are all different energy forms. God communicates to me clearly and says to trust Him and do as He says—all will be well. I dress as He says, with wings. I cross a bridge. I get sucked up into God's protection in heaven. I know birds are safe (protected).*

*My friend Phyllis decided she didn't want Bill, her husband, any more and wanted to go on to husband number three. I am next in line for a relationship, so she introduced him to me on the condition that I find the natural fulfillment*

*of my body . . . be willing to receive love. Bill and I had always been attracted*
*to each other, so this was OK with us. We hang around getting used to the*
*idea, and someone tells us that we need cups to make it official. We head for a*
*ceremony and grab some brownies along the way.*

At first glance, the two sections of the dream appear unrelated. Faye
"groks" (intuitively understands) that all forms are different expressions of
some universal energy. This includes her as well. God then instructs her.
This exemplifies impersonal, masculine, Father energy—"God," whom
Faye sees as masculine in this dream. This supreme authority is reassur-
ing and protective. Following God's instructions, she dresses in wings.
She crosses a "bridge" and is taken up into heaven where birds are safe
and protected.

Crossing the bridge represents a transition in Faye's psyche. This is a
bridge of trust. The action of crossing leads to the ascent to heaven. Since
this is all Faye's inner psychic material (she is the dreamer), we can conclude this part of the dream is about trusting her own masculine possibilities and expressions. The dream says she can trust and respond to her
inner masculine authority, that it is safe to do. In the dream, she knows
birds are safe; birds have wings; she has wings like a bird; therefore, she
is safe.

So far, the dream tells Faye she contains wise, nurturing and masculine
forces that can allow her to soar into "heaven," where she will be protected. The action of surrender to the advice and guidance of these forces will
lead to protection and safety. Then the dream goes on.

The next section states the conditions for success and fulfillment. Faye
must be willing "to receive love." She must allow herself to be receptive
to nurturing and supporting masculine forces. The dream says she must
learn to love herself and re-evaluate her inner relationship with masculine
energies. It is like the first section: trust in the masculine and you will be
fine, you will be fulfilled.

You can imagine how this might be difficult. If you are a woman reading this book, you can instantly relate to the problems involved in trusting the masculine. If you are a man, you can also quickly see this might
not be easy for someone to do. In our society, we have some rigid ideas

and positions about men and women that are not easy to shift. We fail to see that much of what we think men and women are about is an illusion created by our unconscious projections. Faye's dream represents a potential for an inner, personal healing of this conflict.

A third level interpretation of this dream connects to Faye's outer life. Faye has many unresolved issues with her real father. She works as an executive for a major American corporation, a position where she must use masculine modalities to succeed and where she frequently has conflicts of authority with male co-workers and bosses. This conflict is partially an expression of the inner dynamics implied by the dream. The implication for waking life is that she does not trust the masculine, because she is told that she can trust it in the dream. Do you see how this works?

There is a very practical result if Faye can integrate the teaching of this dream. Inner resolution of her masculine and unconscious energies will change relationships with men in the waking world. This will still be true even if her bosses and co-workers continue to be difficult and chauvinistic in their relationship with her. If she can integrate her own internal conflicts about masculine expression, Faye will be able to relate to men in a different way. That will create a more satisfactory result for her.

This is one of the most rewarding and fulfilling benefits of dream work; as we accept and integrate the inner material, our relationship to outer life changes dramatically. We relate to things differently, because we perceive them differently.

Shortly after she had this dream, Faye realized something was changing in her relationship with her real father. She has been trying to achieve this result for a long time. The change is for the better as far as Faye is concerned. Her work situation is also undergoing dramatic change, which excites her.

There is another important image to consider in the dream. This is the need for "cups" to "make it official." What will be made official is the union, the relationship of "Bill" (masculine forces) and Faye. The cup is an ancient symbol of the feminine, appearing in many cultures over thousands of years. A good example is the Holy Grail of the Arthurian legends. The Holy Grail represents nourishment, Spirit, life, mystery and God. In the story, the Knights of the Round Table seek the Grail because it will bring life back to the wasted, desolate kingdom and heal the King. It is a symbol of both the Christian mystery and the spiritual integration and union of masculine and feminine. The cup is man-made, but the form is feminine. Together feminine and masculine provide context for the formless, life-giving feminine spirit.

This image means that union with the masculine (Bill) takes place through action of the feminine (the cups). Getting the cups in order to make the ceremony of the union official means recognizing this co-creative interaction. In other words, there is no conflict here but rather mutuality that can result in fulfillment. The requirement is conscious acceptance of the conditions. In practical terms, she needs to reevaluate her attitudes and ideas about why and how men and women relate.

The brownies are another detail. Brownies relate to a more childlike part of the consciousness. There is a suggestion of the child in the image of grabbing the brownies. Childlike is different from childish. Childlike suggests the freshness of viewpoint and wondrous experience a child brings to its life; childish is quite different, the negative side of the child that expresses unrestrained ego and immaturity. This symbol suggests Faye can open to a fresh and new perspective that will nourish her. It is a subtle directive to allow a childlike newness to come forward in her perception of masculine/feminine relationship.

This dream illustrates one way that the masculine and feminine relate in the unconscious. It implies a possibility of resolution and fulfillment. Integration of the dream message will lead to better relationships with the men in Faye's life. It will change her work relationships and her relationship with her father. In her waking life, Faye has strongly ambivalent feelings about her goal-oriented and logical masculine side and her less structured, feminine side. The dream holds out a promise of resolution about this as well.

Just a little dream, that may portend a major shift in Faye's life!

Here's another dream about feminine and masculine. In this dream, the "sister" who appears does not actually exist. She represents an important part of the dreamer unavailable to him until the time of this dream. See what you think.

# Kevin's Dream

*I dreamed I was at my parents', in my old bedroom that I shared with my brothers. Only my younger brother is present. I am crying because my brother has just told me we have a sister whom our parents have kept secret from us. Then in come our parents, as it is the last day of my visit, and they have come to say good-bye. I hug my father and say, "I am glad to have had the chance to see you." He responded with, "No you're not, you're crying." My response to myself is "Well, that's just how he is." I am mildly surprised by this.*

*He then vanishes from the scene, which changes to another room. My brother and I are talking with mother, asking about our sister. My parents had kept her away at a private school or the like and thought not telling my brothers and I about her was inconsequential.*

*I then meet my sister, who is only one year younger. We catch up on the years, and I am filled with a feeling of completion. So much suddenly fits together on a feeling level, as if something that had been long missing was suddenly found.*

Kevin's dream contains both personal and impersonal elements, mixed together in the symbols of his family members and the sister who does not exist in real life. The dream begins with powerful emotional content: Kevin is crying because of all the feelings he has about the separation from his sister. Whatever she represents must be very important to him, and this is borne out and balanced at the end of the dream when he experiences a feeling of completion and reunion with the sister.

Who is to blame for this separation? In the dream, it is the parents whom Kevin is visiting. In waking life, Kevin blames his parents for a lot of things, especially his mother. Symbolically, in the dream it is their fault Kevin did not know he even had a sister. In Kevin's psyche, the parents represent psychic energies of authority and rule-making. They symbolize suppression and criticism and having to do what they want at the expense of Kevin's own desires. This information emerges when talking with him.

In Kevin's dreaming mind it is not his fault he never knew the "sister." This kind of dream information may easily be overlooked, because the mind jumps to the dream excuse—the action of the dream parents, who never told Kevin he had a sister. That would be a mistake when interpreting this dream. The first level, the level that simply associates dream images with real life people and circumstance, does not know what to do with this piece of the dream because Kevin doesn't really have a sister in waking life.

The second level of interpretation makes an association with feminine, feeling modes and says, "Aha! Because my parents rejected me, I suppressed my emotional, feminine expression (represented by the dream sister). It's their fault for not being sensitive to my needs." The third level message for outer life is that Kevin needs to look at this issue of how he feels very differently from the way he did in the past. He has to take back responsibility for what he feels is missing, and stop blaming his parents.

Like many of us, Kevin has a love/hate relationship with his parents. This is partially a reflection of the lack of love and affection he felt when he was a child. If you had a childhood with little parental affection, you may have a personal experience of what I mean. There is a lot of unrecognized emotional content here on Kevin's part. This is indicated when he hugs his father.

It seems that Kevin doesn't really care much when his father invalidates him in the dream. The father is essentially telling Kevin that he is lying. To whom is he lying? It's Kevin's dream, so he must be lying to himself! Do you see this? The father is saying that Kevin is lying because Kevin is crying. The action of Kevin in the dream is not consistent with his statement of gladness. Something is going on here! The something is that Kevin has blocked off a lot of painful feeling about his real father with a "that's just how he is" approach. This is part of the message of the dream.

Kevin dismisses an intense and emotionally loaded piece of himself with that statement. This is what he does in real life also. When I asked him what he thought about this section of the dream, his response was that he felt he had "handled" his feelings about his father and that these no longer were a strong factor for him. This is not so, but it was one of those times when pushing for a deeper recognition of the dream message was not going to be productive. Sometimes the content of a dream is so loaded that the dreamer can not accept an accurate interpretation.

By negating the father image and suppressing his real feelings, Kevin is negating himself. This leads to serious problems in Kevin's expression of mature masculinity.

The mother figure explains it wasn't important for Kevin to know about the sister. There is not much direct information in the dream about Kevin's mother, but we do see her invalidation of Kevin. It is simply inconsequential to her whether Kevin knew about his sister or not.

This dream mother does not care at all about Kevin's relationship to his inner feminine self, represented by the dream sister. This is true in real life as well. In Kevin's real life, the only person Kevin's mother seems to care about is herself. This piece of information emerges when Kevin talks about himself and his family. Kevin blames his mother for a lot of his unhappiness with women.

We have to be careful here. It would be easy to let Kevin's unconscious jump out and land on his mother where we could agree with it. Not so! Whatever his mother is really like, she is not responsible for how Kevin thinks and feels about the feminine, internally expressed or in the outer world. If we give her that power, we dis-empower Kevin and make him his mother's victim. Kevin is responsible. Unless we take this approach to responsibility, we do a disservice to ourselves and to others.

---

## KEY POINT
Responsibility does not mean fault, blame or guilt. Responsibility means accepting the possibility that in some way, conscious or not, we influence and participate in the situations we feel are not under our control. This does *not* mean we created the situation. It *does* mean we must develop an *ability* to respond consciously to the situation by being aware of our feelings and accepting that we are responsible for how we feel.

---

It may take a while to recognize we are responsible for ourselves and are not the victims we think we are. Most of us walk around in a semi-permanent state of what I call Victim Consciousness. Victim Consciousness means we think and act in ways proving we are at the effect of negative events that happen in life. We think others are responsible for the quality and circumstances of our lives. The consequences are predictable and far-reaching. Blame, anger, misplaced action and personal disempowerment are all guaranteed if we unconsciously think of ourselves as victims.

We may not be responsible for the random, negative events that occur in life, or for the actions of people who hurt us in some way or cause negative changes to take place. But we are absolutely responsible for the way we deal with these events and the way we feel about them. The idea we are responsible for the way we feel has never been popular. It is much easier to blame someone else for bad feelings than to take personal accountability. It took me years of work to turn this simple, spiritual concept into a working reality.

Since we are the ones who are having the disturbing feelings, we are the only ones who can do anything about them. We are responsible for how we feel, not others, regardless of outer events or situations that provoked the feeling response. This does not mean we should repress or manipulate our feelings, simply that we are ultimately the only ones who can affect them. This is really the subject for another book! For now, see if you can consider this as a true teaching.

Back in Kevin's dream, there is good news. This is a dream of resolution, because he establishes communication and meeting with the sister. She is younger than he is, meaning this is not a mature, developed part of himself. That follows, doesn't it? The sister represents possibilities of intuitive expression and emotional depth not available in the past. Kevin has accessed another dimension of self that will compliment and balance his masculine perspective. This can only mean good things for the future.

So far, we have looked at two dreams providing examples of the dreamers' inner relationship with feminine and masculine aspects. In the dreams, new energy is introduced, symbolized by the new relationship in Faye's dream and the sister in Kevin's. Here is another dream showing a different kind of relationship.

# Eric's Dream: Section One

*I am a warrior/knight, dressed in soft clothes and a cape. I am offered all that I need in the way of money and food. The catch is that I have to serve some authority (I'm not sure what). At first it is appealing, but I am suspicious and I do not accept. Because I do not accept, I suddenly find myself being controlled. My will is not my own. There is another heroic figure who is in charge. He is stern, blond, and wears a blue cape. He carries a sword.*

*I also carry a sword, but because my will is being controlled I can not use it as well as I once did. I am not completely under control, but it is only a question of time unless I escape. I am forced to take a sword exercise with others but the swordplay is clumsy, since everyone is under control. I am struggling inside not to succumb to the influence of the heroic figure.*

*Then it is dusk in the dream. I am sitting with a female figure, also heroic with cape and sword. She too is being controlled and we are talking about escape. She is in the same position as I am. We are sitting in some sort of court-yard and we are not supposed to be there. If whoever controls us should sees us there, we will be in trouble. We are trying to think how we can escape. All the time I am fighting the control impulses. I am tired of fighting and almost at the limit of resistance. Once I succumb, I will not be able to break free. The woman is also my lover, and part of the control issue is to separate us.*

There is another section to the dream but let's stop here for a moment. Please take a few minutes to look at the dream and see what you feel about it.

It is clear that the dominant issue of the dream is control. Control of what? This dream is talking about the way Eric sees the masculine/feminine internally. It shows how he unconsciously deals with the relationship between the two.

The heroic figures, man and woman, are warriors, fighters. Eric is also a knight, a noble warrior. Knights, good or bad, fight for Lords and Kings. They are in service to these higher authorities. The blond knight is a mythic, archetypal figure, an embodiment of the energy concerned only with war; he is compassionless and stern. An *archetype* is a kind of universal, over-arching patterning of perception and impersonal content. This archetype symbolizes an aspect of the masculine not concerned with life. It is the energy idealized in the Nazi mythology of the Aryan, Teutonic knight. This figure does not support joy or love in life, but dedicates itself to ideals of loyalty and war.

Eric and his woman companion are also warriors. This shows a correlation and similarity between them and the blond knight. All three are in some way the same. When you and a dream character are similar in some way, you can be sure whatever that character represents is something you need to notice about yourself. However, in this dream, there is also a difference. Eric does not want to succumb to the blond knight, the authoritative and cold symbol of the masculine, even though it offers him money (energy) and food (nourishment). As a result, a battle of wills is joined. Eric is engaged in an inner struggle that will affect the way he expresses and manifests his masculinity in the outer world.

Part of the control issue is to split Eric off from the inner feminine counterpart of his masculine warrior energy. That is one way the masculine gains control in the psyche (of men or women), and it often results in very unbalanced expression in waking life.

In company with the woman companion who mirrors and complements his masculine, Eric has come this far: but now he is in trouble. They are trapped, losing the battle, afraid of defeat and weary. Eric is fighting to maintain the connection to his inner feminine forces. Something more is needed, if Eric is to recover his will.

The masculine symbol of the sword stands for Eric's ability to survive in the world using his masculine strengths. There is trouble here as well. Because of the internal conflict of direction and will, Eric can no longer wield the sword well as he once could. He has become disempowered and ineffective in masculine expression. This could show up in many ways in outer life, including sexual dysfunction.

All of this adds up to an important dream and a crisis in Eric's life. You can be sure this inner struggle and disempowerment were reflected at this time in Eric's outer world. He was ineffective, self-doubting, angry and confused. Things were not going well for him. And yes, symptoms of sexual difficulties were surfacing.

The dream has shown the problem; now it will reveal a potential for resolution.

# Eric's Dream: Section Two

*There is another female figure there, sitting across from me. She is dark haired, fair skinned. She is a friend, and I want her to help us. She would like to help, but is unable to because she is also at the effect of the controlling force. I feel like crying. Heroes such as I am are not supposed to cry, yet something tells me in the dream that if I cry it will help me escape. I resist crying momentarily, but I am so tired of fighting and I know there is little I can do. I begin to cry, deeply. Then I wake up.*

This female figure is a new, different representation of Eric's inner feminine energies. She is dark haired, contrasting with the blond warrior and Eric's blond lover. The contrast symbolically sends a message that she carries a different kind of energy and, presumably, a different kind of possibility. She is willing to help but cannot as long as she is being watched or controlled by the force Eric is fighting. In real life, the issue of control for Eric is partially about suppressing what she represents. This is part of the message the dream is trying to convey. It is his dream and his psyche, and he is the controller.

What is being controlled? The dream now makes it clear in a general sense. The "control" is a symbol of how Eric suppresses strong feelings and emotions through a rigid and simplistic kind of masculine expression. The dream does not specify the exact nature of the emotional issues.

If Eric will cry, he may yet escape. Resisting at first, he finally surrenders, tired of the long and hopeless battle to escape the force overwhelming him. The messenger of salvation is the feminine, and he will have to surrender to expressing his deepest feelings in order to survive. That is exactly what he has learned not to do in his life as a man.

This dream presents the classic battle between concepts popularly, though inaccurately, perceived as "Feminine" and "Masculine." In this limited view, the masculine is not concerned with feeling expressions. It is usually characterized as taking competitive and mental relationships with life in an effort to achieve dominance. The Feminine, on the other hand, is characterized as emotional and internal, centered in a feeling reality. These two ideas do not appear to be compatible. In Eric's psyche these old stereotypes and perceptions must be broken down. Although the perception is limited, it is true for Eric until he changes his viewpoint. It is a lot like the phrase "What you see is what you get."

The problem with traditional and limiting viewpoints defining masculine and feminine is that the viewpoint determines the experience. Eric's traditional viewpoints are basic to his experience of life, or he would not have had this dream. He has now come to a point in his emotional development as a man where the conflict between what he thinks and what he feels is interfering with his life. He faces a challenge of maturation as a human being. Successful resolution lies in potential surrender to his feelings and discovering new options the surrender can reveal. His old viewpoint must go. This can be accomplished by allowing the experience of his feminine self to guide him.

Can you see and feel this?

In each of these three dreams we see a situation of change for the dreamer. In each case a new relationship is being initiated and called for, a different ordering of inner masculine and feminine expression. In each case, a conscious effort to integrate and work with the inner change offers the possibility of a different external experience. The dreams point the way for the conscious mind to expand and explore a different life potential for the dreamer.

One of the mistakes we commonly make when we look at masculine/feminine, man/woman dichotomies is to assume the mask we see is the totality of what we are observing. It takes only a moment's reflection to realize that any man or woman is an immensely complex being, with many different ways of expressing self. The expression of self that we see in the moment is not necessarily what we will see tomorrow or what we saw yesterday. How many possibilities do you contain, for example?

Each of us seems to be a multiplicity of being and possibility, but we forget this. As man or woman, we express our personal and impersonal selves in any given moment. That expression is the result of an exquisite tapestry of masculine and feminine our psyche has woven. Our dreams show us which threads of the tapestry are in need of repair, which colors are dominant, and which parts are unfinished, or still on the loom. This not only helps us to appreciate our own complexity but also helps us see the tapestry others have woven in a new light of understanding.

The interaction of masculine and feminine in our lives has infinite expression. One of those expressions is sexuality. We will explore this in the next chapter.

# CHAPTER 10

# SEXUALITY IN DREAMS

Whenever I conduct workshops in self-discovery and personal growth, dreams are an important part of the work. Eventually, someone always shares a dream with strong sexual imagery. When I ask participants if anyone in the room has not at sometime or other had a powerful sexual dream, no one ever raises their hand. Sexuality is so much a part of human existence it would be inconceivable not to have dreams sexual in nature. Sometimes problems arise when we attempt to understand them.

When you look at a sexual dream you will find that thinking of sex and sexuality precipitates strong, personal, unconscious responses that immediately overlay the actual dream material. No one escapes confusion or projection when it comes to sex! This is a loaded area for all of us. If you have any objections to considering sexually oriented material, you may skip this section and move on to the next chapter. Dreams are often quite explicit when it comes to sex and the images must be explored in order to understand the dream content.

Before we consider individual dreams, I would like to share some thoughts with you. If we want to understand sexuality in dreams, we have to remember that the images are symbolic, like any other dream image. Therefore, by definition an image of sex or sexuality in a dream must mean more than is immediately apparent. Because of our unconscious psychic material, we are usually plunged into a reaction based on the surface image presented to us by the dream. All of our cultural and personal attitudes about sex instantly come into play. But if we treat the dream image as symbol rather than substance, we immediately open up a whole new range of possibility for understanding the meaning of what is presented.

What is sex? Once we get past our natural physical experiences, It is primarily a relationship of energetic forces. Sex is about relationship. By relationship, I mean a correspondence of energies interacting intimately together. There is an exchange of some sort, a blending and fusing that holds the potential for new manifestation. This is true whether we are talking about procreation or quantum physics. It is really forces and energies that are carrying out the interaction.

From this point of view, even the creation of the universe can be interpreted as a sexual interplay of forces. If we really want to understand a dream with sexual content, we need to keep deepening our perspective until we arrive at a place where sexuality is seen as a dance of energies.

---

## KEYPOINT
**Sexuality in dreams must be viewed symbolically to fully understand the meaning of the dream image. The true meaning of any dream containing sexual images cannot be discovered through an interpretation limited to a literal reading of the physical, sexual action seen in the dream.**

---

It is not possible to give a standard interpretation for a sexual image appearing in a dream. For example, suppose the dreamer dreams about having a torrid sexual affair with someone else's mate. It would be superficial and often misleading to interpret such a dream as simply indicating a wish on the dreamer's part to have an affair. This kind of interpretation can get everyone in a lot of trouble! Even if the dreamer physically desired the other in real life, this would still not give us the depth of interpretation we are looking for.

What does this desired person represent to the dreamer? What qualities does he or she possess that beckon? Because we now know the unconscious projects itself onto others, what is it in ourselves that we are seeking to fulfill with the other?

Right here I want to acknowledge the simplicity (if that is the right word) of pure physical desire, sometimes called "lust." There is an instinctual biological desire to further the species, triggered by many different stimuli. It is also possible to be addicted to sexual pleasure. Many books have been written about this. When we consider sex in dreams, however, we can assume that something else besides instinctual physical desire to further the species or simple physical desire is present. It is impossible to talk about sexuality in dreams without talking about feminine and masculine energies. We began discussing this in the last chapter. Each of us contains all possibilities of feminine and masculine expression. This will be a controversial statement for you only if you are locked into a perception of sexuality based on personal gender.

One of the principle ways the human mind perceives and learns is through the experience of comparison and duality. We perceive the world dualistically. For example, you would not know what "hot" was unless you could compare it with "cold" or "not hot." Everything we see and do in our world is ultimately filed away by the psyche in dualistic terms. Think of all the opposites we perceive. Up/Down, Black/White, Young/Old, Right/Left, etc. The list is infinite and includes Masculine/Feminine.

When our cultural value systems and beliefs are confronted with an apparent contradiction of what opposites are "supposed" to be, confusion results. A good example would be the wide range of attitudes and reactions that occur when men display feminine characteristics and women masculine ones. If this is carried on into the sexual area there is liable to be a polarization based on judgment and disapproval by the majority, in turn based on unconscious and unrecognized material.

This carries over into the interpretation of dreams. If a heterosexual man has a "homosexual" dream, he is likely to become so activated by the images that the entire point of the dream message is lost. This is especially true if he has taken on a feminine role in the dream activity. The problem, as always, is superimposing the outer mind's beliefs about life and "right behavior" onto the unconscious, which could not care less.

---

### KEY POINT
**The unconscious mind does not make distinctions based on learned belief systems or cultural value judgments about sexuality and sexual behavior.**

---

This statement also holds true for any other kind of behavior. I want to reiterate that the unconscious is not bound by the behavioral and cultural values we have adopted, whatever they may be.

If this statement is true, then sexual material presented in our dreams is a symbolic message showing us something we are attempting to integrate or unite with internally. This may or may not require action externally. It does require contemplation if any value is to come from the message.

The message of any dream can always be read on several different levels containing progressively more information. When we look at dreams with sexual content there may indeed be a first level that has to do with physical desire. We dream of having sex with another, actual person and in waking reality we desire them. This might not be consciously recognized, or it might be well known to the dreamer. That is valuable to know and is useful information. However, much more is going on, and that is the tricky part when it comes to interpretation. All of our ideas regarding masculine and feminine, as well as our value judgments about sex and sexuality, must be considered if we are to get to the real meaning of the dream.

Let's look at some dreams and see if we can get a better idea of how it works.

## Bill's Dream

*I was in a place like a department store, and I was like a manager. I had been interviewing vendors, people bringing me merchandise (selling). A tall woman came in and asked to speak with me. She had dark hair and was wearing a flowered dress, not particularly attractive. Another man came in and the woman faced him, ran her fingers down her body, and said, "Hello there. Are you ministering to Carol?" She was not attractive or sexy and I felt some revulsion.*

*A woman security guard came in and attempted to eject the woman in the flowered dress, apologizing for letting her slip by her (the guard). The woman said to me, "I guess we can't do business, but thank you for being nice to me." I said, "What is it you are trying to sell?" She said, "Why, myself, of course."*

Before we go through the dream, you may want to try an interpretation for yourself. Although you don't know the dreamer, there is enough information in the dream for you to do a good job. One piece of information for you; "Carol" is not an actual person the dreamer knows, so you don't need to know anything about her in order to fill out details of the dream images.

This dream illustrates some of the ideas I have been sharing with you in this chapter. The sexual content is mild in appearance but strongly present; it contains a message about relationship that Bill needs to appreciate and understand.

The setting of a department store tells us something about Bill. A "department" store has many different departments, carrying different items or inventory. This is a metaphor for departments or compartments of consciousness in the dreamer. Bill is manager of the store: he is the one in charge of all the departments/compartments. He has the ability to "manage" them.

This is the first useful piece of information for Bill in terms of his outer, waking life; he is in charge of what goes on here. He is responsible for interviewing the "vendors" who will provide items for the different departments. He chooses what will be added to the stock and what will not. That is his job in the dream—to select what the store will purchase. The dream is showing him that he gets to choose what his consciousness will stock and offer, like a department store.

Now the tall, dark haired woman enters the scene. She wants to speak with Bill, meaning she has a message for him. A dream character that asks to speak with you is always an interesting figure. Whatever she has to say must be important to him. She represents a piece of an inner dialogue, a character in Bill's inner play. The dream is a stage, so to speak, to present the characters in this inner play.

Another man briefly appears, an unknown figure. He represents an unfamiliar masculine aspect more approachable by the dark haired woman than "Manager Bill" in the dream. This is born out by Bill's revulsion towards her. The woman runs her hands down her body in a provocative and sexual gesture. Haven't you seen this gesture at some time or other? It is usually interpreted as overt sexual invitation, and in our culture is most often associated with "loose" or "wanton" women, or with playful invitation to sexual interaction. It's an invitation to relationship on the inner plane of Bill's dream and of his psychic landscape.

She greets the man and asks him if he is "ministering" to Carol. This is puzzling because Carol is a name that means nothing to the dreamer. We are looking at a hidden part of the inner play. "Ministering" is clear enough—to minister to someone is to care for his or her needs. The name Carol is a play on words, like the word care. Care/Carol. The dream is asking Bill if he is taking care of some feminine aspect of himself. This is an example of how the dreaming psyche can make a point through the sound of a word or words.

---

## KEY POINT
**Dreams often make a point through a play on words. This could be a written word, the name of a person, a word that sounds like something else or any image that when spoken aloud sounds by association like something else**

---

Bill does not find any of this attractive. In the dream, he does not see her as "sexy," meaning he does not want to engage in any intimate exchange with her. He doesn't want to relate. In fact, he feels revulsion.

Revulsion towards what, or whom? In the dream, it is toward this female figure/messenger. Bill's revulsion means he does not want to have anything to do with her or what she represents, and he is not interested in Care/Carol. He does not want to deal with the issue of caring for or nurturing the feminine side of self.

In comes a woman security guard. What a wonderful symbol! A female aspect that "guards" security. A watchdog and authoritative symbol, on the lookout for other feminine aspects that might bring disturbing news and breach "security," i.e., endanger the status quo.

Who is the principal feminine authority in our lives? Would all the people who thought "Mother" please raise their hands? In Bill's case there were many such figures, starting with his mother and including his first wife. This dream is pointing out to Bill that he perceives life based on the ideas of a feminine "guard" who is in charge of his "security." That's all right for children, but might not be an attitude that serves him in his present, adult life.

Are you following the interpretation so far? One difficulty people have with this work is accepting the idea there are distinct parts of self with different "energies" and differing agendas and points of view. We tend to think of ourselves as single beings with a viewpoint that is "ours." In reality, we are many-faceted beings, the facets combining to make up our unique personality and totality. If you don't believe me, just think of all the times you have been inconsistent or have changed your mind about something because you find yourself in a new situation. Different parts of you respond to life in different ways. Dreams show us the many facets of ourselves that we contain. By seeing what those pieces are like, we learn more about who we really are.

Bill's security guard represents a well-established inner authority guarding access to the "manager." To sell something to the manager, the vendor must get past the guard. We might wonder what has been turned away by this guard in the past.

The guard apologizes and tries to throw out the intruder. The woman then says, "I guess we can't do business, but thank you for being nice to me." This means the timing is not right for Bill to get the message or understand what she represents. "Being nice" means Bill has allowed her (and what she represents symbolically) to get past the guard. That's progress—at least Bill has now seen her.

The ending is classic. When Bill asks her what she is trying to sell, she says it is herself. Remember that Bill is the buyer and gets to choose what the store will stock. Do you think this means she is a prostitute? Of course not—she is trying to get Bill to integrate and appreciate a new and different aspect of his own consciousness. She is trying to get him to interact with the feminine in a new way. This implies change, but Bill is not interested.

In waking life, Bill needs to take a look at how he controls and regulates his behavior. The chances are he will find he acts out patterns of decision-making and behavior based in mother-complected and childhood dynamics. These are not fulfilling patterns for an adult.

We have definite ideas of what is masculine and what is feminine. We cannot get very far into dream work without looking at these ideas. Anyone who pays attention to current events knows there is a great deal of debate and disagreement regarding the roles men and women are supposed to play in society. This upheaval is worldwide; change is in the wind and often it is not welcome. Each society deals with the change in its own way. On the one hand, we see conscientious acceptance of change, with some resistance, as is found in Scandinavian culture. On the other hand, change may be met with rigid repression, as we see in a country like Afghanistan.

Our particular culture and upbringing indelibly stamps traditional ideas onto our psyche about how men and women are supposed to behave. Cultural ideas are established over hundreds or thousands of years. In our waking lives we act out of our understanding of what the roles are "supposed" to be.

The unconscious, however, is not subject to these cultural imperatives and can present the full range of possibility inherent to it. The struggle for expanded consciousness is to energize as full a balance as possible, so we may reap the reward of a life that lives up to its inner potential. To do that we must honor as much of ourselves as we can see. Dreams provide one avenue for discovering an expanded vision of self.

Over the years, I have developed a framework for looking at masculine and feminine that makes sense for me. I have tested the viewpoint many times, but I always come back to the same conclusion. It helps my understanding and seems both intuitively and spiritually correct to me. I offer it here to you, as a way of trying to understand a mystery ultimately not susceptible to definition. Please remember I am discussing the relationship of forces and energies, not individuals.

# The Roles of Masculine and Feminine Forces

The masculine provides a *context* for the feminine to express. Masculine energies define form and produce action in the external. The feminine provides *content* and *direction* for the masculine. Feminine energies bring inspiration. Creation requires a nurturing by the feminine, leading to form, expressed through the energies we label masculine. Feminine energy without the masculine is unable to take form and remains potential rather than manifested. Masculine energy without the breath of the feminine is essentially sterile and anti-life. Each is incomplete and unable to reach its full potential without the other.

In life, everything is a continuous dance of these masculine and feminine forces. They appear to us in dreams as the characters, male and female, of our inner play. Androgynous figures, that seem to be a fused energy of both, represent certain integrated parts of our psyche.

When we view sexual activity in our dreams we are viewing this dance with our inner vision. The dreams show us what is actually going on in our unconscious and how we feel about it. They will accurately reflect to us our fears and successes, our triumphs and defeats, our progress or regression in terms of achieving inner harmony and a balanced expression of the dance.

Here is another dream, difficult for the dreamer to share, because she felt so vulnerable to what she saw in the images. She said she was scared and felt ashamed because of the images in the dream and because of what she thought the dream meant.

The words people use to describe their feelings are very revealing. Their choice of words and the quality of their voice can tell you which of the many aspects inside them is doing the talking. If you pay attention to your own choice of words and the corresponding feelings, you can discover what I mean. This is valuable information. "Scared" is the word a child would use, and it tells me that the dream will reflect a younger stage of psychological development.

This dream occurred during a ten-day residential conference I was conducting. During a conference there is always a period of silence and fasting. This period of inner work is a very powerful experience for the people attending. Dreams tend to intensify and present psychic material that might not be as readily available in a different state of consciousness.

## Debra's Dream: Section One

*The dream starts when I am in the fasting and silence period. It seems as though there is a lot of commotion going on. In the other room, Gloria and Fay have a radio alarm that goes off. They don't shut off the radio. I can hear the news on the radio. I was annoyed they didn't turn off the radio. I left and came down the mountain and back to what felt like my home.*

The setting of the dream is during the conference, in present time for Debra, so what happens in the dream is likely to be related to present time as well. Gloria and Fay are two women who are somewhat older than Debra, although not "elders." They both have authoritative positions in the outer world and carry a sense of maturity in dealing with life that Debra admires.

The alarm is exactly what it appears to be: an alarm, signaling something that demands attention. After the alarm, the radio presents the "news." This is something Debra needs to hear and the information will be "news" to her conscious mind. She does not really want to hear it though! She leaves the conference and goes "home," to the place where she lives. "Where she lives," "home," is a symbol for the way she relates to life. It is the place where she connects to herself. It is the context from which everything is explored.

Can you feel this? Feel into the meaning that "home" has for you, and then go beyond that to the symbolic meaning.

# Debra's Dream: Section Two

*I come to my old home. This is my mother and father's home. There is a lot of commotion here, and I forget to maintain the silence and fasting. Then I remember, but it is really hard. I can't seem to communicate to my parents about the silence and fasting, so I end up breaking it.*

Now we have more information. The "home" Debra goes back to is the home of her parents. If you were interpreting, what meaning would you give to this image?

This section tells us that the message of the dream concerns a context of thought and perception established during her childhood. Something in Debra's present awareness is linked to that earlier time. The appearance of parents and/or their home in a dream signals that the material contained in the dream is in some way related to early stages of development.

When I asked Debra what the silence and fasting meant to her, she answered that it was her "true self." To her, the silence and fasting are a way to get in touch with her authentic self. In the dream, we see this is not something she can maintain in her parents' presence.

Does this sound familiar to you? How many of you have difficulty maintaining your usual sense of self around your parents?

For the second time in the dream, there is a lot of commotion going on. The commotion is in Debra's mind. Something is stirred up in her and she cannot maintain her sense of self amidst the turmoil. Debra said it was her mother with whom she was unable to communicate in the dream, who cannot understand Debra when she tries to communicate her sense of self.

If the dream had ended here, Debra would have a lot to think about, but we have not yet gone far into the dream. This particular dream contains a good deal of useful information on the first level of interpretation. It tells us a lot about Debra's relationship with her mother and how she feels about it. It tells Debra she has unresolved issues needing attention. The next level of interpretation suggests Debra must recognize that her own internal and parenting energies are not in accord with her self-expression. She does not connect with the part of herself that mothers and nurtures. Okay so far?

# Debra's Dream: Section Three

*There is a feast going on. It feels like a big family ceremony. Like a wedding or a big family reunion. Then I forget to keep the fast going. At that point, I real-ize that I will have to leave. I start to go back up the mountain. I even leave without telling my mother because I just can't communicate with her. I go back and as I am going back I see a bunch of people being led blindfolded by a leader. I think the group is from the Dharma center. It's some kind of initiation or test for students and the leader is guiding them through. They have to cross a stream blindfolded. I overhear some of the words that the leader is speaking but it doesn't seem right to me, it doesn't seem true.*

At this point, we have not encountered the sexual parts of this long dream. When we do get there, it will be easier to understand if we have the entire dream to look at. Dreams are often sequential in their pres-entation, so that each section follows upon the one that has gone before. The more remembered by the dreamer, the more we can see the rela-tionships between each section.

The feast at "home" proves too much for Debra's desire to keep fast-ing. The fasting, like the silence, represents something Debra wants badly, a sense of self as authentic and true self. She cannot maintain it in around her family. The kind of nourishment (food) that exists in the context of the family setting is not what she needs. She realizes she will have to leave and does so, recognizing it is useless to tell her mother.

So far, the dream has told her that she has serious and unresolved issues of nourishment, family and self-identity. These issues must be addressed to establish her true independence as an adult. Although she is married and long past physical childhood, she is still expressing childhood dynamics that are affecting her present life.

She heads back to the mountain, back to the conference, thus affirm-ing her desire to back herself up. This is a good sign in the dream, and shows she is committed to her own growth and independence.

As she walks, she sees the leader with the blindfolded students. These students represent part of her that literally cannot see what's going on.

She does not trust the leader. What he says sounds wrong to her, indicating that the path of teaching he represents is not the correct one for her. The Dharma Center is Buddhist. In the past, Debra has spent some time there, but it feels rigid and incorrect to her. The students have to cross a stream. Debra feels the stream represents some kind of feminine energy (this came from the dialogue with her about the dream). She is not comfortable with this blind crossing.

## Debra's Dream: Section Four

*Then I am in a bedroom in a big house. It's an old two or three story farmhouse. I'm in the bedroom with Jack. We're going to have a private session to work on the blockage of my second chakra and the womb area. Jack is working with his hands, doing energy work and massage. We look into each other's eyes and discover that there is a sexual attraction and that it is mutual. There is a sense of release in knowing that we have both been feeling these energies but didn't know it was mutual.*

*We start to kiss passionately and roll off the bed. Jack doesn't look like himself, he is thin faced and looks more like the red figure on the tarot card, The Wheel of Fortune, demonic, more that look.*

Part of Debra's feelings of shame about the dream have to do with Jack as a real person. Debra's first reaction is to confuse the actual person with the dream figure. Jack represents many things to Debra, including teacher and healer. She has done a lot of work with Jack in waking life. When talking about the dream she said she had a sense that the work "Jack" was doing in the dream was necessary for some inner healing, and that this required a masculine energy.

The second chakra is associated with sexual energies. In real life, Debra was unresolved about having children and was experiencing frustration in her sexual activity. The dream states that there is a "blockage" of sexual and reproductive energy. The symbol of Jack, if correctly interpreted, may offer a clue to the source of that blockage.

The Tarot card she mentions shows a central image of a mystical wheel.

On the bottom of the wheel is a somewhat demonic looking figure, red, with semi-human features. For Debra this is a "Demon Lover." The Demon Lover is an ancient figure in myth and story. Psychologically it can often be related to the father. For an excellent presentation of this relationship, please refer to the book *Addiction to Perfection* by Marion Woodman, published by Inner City Books.

The changed appearance of Jack in the dream tells us the dream is not really about Debra's attraction to Jack the person. It is true she is attracted to the real person, which disturbs her in real life, but that attraction is based on the unconscious material symbolized in the dream. Jack carries specific qualities that trigger unconscious associations Debra contains.

# Debra's Dream: Section Five

*Jack's body was very skinny and his penis was very small. It seemed like there was a large hole that I could see at the end of it. Jack got up and said that he would go and relieve himself first, so that he wouldn't come too soon and it would all be for me.*

*Jack comes back and we start making love. We're on the bed now. I notice that there are two girls sitting outside the window on the roof. They're between eight and twelve years old. Pre-adolescent. I don't want them to see me. They feel like tattle-tales. I go to shut the window, pull the curtains. I go back to bed and then the curtains open. I go back to the window, shut the curtains, go back to bed, the curtains open again. This goes on and we keep getting interrupted.*

*Then one of the girls is inside the room. She's watching. I open the window and stick her outside the window. I close it up and lock it. Then it starts to rain outside. I go downstairs to lock the front and back door so they can't get in again.*

This section is taking Debra farther into her unconscious. The size of Jack's penis is contrasted with the large hole at the end of the organ. Something in her wants to diminish the power of this figure, yet the large opening suggests just the opposite. There is also something in Debra that wants total involvement with this figure, "It would all be for me." All of the sexual "essence" of this figure will be hers.

But something is interfering here. The two young girls are watching, and no matter what she does, Debra cannot keep them from seeing what is going on. She is afraid they will tell on her. They represent younger aspects of Debra, and this section tells her the message of the dream has something to do with a pre-adolescent stage of her development.

The window cannot be kept closed. A dream window often represents seeing something through a filter of crystallized emotion, rigid patterns, or feelings held in check. A window is a barrier. The girl characters are constantly removing the barrier, exactly what Debra does not want. Finally she locks the window and shuts them out. She goes downstairs to make sure they cannot get in. Going downstairs in a dream is sometimes a signal one is going more deeply into the psychic content of the dream.

The second and third stories of the house where she is having sex with Jack are analogous to sexual/emotional areas of her psyche. It is also a farmhouse. Farms grow food, so this house is a symbol of an overall theme of nourishment (or the lack of it). The farmhouse provides the context for the sexual action.

## Debra's Dream: Section Six

*When I go down into the kitchen there are all these people. Women and children, all these people running around. I have a robe on. I'm shocked to see all these people and I ask one of the women if it's usual to have so many people here. She says, "Oh, yeah, there's always lot's of people here."*

*It's a really big kitchen, enough room for communal cooking, a big center. There is another woman there who does not feel like one of my relatives and she is pointing out her kids. I have a feeling that some of the people are my more distant relatives, cousins and aunts. I say, "I didn't realize, I haven't been home for so long."*

*Then I walk back to the parlor/living room area and there are two men sitting dressed in dark suits discussing worldly affairs, smoking. Then Jack is there on the couch. Now he is much fuller, more handsome—he has a robe on, silky, a silvery color. His legs are open and his penis and organs are showing. His penis is real large.*

*I'm shocked and say, "What are you doing down here, cover yourself up, they'll know what we're doing." Jack just sits there with a smirk on his face. I know that we're not going back upstairs. I feel so embarrassed and shameful.*

This is the end of the dream. The kitchen feels to Debra like the place where all the women's work is done. It is full of people from whom she feels distant, although they are relatives. She is detached from these busy women and children. They represent a whole cycle of maturity as woman, including the process of children and mother. This scene relates to the beginning of the dream and the estrangement she feels from her mother. It comments indirectly on her reluctance to have children. The kitchen is the domain of the mother. It is the place where food is prepared—nourishment again! Debra is estranged from this process.

The parlor/living room, on the other hand, is the territory of the men. Debra learned this cultural value while growing up. The parlor is the domain of the father, a clue that can help us find the meaning of the dream. The room is full of authoritative, worldly, masculine figures, talking and smoking. It is Victorian in concept. There is a distinct separation between the men (man) and the women (woman). Here is Jack again, shockingly displaying his huge phallus and smirking at her. Now Debra is terribly embarrassed and ashamed, as everyone will know what they (she) have (has) been doing.

Please take a moment here to pause and think about what the dream might mean. Although the dream content is highly charged and difficult for Debra to look at, understanding the message is crucial if she wants to move into an expanded sense of self as a woman and as a sexual being. What do you think the message is? What is the dream mainly about? You have all the clues before you to make a good stab at the correct interpretation.

If we look at the dream as a whole, several important points jump out at us. Before you read the list I have made below, you may want to make a list of your own of the most important images or events contained in the dream. Look back at the dream and just write down whatever images or thoughts seem significant to you.

## A LIST OF IMAGES/EVENTS/THOUGHTS
## ABOUT DEBRA'S DREAM

○ Jack is an authority figure and teacher

○ Sexual interaction; Debra's feelings about it in
   the dream and when telling it:
   a. starts passionately
   b. interrupted and frustrated
   c. embarrassed and ashamed at end of dream

○ Goes back to parents' home

○ Can't communicate

○ Feels like she can't maintain sense of self

○ Lover is somewhat demonic

○ Wants it "all for her"

○ Confusion and commotion with all the women
in the kitchen

○ Young girls interrupt her

○ Embarrassed by sexual display in the parlor,
   where the older men are

The main clues are these: the childhood association, the fact that she cannot communicate with the mother, the sexual display is embarrassing when the older men might know about it, and the young girls interrupt her with Jack. It is also important that she sees Jack as an authority figure. When you put these together, what do you get?

This is a dream of incest and frustrated sexual expression in relationship to the father, bound up in the childish part of her psyche. It is also a dream of the way Debra sees herself in relationship to her mother, although this is not immediately obvious.

For incestuous energies to be active and present does not necessarily mean acting out incest physically. No human escapes the conflict that arises in the psyche over sexual attraction to a parent. Without getting too far into the psychology of this, let's keep it simple and say that we are all attracted to the parent in this way, although it may not be consciously realized. This is human and natural.

Children are sexual beings, although adults prefer not to see this. The fact that children's sexuality is immature, uninformed and unconsciously expressed in no way limits the essential power of the sexual energy they contain. If you are familiar with the work of Sigmund Freud, you know he emphasized the immature, repressed and powerful sexuality of the child as a root psychological cause of many problems. Freud was well aware of the unconscious, incestuous patterns we all carry. One of the cornerstones of Freudian work is recognition of unfulfilled and primal sexuality rooted in an infantile, unconscious and childish desire to possess and control the parent, while pushing aside the rightful spouse.

Problems arise in the adult because in many ways the core of our psyche cannot recognize the difference between mate or lover and parent. We bring the unfulfilled expectations and wants that we experienced with our parent to our intimate relationships. This is not a new idea, although it is not always a popular one.

We may unknowingly project this impossible situation onto our sexual partner. This creates inner (and usually unconscious) conflict because of the taboos placed on incest, in turn leading to unsatisfying and frustrating relationships. The resolution of this kind of problem demands honest recognition of the incestuous attraction. You can see how this might not be easy to do! More than recognition is required. Healing cannot take place unless we can learn to appreciate, without judgment, the very thing that brings up the feelings of shame and embarrassment. In other words, we have to stop blaming ourselves for having taboo feelings and thoughts, appreciate that this is simply part of being human and move on. Not easy to do, but it *can* be done.

Debra's dream is showing her the problem. The solution is not shown, except by implication. Understanding the implication of a dream comes when you hit level three. A level three interpretation brings out the hidden meaning of the dream and, by implication, points the way to action or solution. It is the fullest level of understanding. Since Debra now knows she has a problem centered on an unconscious attraction toward her father, she can take steps to do something about it if she wants to. That might require time in therapy to resolve the feelings.

When Debra first told me the dream, she said she felt somehow that it was about incest. She had not yet analyzed the dream, and was overwhelmed with embarrassment about the sexual material. Debra can remember only two times in her life when she felt she had her father's full and loving attention. He was essentially unavailable to her. This is painful to her. Jack is a strong male authority figure who is "safe"—he is supportive of her and he will not take advantage of her sexual attraction towards him. This creates the freedom for Debra to look at the material in the dream with less emotional baggage. First, she has to see it is not a simple matter of physical attraction for a man who is not her husband.

Debra's mother taught her that genitals were "dirty" and should be hidden. Debra is imprinted with her mother's attitudes towards sexuality. She is full of ambivalent feelings about her sexuality and role as a woman. She is angry with her mother and is only beginning to recognize this. She is experiencing a classic conflict between physical desire and sexuality and the thought that sex is wrong, dirty, and forbidden. The main object of her childish desire, her father, is unavailable to fulfill these needs. She is stuck in an endless loop of frustration unless she has the courage to take on understanding, acceptance and forgiveness of herself.

You might need a mental break after this! Remember that the title of this book is "What Your Dreams Can Teach You." Superficial readings of dreams are fun but they do not teach you much. What dreams can teach you is more of who you are. As you learn more about who you are, you have more options for life and living available to you. Since dreams are an interface with the unconscious, it is impossible to do meaningful work with dreams without entering the realm of psychology. The good news is that you do not need to be a psychologist to understand your dreams. You only need a willingness to feel honestly into the images and make a commitment to trusting your intuition. As you work with dreams, your connection to intuitive understanding grows steadily, and this will spill over into other areas of your life as well.

Now we will take a short dream with strong sexual content and use the worksheet approach presented earlier to see if we can understand the meaning.

## Gloria's Dream

*The scene is a bedroom. Two Mexicans are raping another smaller male Mexican. I don't like what's going on. Someone comes into the room and talks to the smaller one. He keeps saying he doesn't mind what the other two are doing to him. There is blood on the sheets. I watch the scene and feel sick.*

On the following pages are an example of how we might use the worksheet with this. You may want to go ahead and do this on your own before reading what I have written.

# DREAM WORKSHEET

**1. Write down and review the dream (see previous page).**

**2. The images or events in the dream that I feel are the most powerful are:**

- two Mexicans raping a smaller one
- blood on the sheets

**3. I feel that the most important image is:**

- the rape scene
- smaller man says it's OK with him

**4. The way I feel about this image is:**

- sick
- unable to do anything
- somehow want to watch

**5. This image reminds me of: (put down anything, no matter how unrelated it seems, which comes to mind)**

- men are cruel
- looks very painful
- violation
- sex is painful
- men are animals
- I wonder how that feels
- why doesn't he complain
- I don't like it

### 6. The next image I feel is important in the dream is:

- blood on the sheets

### 7. The way I feel about this image is:

- frighténed
- messy
- something about this is important
- I don't like blood

### 8. This image reminds me of:

- women have periods
- women are vulnerable
- sex is messy and violent

### 9. Another image I feel is important is:

- the small Mexican telling another man that he doesn't mind what is being done to him

### 10. The way I feel about this image is:

- doesn't make sense
- he must like it
- disturbs me
- how can he like it

### 11. Any other details I now remember are:

- no others

**12. I feel that the dream is about:**

- something about sex
- how I feel about men
- how I feel about sex and men

**13. Another thing about the dream is:**

- I want to watch even when I feel sick
- the dream is saying that the way things appear isn't what is really going on, or what I think is going on

**14. The way I feel about this dream is:**

- the dream is important for me to understand but I don't want to look at it

**15. Some other thoughts that occur when I review the images of the dream are:**
- I feel both attracted and repelled by the images
- I'm very ambivalent about sex

**16. Review what you have written.**

**17. When I ask for help from within about this dream, I sense that the dream is about:**

- my feelings towards sex and men and some inward conflict about men and masculinity

## 18. My interpretation of the dream is: (from the Dreamer Within)

The dream is about conflicts of sexuality in the dreamer's consciousness. She has deep distaste and fear about expressing sexuality. She feels that men are uncaring, unfeeling and violent, and that sexual penetration by a man is a violation. At the same time, she knows this is not the only viewpoint. Because it is a masculine figure violated in the dream, she can assume there is a conflict about surrender to sexual energies and actions, based in a masculine perspective.

The dreamer carries strong masculine energies of control and dominance. To surrender this role in the sexual act is very difficult for her. The dream tells her this is possible and that no harm is done by this surrender.

The blood on the sheets represents life and sacrifice. The sacrifice is the act of surrender to the strong masculine and sexual forces. The Mexican figures indicate this is an area foreign to her: from another country, so to speak. This means she is not consciously aware of how this conflict arises within her.

Problems she may experience in expressing herself sexually have roots in the masculine orientation towards life she has adopted. This hinders her full expression as a woman. Because the psychic material is not recognized by her conscious mind, she has a strong tendency to blame men for her frustrations. This carries over into her outer life and is a result of projecting the unconscious material outward onto the nearest masculine screen available.

How did you do with your interpretation? This is very confrontive material for Gloria. If the interpretation above is correct, it reveals a relationship with sexuality neither satisfying nor fulfilling. It does point the way towards change if Gloria can shift her viewpoint. That will not be easy, because it demands acceptance and appreciation of masculine aspects within as well as without. On the one hand, she identifies strongly with masculine modalities and uses them to achieve success in the outer world. On the other hand, she intensely dislikes those same modalities as men in her life reflect them back to her.

You can see in a dream like Gloria's or Debra's the revealed consciousness of the dreamer. It is essential to shift into a centered and appreciative perspective when looking at dreams with such highly-charged emotional content. This is true whether it is your dream or another's. Be gentle and non-judgmental with yourself and others, for we all contain vulnerable and difficult areas. Dreams of sexuality reveal the primal psyche. They require the objectivity of heart-centered compassion for genuine understanding.

# CHAPTER 11

# SERIAL DREAMS

Serial dreams are distinct from what I call "progressive" dreams. Progressive dreams occur over a long period, sometimes years, and focus on similar psychic content. They show development of a theme, a progression (or lack of it) in the dreamer's consciousness, and present periodic updates on the subject. Serial dreams, by contrast, are like the old movie serials. They present a complete section of the story, with each new dream picking up exactly where the previous dream left off.

I don't know many people who have had this kind of dream. If you are a dreamer who has had this experience, I would like to hear from you. You can find contact information at the end of the book.

This kind of dream is particularly interesting to me. Serial dreams show the complexity of the psyche in a different way. Something in the dreamer has a coherent and long tale to tell. It decides that the best way to present the material is over a period of several days, in a consistent sequence exactly like the presentation of a storyteller. Sometimes, like the old serials, the dreamer is left with the knowledge more is to come and that the present sequence is finished for now but will pick up again at some undetermined future date. You know how the trailers in the movies say, "COMING SOON TO THIS THEATER . . ." Serial dreams are sometimes like this.

I think serial dreams are particularly important for the dreamer. Why else would the consciousness take the time to elaborately play out the message with such detail? The following dream occurred over a period of two weeks. There is often a day or two between segments of a serial dream. The woman who had this dream is an experienced dreamer and has been consciously recording and working with her dreams for years. She remembers her dreams in great detail. She is also psychically sensitive and has had difficulty integrating this into her outer life.

This dream presents some interesting material. You will have to watch out for any traps your psyche springs on you regarding the content. Remember that a basic rule of interpretation is that you must watch out for projections of your own unconscious material upon the dream. Ready? Here is the dream.

# Cassandra's Dream: Episode One

*When the dream begins, I find myself in the central marketplace of a small village. The village looks like one you might find in Egypt or Morocco. The people are dark-skinned and are wearing long, loose robes. People from all the surrounding countryside have gathered for market day and the central square is crowded and noisy. I'm there because I am on a trip led by a male teacher and a woman teacher. I'm traveling with about twenty people in the group and we are exploring the market.*

*It's very sunny and hot, and the air is filled with dust and spicy smells. Everyone seems to be moving around the square in the same direction as they look and barter for things. I join the flow of people.*

*Then I see coming towards me a tall, thin, dark-skinned man dressed in white. He and a smaller group of people are moving in the opposite direction to the other people in the market. As he comes abreast of me he turns, stops, and looks directly at me. In this moment I feel a compulsion to turn and follow this man. In fact, I feel that I am meant to go with him. But I hesitate. I'm afraid that if I go with him I won't be able to rejoin my tour group. The crowd pushes against me and carries me away from the man.*

There is enough in this first segment of the serial dream to provide plenty of information by itself. The setting is a Central Square and marketplace. This suggests that the theme of the dream is a "central" issue for the dreamer. A marketplace has many possibilities. In a market, we can pick and choose between many items, objects and foods. It is a place of option and choice. She is touring under the guidance of a male teacher who is in real life a well-known and respected leader in metaphysical circles. There is also a co-leader, a woman present. The woman is not identified. She represents a balancing, teaching energy. These figures symbolize the path Cassandra has been following in her personal, spiritual development up to this time.

The idea of a path is emphasized by the way everyone is moving around the square, all in the same direction. The hot, foreign scene indicates the content and message of the dream is not familiar to her. It also contains a lot of energy (hot/heat). There is a lot of commotion about her, a press of people, symbolic of a multitude of ideas and viewpoints.

A strange and commanding figure appears, dressed in white and followed by a much smaller group of people. This figure is moving in an exactly opposite direction to the rest. He represents, among other things, something that follows its own path and does not move "with the crowd."

The figure stops before her and she feels strongly she should go with him. Although she wants to go, she fears losing the group she is with. This means that if she follows whatever this figure represents, she will not be able to continue on as before. This is a figure of transformation and change. Then, in her hesitation, she is carried away by the crush of people (her ideas and viewpoints, agendas and older ways of seeing that do not relate well to this figure). This accurately shows the current, dominant way she relates to this new energy at the time of the dream.

This figure would be described in Jungian terms as archetypal: it is called "The Messiah." The Messiah and other kinds of archetypal images will be discussed later. For now, think of archetypal figures as representing psychic energies and patterns of behavior universal in human experience and consciousness. These figures occur, in various guises, in all human cultures. When one of these figures appears in a dream, we know the dreamer is dealing with fundamental psychic material. Something in the dreamer resonates intensely with what the figure represents. Such dreams are particularly important.

The segment ends here. It is introducing the dreamer to a new and disturbing energy. Future sections of the dream should take her into a further interaction and relationship with the unconscious material and develop the symbolic story. That is what happens, as we shall see.

The messiah in human culture is the figure who brings the true and divine word to man. If one follows the messiah, everything will change. The messiah brings the call to God and Spirit. If Cassandra heeds this figure she cannot go on as before, and her psyche knows this. So, she hesitates.

# Cassandra's Dream: Episode Two

*In the next dream, I find myself walking through the back streets of the village. The streets are very twisting and narrow and the earthen walls of the homes are close around me. I come to an opening in the wall to my right that opens into an inner courtyard. The courtyard is small and square with a bare, earth floor. Opposite me is a wooden door set into the wall and beside it a bell cord.*

*I step into the courtyard and I sense that behind me the male and the woman teacher from my tour group are standing in the doorway. At this moment, something compels me to reach up toward the sky. As I look up I am looking directly into the brilliant sun and I cannot see what I'm reaching for. But my hand grasps something and I find that I am holding a white feather. I know this is a sign I have come to the right place. The man whom I am meant to follow is waiting for me on the other side of the door.*

*I go forward and pull the bell rope and hear the bell ring. Then a small panel in the door is flung open and a very strange character peers out. He is small and hunched, and one eye is scarred. He is dressed in a dirty white robe and a turban. He squints at me and says, "What?" There is about him the feeling of a trickster or a magician and I hesitate. But I know that what I seek is on the other side of the door, so I say, "I've come to talk to him." I feel almost breathless as he pulls the creaking door open.*

Let's take a look at this dream, using the techniques for interpretation presented so far. If we use the worksheet, we can get a good sense of what is meant.

# DREAM WORKSHEET

**1. Write down and review the dream (see previous page).**

**2. The images or events in the dream that I feel are most powerful are:**

- the blinding sun
- the man with the turban
- the inner courtyard
- the white feather
- teachers behind me

**3. I feel that the most important image is:**

- the man with the turban

**4. The way I feel about this image is:**

- surprised
- unsettled
- I have the right to go by him
- he's a guardian of the door
- he's not trustworthy

**5. This image reminds me of:**

- Sinbad the sailor
- magical
- old movies about strange people in secret places
- *Ali Baba and the 40 Thieves*
- a guard

**6. The next image I feel is important in the dream is:**

- teachers behind me

**7. The way I feel about this image is:**

- like parents
- support me
- surprised they're there
- they're behind me
- good about it

**8. This image reminds me of:**

- parents again
- something in back of me

**The next image I feel is important is:**

- The blinding sun

**The way I feel about this is:**

- very bright
- warm
- attracted
- right to go for it
- lots of energy
- can't see what's there
- overpowering

**This image reminds me of:**

- Religious painting
- nature
- Greece in Summer
- good place
- powerful energy
- God

**The next image I feel is most powerful is:**

- The inner courtyard

**The way I feel about this image is:**

- secret place
- hard to find
- comfortable but strange
- like the simplicity
- feels right
- hidden

**This image reminds me of:**

- mysterious
- calm and centered
- an entryway

**The next image I feel is important is:**

- the white feather

**The way I feel about this image is:**

- don't know
- it means something
- strange thing
- pretty

**This image reminds me of:**

- birds
- white dove
- spirit symbol
- a message
- a key

**9. Any other details I now remember are:**

- no others

**10. I feel that the dream is about:**

Finding something inside me that knows a secret. Something about this I want to know. This man is important to me. There is something that guards the way. It's not trustworthy, but I can pass.

**11. Another thing that the dream is about is:**

- search for connection to God

**12. The way I feel about this dream is:**

I feel excited and like there is more to come. I feel good about the dream. I feel special.

**13. Some other thoughts that occur when I review the images of the dream are:**

- this is an important dream
- I am excited
- I am a little worried
- the guard bothers me

**14. Review what you have written.**

**15. When I ask for help from within about this dream, I sense that the dream is about:**

- something about the spiritual quest and my choices to pursue it

**16. My interpretation of the dream is (this interpretation comes from the Dreamer Within—since it is impersonal, it often presents the interpretation in the third person):**

The dreamer is ready to begin the exploration of a new spiritual teaching energy, bringing guidance and knowledge she has been seeking. She must watch out for the illusions her mind can place between her and this inner awareness (the trickster figure), but she knows how to gain access to it. She is supported in this task by previous spiritual work, represented by the teachers she has traveled with in the past.

The key to accessing the new guidance resides in her willingness to feel into the energies of life and creation. Although she cannot see how this is to be done, this is only a problem for her outer awareness. If she will find a protected, simple and still place within, she will be in the right place to feel into the energies here represented.

She must trust her abilities and hold firm to her intention to be with this inner guidance.

Did the worksheet help clarify the dream for you?

## Cassandra's Dream: Episode Three

*In the next dream, I find myself walking along a dusty country road outside the village. I am with my travel group but they are far in front of me. There are trees along the side of the road that offer some shade. It is early morning and still quite cool. Again, walking towards me I see the tall man with his small group of followers. They are talking and laughing. I stop in the middle of the road, directly in front of the man. He has an interesting, angular face and dark eyes that are full of life. As I look into these eyes, I instantly know that this man is something beyond the merely human. I say, "You're the one." By this I mean that he is one of the great teachers of all time and that his teachings are a translation of the divine to the level of human understanding. Because of the impact of these teachings, history will be changed. People will learn to live in new ways, but people will also die and whole nations will be swept away. I see in his eyes the knowledge of all these possibilities and I also see that this will not alter his course. I turn and follow him.*

So far, the dream has taken Cassandra progressively deeper into her involvement with this teaching figure. First, she saw him, going a different way, in the crowded marketplace. She hesitated and was swept along by the "crowd." Then she found a quiet, hidden place where he could be found. She was shown that she has support and access to this energy. Now the dream takes her to the next step: recognition of the importance this symbolic figure holds for her.

She is far from the village and the crowd; something is taking her out of her old way of seeing things and placing her into confrontive and direct relationship with the new. She has become separated from the "travel group," the context of a different teaching. The travel group also emphasizes teaching as exploration. The group coming toward her is happy and laughing. They represent a new possibility, appealing and welcoming.

Cassandra sees this is a connection to the divine. She is made aware that this means upheaval for her. "People will die and whole nations will be swept away." This kind of statement fits with commitment to the messenger of Spirit, and means nothing short of total change. Nothing will be the same. This result is inevitable, inherent in the process. She recognizes that following this energy will lead to transformation.

## Cassandra's Dream: Episode Four

*I find myself sitting by a campfire somewhere in the desert. The teacher is sitting directly across from me on the other side of the flames. Around the fire, his group of followers is sitting in a circle. It is night and the sky is full of brilliant stars. The air is cool, but there is a soft, warm, almost magical breeze blowing from behind the teacher. The group is talking and laughing softly.*

*Suddenly the teacher looks directly across the fire at me and it is as if no one else is there. He asks, "Are not the stars beautiful, the air full of promise, the desert ever changing and yet still perfect?" This description is so wonderfully apt that all I can say is "Yes." He touches the fingers of one hand gently to the earth and the other hand gestures toward the sky. He says, "You have created all this. Pay attention."*

Time has moved along in the dream. When she met the teacher on the road it was morning: now, it is night. This emphasizes the developing progression of the theme. Now the old group is completely gone and Cassandra is linked to the new possibility. The fire is a dream change in form for the energy represented by the sun in the earlier segment. It has been brought down to a human level, a friendly and serving level. The circle represents wholeness and completion. There are no more squares, as there were in the earlier segments.

A square can represent the logical processes of the mind; a circle carries a completely different feeling. The circle is also an ancient symbol of the feminine and of union and wholeness.

Now we arrive at the essential teaching of the dream. What is it that this numinous messenger of Spirit has to teach her? What is the message he brings that can sweep away nations?

The teacher tells her she is responsible for creation, the earth, the sky,

the stars, and all the beauty of creation that surrounds her. He is affirm-
ing her innate divinity. At the same time, he is reminding her that she
must pay attention. This is an injunction to pay attention to the way she
views life and to the actions she takes because of that viewpoint. In other
words, the dream is saying she creates life through her perception. More,
this will determine her experience. The implication is that she has not
been paying attention, or might forget to do so. Cassandra is being told
to affirm the divine perception of life and creation. She is reminded that
this is her task.

If any of us actually does this, it creates a vast upheaval in the way we
relate to the world. It is not enough to pay lip service to the idea that we
carry the spark of divinity, nor is it enough to say we love life. Only a shift
to an inner place that knows with certainty it is so will make it true outwardly on the physical plane.

With consciousness comes responsibility in a more expanded sense.
With consciousness of our connection to the divine comes a sea change
in our relationship with life. Certainly, nothing can be the same after that.

When Cassandra related this dream, she was caught up in her own
unconscious desires to have a real, physical Messiah appear and guide her
safely home. Her inclination was to see the dream as prophetic in nature.
She was just about ready to fly off to Egypt or Morocco! If you had this
dream, what would you think?

The desire for the appearance of the Messiah is one of the great, psychic streams running through human consciousness, particularly in our
Western tradition. It is also found in the East. (There is currently a powerful image of a new messiah in the collective unconscious, triggered by
the changing of the millennium.)

There is a trap here for the unwary. Dreams of figures bringing divine
messages must be looked at carefully. There is an element, perhaps, of
*compensation* present. Some dreams will present ego-enhancing material
in order to strike a compensatory balance with an unsatisfactory outer
life. If we have a dream singling us out for divine attention, such as this
one, it is a good idea to go slowly.

This does not mean the message of the dream is invalid. It does mean
we have to take time to notice if such a dream makes us feel special and

important. Cassandra, in her waking life, wants to be special. She is attracted to shamanistic work and the specialness of initiated and mystical states. Her dreams frequently have her interacting with strange and mythical figures. She has practically a full range of archetypal figures appearing from time to time in her dreams!

Cassandra needs to pay heed to the message the dream presents and at the same time watch for how her psyche might trick her into misinterpreting that message and distorting it. This is what is symbolized by the figure with the turban who guards the door, another archetype, named appropriately "The Trickster."

If you have a serial dream, treat each section separately and arrive at an interpretation unique for each segment. When you piece it together, it will make sense to you, just like a movie. Sometimes the editing can be a little rough, but the story is there, nonetheless.

# CHAPTER 12

# DREAMS OF CATASTROPHE AND WAR

As we move along in our exploration of different kinds of dreams it is predictable that "neat" classifications will start to break down. Our outer mind would be happy to have all dreams nicely compartmentalized, so that we could determine right away what it is we are dealing with when we have a dream. This is the approach often taken in books about dreams. One looks for an important image and then consults a list that says the dream is about x and z. The mind is outwardly satisfied by this logical approach.

If you have been following along with me, you know by now that nothing is ever that clear or simple in the unconscious. A dream always contains material expressive of our inner conflicts, activities and triumphs. The reason to work with dreams is to gain a better understanding of self. As we see more about ourselves, we gain the possibility of more freedom and options for personal expression. We develop the ability to choose how we will relate to life, with more satisfaction than we had before.

A dream of natural or man-made catastrophe or war never means just one thing. It would be simplistic to say that the dreamer is experiencing an inner conflict, for example. One can be sure there is an inner conflict, but what is that really about? There can be elements of conflict with authority, expression of sexuality, denied and repressed emotion, family history, compensation for feelings of disempowerment, unexpressed rage, fear of life and a desire for inner change, just to mention a few possibilities.

This chapter takes dreams of catastrophe and war and attempts to provide some guidance about them. The material might as easily fall into another category, such as death and transformation. At this point in our journey, the categories start to overlap.

It always amazes me to see how easily people who have this kind of dream slip into the trap of projecting the dream onto outer reality. A woman I know dreamed of a dam bursting above the town where she lived, and made waking plans to move away to avoid the flood. This is a true example from my experience. She made the mistake of confusing her inner world with the outer, and saw the dream as prophetic. It was indeed prophetic, but not in the sense that she thought. The dream portended a major shift and the release of repressed emotional material she had figuratively "dammed up" for years. Interestingly, after she moved she ended up in a town where she again lived below a dam!

Dreams of nuclear holocaust are sometimes seen in this way. The primal fear of annihilation activated by such dreams finds ready confirmation in the evening news and the genuine danger existing in our world of such an event. The dreamer then begins to act out of that fear, seen by the outer mind as an immediate threat brought to its attention by the dream. This leads to a skewed relationship with life and reality.

The error of interpretation is always the same; we impose the values and beliefs of our outer mind onto the complex symbolism of the unconscious, and project the unconscious outward onto our waking life. This has been pointed out previously, but bears repeating. My experience has been that we need constant reminding of this ever-present trap when looking at dreams. I have been working with dreams for many years, yet I still get caught in my own material now and again, especially when the subject is "loaded" for me.

When we dream of war and disaster, we are looking at a time of inner upheaval. The actions we take or experience in the dream tell us how we are dealing with this upheaval and can reveal the underlying cause of the upset. War is an instrument of change, as is flood or famine. There is always a change being called for in some way when we dream of these disasters. Usually we do not welcome change and we will tend to resist it.

We feel threatened in the external world when something looks like it will go against our wish to have things the way we think we want them. The threat can be perceived as a person, group, event, an act of nature, or anything else offering a challenge to the status quo of our personalities. Internally our dreams reflect the confrontation with whatever energies of change are being called for.

Dreaming of war is to dream of internal conflict and the destruction of something representing an older, established perception of life. If we can interpret the meaning of the dream, we can identify the conflict with accuracy. Once identified there are steps we can take to resolve it.

The following dream is a good example of imagery showing both war and natural catastrophe as symbols for the inner conflicts of the dreamer:

## Barbara's Dream: Section One

*I am in a parking lot of a shopping center and I'm walking between two cars when a huge airplane flies over (very low) making a loud, terrifying sound. I crouch between the cars and watch it fly away. As it does, it drops bombs. I look around and in the distance other planes are dropping bombs. Fires are starting. The man I am with yells for me to get in the car and we take off down the street. The streets are full of cars by now and people are fleeing, just as we are. Accidents are happening all over.*

This section presents several important images. The rest of the dream will develop the meaning of the images and give Barbara specific information.

The first thing we see is that the threat and confusion is general. Whatever this dream is about, it concerns Barbara's whole being. Her dreaming psyche could just as easily drop bombs on her, but leave everything else intact and normal! But bombs are falling everywhere, above and in the distance. Fires and confusion break out. The entire community is fleeing and this causes accidents.

This is a message in itself. It reads: FLEEING FROM THE SITUATION IN PANIC LEADS TO ACCIDENTS! Accidents are random and uncontrollable events with negative consequences. This is what she can expect if she does not pay attention, not only in the dream but also in her outer life. It tells her she is currently fleeing in response to a problem, i.e., she is not dealing directly with some situation in waking life. She is not able to deal calmly with the situation. That is predictable if she feels deeply threatened for some reason.

The airplane is a huge, impersonal and terrifying force. She is clearly not in control here. Something stirred up in her unconscious is asking for attention by way of this dream.

Barbara at this time was doing a lot of personal exploration and was beginning to get glimpses of feelings not allowed expression for many years. Mostly these were of loss, anger and frustration, involving her early childhood and adolescence, and her passage towards womanhood.

The dream figure that yells at her and tells her what to do to escape is masculine. Perhaps there will be more information about this later in the dream.

## Barbara's Dream: Section Two

*We somehow manage to get through the traffic and we head into the mountains. When we get to the mountains my companion knows of a house we can go to. He shows it to me but we don't go right in. He says we need to see the neighbor first. We are talking outside with the neighbor when something drives us into the house. There is a husband, wife, small child, the man and me. We are in their house in a corridor lit by a bare light bulb and we are discussing what to do. I have a feeling we ran inside because of looters and people running through this residential area.*

*While we are talking, I produce a newspaper that tells of the coming tidal wave—a result of the heavy bombing. The map in the paper shows that the coast will be inundated, as well as a great deal of the inland areas. My companion grasps the implication at once and tells me we must leave.*

Pull out your worksheets and let's see what comes up. You do yours and I'll do mine. See if we come to a similar conclusion or reading for what we have so far. Here's mine:

# DREAM WORKSHEET

**1. Write down and review the dream (see previous page).**

**2. The images or events in the dream that I feel are the most powerful are:**

- "head into the mountains"
- house of refuge
- nuclear family in house with dreamer and companion
- newspaper about tidal wave

**3. I feel that the most important image is:**

- the newspaper

**4. The way I feel about this image is:**

- wonderful image of "news" and event
- tells her something she needs to know
- warning

**5. This newspaper reminds me of: (put down anything, no matter how unrelated it seems, that comes to mind)**

- Edgar Cayce prophecies
- a dream I had years ago
- overwhelming event

**6. The next image I feel is most important is:**

- the family group

**7. The way I feel about this image is:**

- no safety
- nuclear family; family equals nuclear, nuclear war, disaster
- vulnerable

**8. This image reminds me of:**

- *Night of the Living Dead* (movie); all vulnerable to unstoppable and dangerous forces
- must be important to dreamer
- my own thoughts about family

**The next image I feel is important is:**

- house of refuge

**The way I feel about this image is:**

- not really safe—only temporary
- something about the neighbor first

**This image reminds me of:**

- not sure

**The next most important image is:**

- "head into the mountains"

**The way I feel about this image is:**

- mountains are masculine

- mountains are higher up
- mountains are more difficult to live in

**This image reminds me of:**

- place to get away

**9. Any other details I remember are:**

- none

**10. I feel that the dream is about:**

- the dreamer's way of dealing with the problem; big change coming for her; change already initiated and beyond her control; something about family and parents

**11. Another thing the dream is about is:**

- the dreamer's relationship with the masculine

**12. The way I feel about this dream is:**

- very important dream

**13. Some other thoughts that occur when I review the images of the dream are:**

- she's got a problem here
- she can't go back

**14. Review what you have written in response to the questions above.**

**15. When I ask for help from within about this dream I sense that the dream is about:**

The dreamer's way of dealing with change: a need to see something about the way she relates to life. She is on the run.

**16. My interpretation of the dream is:**

This section of the dream shows that the dreamer relies on masculine modalities for dealing with crisis. She seeks a symbolic place of refuge that must be viewed from a different perspective (the neighbor) before it is accessible, but she is driven to it without understanding, by the impact of events. The neighbor is a symbol showing she is actually quite close to understanding and gaining access to the refuge. The refuge is a symbol of energies centered on her childhood and family. This is the significance of the family grouping in the house. Responses for dealing with life established during this time of childhood are inappropriate for her present situation.

The newspaper tells her it is too late to avoid the coming upheaval and that she must take steps to prepare for it. Her strong masculine aspects have an ability to handle the situation, and she must leave the "family" home if she is to survive. However, she is too much under the influence of these masculine properties. Balance with the feminine is not indicated in the dream.

This is further born out by the image of flooding. The flooding represents an overwhelming force, emotional and feminine in nature, that will reshape the inner landscape. This is a force of dissolution of older perspectives and responses.

Did we come up with something similar? If you did not, remember that we are practicing here. It is OK to not understand dreams! Also, you may have a different insight and perhaps a different interpretation than I do. Trust what you get and take it all with several grains of salt. Eventually, if you keep working, you will develop a sense of certainty about dream work. You will know when you are right in your interpretation, when you are doubtful and when you can't do it at all.

It was interesting for me when I did the worksheet to see the associations that surfaced for me: *The Night of the Living Dead,* the Edgar Cayce material and a dream that I had not thought about in many years.

The movie mentioned is a grade "B" horror film you may have seen, a film that seems to speak so directly the mass psyche that it has achieved cult status. Much of the action takes place in a house attacked by zombie creatures brought back from death and uniformly hostile towards the living. There is relentless pressure by these creatures as they attack the house. The association in my mind is one of "no safety" in the home. The worksheet reveals as much about my psyche, perhaps, as it does of the dreamer's! That is a side benefit of working with dreams.

The Edgar Cayce prophecies have to do with a widespread inundation of the United States and the world, causing great change and upheaval of the established order. The dream that re-surfaced for me was about flooding and prophecy; I will share this with you later, in the chapter about prophetic dreams.

Perhaps you have realized by now that the worksheet is more than just a tool for working with dreams. It is a mirror of your self. The associations you write down may have to do with the dream; they may also have to do with your own psychic material. Your attitudes, conscious and unconscious, will be revealed about any subject suggested by the dream images. In the section of Barbara's dream that we looked at above, my personal material about home and parents must be taken into account when I assess the accuracy of my interpretation. If I know what that material is or at least know it is there, I can then separate that which is mine from that which is the dreamer's.

Do you follow me on this? In other words, if I know I have unresolved issues about parents and safety, I have a chance to recognize when that might get in the way of a successful interpretation. I have a better chance of seeing Barbara's dream clearly.

Most of the time when people interpret dreams they have not done this work of observing self, unless they have spent time in therapy or are professional therapists or analysts. The result is an inaccurate interpretation. This principle also holds true for other methods used for attuning to intuitive information, such as psychic readings, tarot readings and interpretation of the *I Ching* (the Chinese Book of Changes). The principles of dream interpretation presented in this book can be applied to these other methods: that's a bonus you get from doing dream work.

## Barbara's Dream: Section Three

*The next thing I know, I'm at the bottom of the mountain. I don't know how I got there. Chaos is raging about me and I begin my ascent back up the mountain. There is a stairway hewn out of the rock and I am able to get up the mountain easily. When I get back to the residential area, I find the house and my companion. He has a boat—a very small boat—and he says the only way to safety is to get in the river and go. We get in the boat and he accompanies me for a short distance. Then, he gets out of the boat and into the water. He tells me to go ahead, that he will catch up with me later.*

In this section, we get some emphasis and some advice. In the previous section, her male companion told Barbara she must leave the house: then suddenly she was plunged back into chaos. The dream lets her know how she really feels about leaving what the house and family represent (i.e., letting go of perceptions and behaviors unconsciously based on childhood dynamics that no longer serve her). In her mind, this will lead to chaos. The mountain is masculine in feeling and offers a safer place for her. Leaving the mountain—leaving a masculine perception of how to handle challenge, stress and danger in her life. Leaving the mountain—a descent into chaos. This is the chaos of the feminine forces. The contrast between the two places in the dream gives us this information, and it is a third level interpretation to see the contrast between mountain and chaos as masculine and feminine.

She climbs back up the mountain by way of a ready-made stairway. This is how she has done it in the past—gone back to the house with the family (gone back to earlier and well-established patterns of perception and behavior). This way is well established through practice and habit.

Can you feel how this represents a pattern of behavior in her psyche? This is a difficult dream and Barbara found it quite confusing when she worked with it. The key here is the sequence and the image. We have to learn how to pay attention to the sequence. The sudden transition back into chaos is confusing to our outer mind, which prefers orderly transitions. The sequence provides the clue for understanding: told to leave house, leads to chaos, leads to re-climb mountain, leads back to house (the established way of dealing with the situation). She is stuck in an unproductive pattern of behavior that has to change. In the dream, Barbara is told there is only one way to safety—via the small boat and getting into the river. The old pattern of behavior leads back to the same place and she will have to do something different if she is to find safety.

The small boat means she is not confident of success in this venture, but at least she has a vehicle for the journey. Success and safety means getting into the river. The river does not feel safe to Barbara, as we shall see. The boat is not a large or stable vehicle. The river represents a natural force not under her control. It must be met on its own terms. She will have to surrender to it.

The masculine companion leaves her and she has to go on. This indicates she is capable of doing whatever is called for without help from what the figure represents. She doesn't need him to move to safety. She is being encouraged to develop her own inner resources.

## Barbara's Dream: Section Four

*The water is moving fast but it is fairly smooth. It looks like a roller coaster ride—with water where the tracks should be. There is a framework ahead of the boat, like a trestle, that I have to pass through. I'm afraid I will catch my head on the frame and get knocked out of the boat or even killed. The first plunge comes up and I'm scared. I can see the girders ahead and I close my eyes.*

*I pass easily under the framework and the boat flows rapidly down the slide. It's not as dangerous as I thought. I continue down the river and through additional sluices, encountering no trouble along the way.*

The important images are the river and the trestle-like framework. "Like a roller coaster ride," means just what it says. When we are dealing with highly charged inner material, it can feel like a roller coaster! We experience an unsettling series of ups and downs not under our control. Ever ride a big one? Personally, I dislike them—they scare the heck out of me and make me feel ill. You might guess from this that I do not like being out of control, and you would be right!

The river is taking Barbara along. Ahead looms the "framework" that looks like a trestle. A trestle is a way to cross an obstacle—it carries something across the obstacle, usually a vehicle or roadway of some sort. What do you think this means? Framework—trestle—structure for getting over obstacle (river). Obstacle—river—uncontrollable flow that can lead to safety. This is frightening but turns out not to be as dangerous as she thought. Following the flow leads her to safety; but following the flow also leads her on a roller coaster journey she fears will injure or kill her because it may lead to a collision with the framework.

The framework/trestle represents structure Barbara has created to deal with her life, the way she has done it in the past. Up to this point in life she has followed a path that avoids the natural, inner flow represented by the river. She deals with this inner flow through avoidance, by staying out of it and using the framework she has erected to bridge over it. She is terrified by the possible confrontation between the flow of self and the structure she has built to avoid self.

The river is also associated with the flood predicted in the newspaper that will inundate things, i.e., inundate her psyche. This is not stated directly in the dream, but is a third level of interpretation. The relationship between flood and river has to do with the fact that both are uncontrollable and dangerous images of moving water. They both stand for the same thing. However, Barbara can pro-actively engage with what they represent if she chooses to. That is an essential point the dream is trying to make.

Once she manages to get past the obstacle symbolized by the framework,

Barbara encounters no trouble. The trestle/framework she used in the past to avoid the water has become a hazard rather than something to help her.

# Barbara's Dream: Section Five

*The scene changes to somewhere inland. I am reunited with the man and we are entering a town where the scenes we fled from earlier are being re-enacted. I am tired, fearful, and very wary.*

This is the final section of the dream. Barbara is not getting resolution here. Even inland, she cannot escape the chaos. It is like the saying that you can run but not hide. This emphasizes the difficulty and importance of the dream material. She is back where she started, faced with the entire sequence all over again. The dream reveals the problem, explains how she has dealt with it in the past and shows her how to take on the resolution. It emphasizes that there is no resolution (symbolized by the journey down the river) until she gets the message.

Resolution for Barbara, if there is one, will occur in the future, not now. For the moment she is still caught up in the repetition of conflict and chaos, and something in her is very tired of all this. Until she makes the shift of perception called for, she can expect more of the same.

Often in a dream of war, the dreamer finds him or herself attacking and killing some enemy; it is the nature of war, after all. In Barbara's dream the enemy is an impersonal and terrifying energy, represented by the airplane. This shows she does not yet understand exactly what is upsetting her. If she shot the airplane down or destroyed it, this would be a different kind of relationship with the "attacking" force than is actually shown in her dream.

If you find yourself at war in your dreams, notice whatever you can about the attacking figures. Are they men or women? Are they strangers or people you know? What is your response to the attack? How do you feel in the dream about the action taken in response? Were you successful in stopping the attack or were you overwhelmed? Is the war over, just beginning, or well in progress?

If an atom bomb goes off in your dream it means a powerful, inner force of change has been unleashed or is contemplated in some way. It makes sense to see if you can get a feeling for what the change is about and to notice how you feel about it. What atom bombs, floods, great storms, war and plagues have in common is that they are all impersonal and uncontrollable, essentially dangerous and life threatening. They are also, however, instruments for growth and change. If you do not believe this is true, think of how Europe, Asia and America were changed through the cataclysm of World Wars I and II (one war, really, with an intermission).

If you have ever been in a great storm, you know that a sense of huge and uncontrollable forces and the possibility of death are powerfully present. During a big hurricane, for example, it is possible to feel exhilaration and an intense sense of life, stimulated by the incredible display of nature. That requires passing into a different relationship with fear so that you can simply be present during the event. Making that shift also allows you to take the right actions needed, because you are no longer reacting out of fear. The same principle applies to understanding your dreams. The challenge with these kinds of dreams is to take on the feeling of the content and honor it without getting emotionally caught up in its power.

If a catastrophe takes place in your dream, what is its nature? Is it spontaneous or are you attacked, as in Barbara's dream? The kind of disaster that occurs offers many clues for understanding the meaning. A big storm coming or in progress tells you upheaval of some sort is on the way. This may make you nervous but does not necessarily have negative consequences. Watch out for the traps of your fears and preconceptions about things like big storms.

If characters appear in your dream, they will offer valuable symbolic information about the nature of the issue upsetting you. The first clue will be related to gender, which will give you a basic idea about the way that particular aspect relates to the overall problem. Are these masculine or feminine characters supportive, destructive, indifferent, confused, frightened, allies or enemies? How do they look? What kind of clothes are they wearing? How old or young are they? What do they say?

Always ask yourself these questions, if they are applicable. Every detail of your dream is important. Every detail contains a clue. Ask yourself, what is it that threatens me in the dream? Why do I want to flee or kill, surrender or watch, ignore or blow up? Why do I want to take the action I take?

The first level of interpretation relates to the activity in the dream and whatever the familiar association is. The second level reads the symbols and derives a whole new content of information. The third level requires an intuitive leap to understanding that reaches the meaning and implication and goes beyond logic.

Don't let the violent and often frightening material of dream wars and dream catastrophes scare you away from understanding.

# CHAPTER 13

# DREAMS OF DEATH AND TRANSFORMATION

Although I did not plan it this way, I find I have gotten to Chapter 13 and the subject is death and transformation. Thirteen is a number of transformation. It is the number of the death card in the Tarot. We all know of many superstitions regarding this number. Have you ever been in an office building where they pretended there was no thirteenth floor? Numbers on the elevator in such a building go from twelve to fourteen.

If I had a dream of a building with no thirteenth floor, I would be very uneasy. I would interpret it to mean I was avoiding some important issue of inner transformation and skipping by it. It may occur to you that labeling the thirteenth floor as number fourteen does not change the real nature of its location! It is still the thirteenth floor no matter what we call it. In addition, all other floors past that point are now inaccurately identified.

Our conscious mind is constantly attempting to change the nature of reality by labeling it as something different from what it actually is. We are always trying to categorize reality and make it fit our preconceptions or personally desired version of what is real. If there is a problem with making reality fit, or an incongruency, our first response will usually be denial. Sometimes by labeling something as other than it is, the problem seems satisfactorily handled, but this is an illusion. You can see examples of this every day by following the antics of the politicians and their spin-doctors, who often seem to be living in a dream.

Reality has a habit of challenging our personal illusions. When faced with a conflict between belief about reality and reality itself, we become confused. There are only three possible responses in such a situation. We can go into denial and paralysis of action, disempowering ourselves, leaving us at the mercy of whatever winds of change are blowing. We can retreat more strongly into the old belief system, in an effort to avoid the change being called for. We can embrace the new reality, at the expense of what we previously believed to be true.

I have been privileged to work with people who were very ill, facing death within a well-defined time frame. These folks knew they had six weeks, or sixty days or six months left to live. They also knew, some of them, that they might survive against the odds if they could find a way to release psychic and spiritual healing energies. These people always had dreams indicating what was really going on with the disease. The story of George and his brain tumor, given earlier, is an example.

Invariably, these terminally ill people were challenged to change some cherished viewpoint of life and their participation in it. Their dreams often pointed the way to the needed change. My experience has been that the dreamers got better when they understood the message and acted upon it. At the least, the quality of the time left to them changed dramatically for the better.

One does not have to be ill and near death to dream of death, nor does a dream of death necessarily mean physical death is on the way. Usually a dream of death, especially our own death or that of a loved one, throws us headlong into reactive responses reflecting our fear of annihilation, loss and personal extinction. In this frame of mind, it is not possible to arrive at an accurate interpretation.

Death as a symbol stands for transformation and irrevocable change. Whatever is dead or dying, symbolically speaking, will not spring back anew. But like the mythical Phoenix, something new may be born from the ashes of the transforming fires. The new possibility has its origin in the death of the old form. Until the old form is swept away the new manifestation cannot occur. Death means transformation.

Nature is full of symbols of transformation. The butterfly is one well-known example. Another is the snake, which renews itself by shedding its old skin. Without the shedding, new growth is impossible. You can probably think of other examples as well.

*Transformation* is a word sometimes taken lightly. This is a mistake, as transformation means nothing less than the death of something old so that something new can emerge. Make no mistake—if you consciously pursue transformation of self and self-understanding, you will have to let go of ideas and viewpoints you hold most dearly. These will not go easily.

When we approach transition points of transformation in our lives, dreams give us fair warning and good advice about the change. Dreaming activity may often increase considerably, or at least the number of dreams we remember. Sometimes it may take years to realize a transformation shown in dreams, understood only in hindsight. Other dreams deal with immediate or imminent change, already upon us.

It can be said all dreams are in some way concerned with our inner transformations, since we are constantly changing and experiencing new input and stimuli. In this chapter, though, I want to concentrate on dreams that clearly indicate a major change at hand, foreshadowing something with permanent effect. Perhaps as we look at some dreams of this sort we can get an idea of how to understand our own experiences of change.

Here are two dreams from the same dreamer, spaced some time apart.

## Carl's Dream: Number One

*I am looking at a coffin. The room is lit by daylight. Somehow, I know that the Feminine is in the coffin. Then I am in the coffin, which is closed over me and sealed. It is still light in the coffin, I can see perfectly. For a moment I panic, then I realize that I can get out of the coffin. I take out my little pocketknife and I work it around the edge of the lid and the casket. This is how I will be able to open the lid. Somehow, I can then see the outside of the coffin although I am still inside. I can see the point of the knife coming through as I work it around the edge. It rips through the lining of the coffin from the inside. The lining is pushed out a little by the action of the knife. The lining is a lovely, pale blue, perhaps silk.*

You can't ask for a better symbol of death than a coffin! But what is this dream really about? What is contained in the coffin, what has died? Remember that death as a symbol means transformation, a change of form and perception, leading to a new reality.

Carl knows that the "Feminine" is in the coffin, with a capital "F." Whatever his ideas and beliefs about the feminine are, they are in that coffin. Then suddenly he is in the coffin. Briefly he panics, trapped in the coffin with the feminine. To get out of the coffin he pulls out his knife and begins to work it around the lid. The knife is a masculine tool. Carl uses a masculine mode to free himself and get out of this situation.

He is also detached from this process, watching it from the outside while it is going on. The implication is that he is emotionally separated from what is in the coffin and what it represents. A second level interpretation focuses on the association of death, the feminine and confinement in a place associated with death. Carl feels trapped by the feminine in a way like death to him. He uses masculine ways to escape.

This is an interesting dream because it taps into collective images seen over centuries, symbolized in the work of the Alchemists. Alchemy is considered a pseudo-science, at best a precursor of modern chemistry. Nevertheless, the science of the Alchemists was really the science of the soul, an effort to understand spiritual truths and apply them in the daily work of the seeker.

The spiritual theme is beautifully symbolized in many written works from the thirteenth to the eighteenth centuries. These texts are full of death and rebirth symbols signaling different stages of spiritual growth and realization. The symbols have many variations, but always reflect the same underlying themes. One important symbol in the evolutionary sequence of spiritual development is an image of masculine and feminine forces (king and queen) buried in a coffin.

These figures have many layers of meaning, but could broadly be said to represent the relationship between the ego, or personal self (the king) and spirit and the life-giving transpersonal self or soul (the queen). In Alchemy, this symbolic stage of development was a precursor to union of the two opposites and the emergence of something new that combined the qualities of both. If we consider this body of alchemical work, we can interpret the dream to mean Carl is not yet ready for the union of masculine and feminine, the next step in the sequence of growth. He aborts the process, escaping from the coffin by using his familiar masculine tools. These tools are not as powerful as they might be, shown by the small size of the pocketknife.

Jung was fascinated by the work of the alchemical philosophers. He saw in their obscure theories and intricate symbols a vindication and confirmation of his own work, arrived at independently through the inner, transforming fires of his own journey. If you are interested in learning more about this very full subject, there are several good books available to explore. Some are listed in the bibliography at the end of the book.

I hope you are beginning to see how many times our dream material often relates to the balancing of feminine and masculine energies, in their many possible manifestations. It is not that one or the other is better or more important than its counterpart. Rather, we need to appreciate and consciously incorporate both, so we can experience a new dimension of wholeness and expression in our lives. Each of us will have unique challenges as we try to achieve this balance.

Here is the second dream Carl had, some time later, illustrating the theme of ongoing transformation. Based on his earlier dream and others he has had, it is a good assumption that this new dream also relates in some way to the integration of masculine and feminine. See what you think.

## Carl's Dream: Number Two

*I am with a group of people in a building. It is night. I am on the second or third story in a large room. There is a large, open window, no glass, just a large, square opening. I am looking out at a dark forest with tall, old pines. It is black out, a storm is rapidly approaching. I realize there is going to be a lightning strike, and move quickly to a different part of the room. The lightning comes with a terrific crash and rumble and strikes the base of a large tree outside. It is not far away, perhaps twenty or thirty feet. The lightning is sustained in duration and awesome in its display of purple-red-white light. It branches at the tree and seems to surround it at the bottom. It is very powerful and luminous. Awesome is the only way to describe it.*

*I look at the tree, which is still standing after the strike, and it is as though I can see into the heart of it, where there is a deep, red glow. I know that the tree is burning inside and will be destroyed. There is more very loud rumbling and crashing and I think there will be another strike.*

This is a dream of transformational initiation. The dream takes place at night, looking out into the dark forest. The feeling is one of something old, ancient and primal. It is one of those dreams that signal a long-term process. The tree is still standing after the strike, but we know it will eventually be destroyed as the fire burns. The transformational fire ignited by the blast has not yet consumed what the tree represents. The tree is a symbol of something in the dreamer's psyche, but the dreamer does not know exactly what that means.

The setting is masculine in feeling: a large room, a square window. A storm is coming. The storm represents an upheaval of beliefs and ideas for the dreamer. As with dreams of natural catastrophe, we are seeing the uncontrollable power of natural forces. The storm is gathering for Carl.

The window is open and large and looks out on a dark forest. The absence of glass shows there is no barrier between the dreamer and the events outside. Because Carl is inside the room, he is somewhat removed from the ferocity of the storm but he is not fully insulated or separated from it. If there were glass in the window it would indicate a detachment or insulation from the events, a separation. That is not the case here, and this means Carl is already involved with the material. This is similar to the earlier dream where Carl was standing outside of the coffin watching himself work his way out. He was both in and out of the coffin, both detached and involved.

When the storm arrives, the transforming energy of the lightning blasts the tree at the base. The tree symbolizes a strong, old and powerful relationship with life. It is old growth, old perspectives, well established and therefore central to Carl's viewpoint about life. It is a life symbol, a living tree. It is a masculine symbol. This tree represents something fundamental for Carl.

The tree could represent a masculine relationship with natural forces. If this is what is being destroyed (destroyed—transformed) by the lightning, the implication is that a new kind of relationship, perhaps more feminine in nature, must be initiated. It could also signal a rebirth of the masculine, but the clear meaning will not emerge for some time.

The dreamer does not know what this dream means. It is also clear at the end of the dream that more is to come, but what that will look like is not shown. That is consistent with a long-term transformational process. We usually know what has been transformed only in hindsight.

The dreamer can see into the heart of the tree, glowing and burning. The transforming lightning has gone straight to the heart of things. Perhaps we are looking at a symbol of the transformative heart chakra energies. When the heart ignites, old beliefs and structures are inevitably destroyed, since life does not at all look the same from the perception of heart appreciation. In my workshops, I try to guide people into an experience of this transformational energy.

The people in the room represent other parts of the dreamer's consciousness. He moves away from the strike, indicating reluctance to participate in what the lightning is symbolically initiating for him.

To sum up, a dream such as this heralds permanent change taking place in the psyche. There is no indication as to where the change will lead.

The person who had this dream actively pursues self-discovery and exploration in his waking life. To Carl, transformational energies are tangible realities. One thing is for sure; the dream represents something already initiated for the dreamer over which he has no control. He is symbolically dealing with forces beyond his comprehension, emphasized by the dazzling display about the base of the tree when the lightning strikes. I predict it will take years for the full meaning of this dream to emerge.

---

## KEY POINT
**Sometimes dreams present imagery indicating the beginning of a long-term process not fully understood by the dreamer. It can take years for the full meaning of this kind of dream to become apparent.**

I have often seen dreams where powerful changes in the dreamer's psyche were foreshadowed by the image of a huge storm. The storm signals that the process of change is on the way or already engulfing the dreamer. If you have a dream like this, see if you can identify some area of your life where you feel threatened. If you seek, you will find. The key to using the information of the dream is to see it as just that: information. Once you know what the change portends you can take steps to adjust to it.

None of us are comfortable with change, and frequently we hate it because things will not be the same when the transition is over. Once transition is initiated, our choices become limited and ultimately come down to whether we accept the change or not. It is a good idea to surrender gracefully and get on with it. If we do not see clearly what is being called for, that's all right—something in us knows what needs to be done, and the task then is to be patient and observant and let things work out. This can be difficult, but we really don't have a lot of choice about it.

Images of transformation and change appearing in dreams are not always as dramatic as the example given above. Very frequently, images of buildings and structures in various states of repair or demolition, construction or renovation appear, symbolic of internal change. Sometimes the dreams give specific information of what is changing. Other times they show initiation of change without saying exactly what it is about, as in Carl's dreams above.

I remember a series of dreams I had several years ago, just before a major shift in my perception. The change was principally about opening to an entirely different experience of God and Spirit, and about my relationship to life. It was a renovating and unsettling change, foreshadowed by my dreams, which were full of images of buildings, foundations, renovations and new construction.

The first dream involved the demolition of an elaborate church. The church was a symbol of the belief structure I had built up over my life concerning God and Spirit. Dreams that followed over several months showed the clearing away of debris left by the demolition. This was followed by new construction: new foundations were laid and walls erected. These dreams were prophetic, because I later had an experience leading to the collapse of my old spiritual belief system. I felt very uneasy during this period. I felt considerable stress regarding the work I was doing at the time, which was deeply interelated with my spiritual beliefs.

After the collapse of my beliefs I could see in hindsight what the dreams had been indicating. While the dreams were going on, I only knew that this area of my psyche was undergoing change. It was not possible for me to know exactly what the change was until it happened.

Here is another dream using an image of a building as a central symbol for something in the dreamer's psyche. As you read the dream, feel into the images and see if you can understand what is going on. It will probably be clear to you on the first level.

Since you have come this far with me, by now you have absorbed quite a bit of information about working with dreams. Notice that you have already learned quite a lot about dreams and are, hopefully, better able to get the overall meaning of a dream. The hardest part is to get the theme. Once you have identified the theme, you can turn your attention to the details that fill out the dream and give more information.

## Kevin's Dream

*I am in an apartment, upstairs in a barn. There is a farmhouse nearby, and I rent from the owners. The buildings are in the midst of the land surrounding the farm, East, out near the interstate highway. I start frying a couple of hamburger patties but then leave on a trip in my car with a woman. I have a little concern that the hamburgers will burn while I'm gone. However when I return I find that they are still all right.*

*I have returned alone and go to the ground floor of the barn, which has large open doors North and South. The east wall has a large flapping section through all of which much light is entering. In the recent past, I have been here rearranging boards propped here and there for added structural support. There is now a sign posted to the effect that any more rearranging or addition of structural members will result in a collapse of the building. The openness and disintegration of the building suggest that it will not remain standing for long.*

Take a moment to feel again into the images. If Kevin were asking you to help him understand his dream, what would *you* tell him and what would you ask him?

Of course, you already know the dream must have something to do with transformation since it is placed in this chapter. But wouldn't you have known this dream was about coming change anyway?

The sign tells us right away that no matter what else the dream may be about the collapse of something is imminent. Although Kevin has been rearranging and propping up the symbolic structure of the barn in the past, anything else he might do along that line is not going to help!

A first level reading of the dream ignores most of the beginning section entirely and zeros in on the warning about collapse of the barn where he lives. Remember that Kevin has his apartment in the upstairs of the dream barn. If the barn goes so does his living space. Is it getting a little clearer for you?

At this point, we could stop and Kevin would have useful information. He would know that something he had shored up and rearranged was now about to collapse. He might come up with an idea of what was collapsing in his waking life. It might be a relationship, for example, or he might be ready to quit his job. A project dear to his heart might be about to collapse. By talking with Kevin, we might see exactly what was going on. If you had this dream, you might see what was going on.

Let's go a little deeper, to the second level, and see if we can get some more information. If we go back to the first section of the dream, several things stand out. The apartment Kevin lives in does not belong to him. He rents it from the owners of the farmhouse. The dream is set on a farm. A farm produces food; food is a symbol for the essence of nourishment. Kevin lives in the middle of a farm that he does not own. Put these images together, and we can see the dream is telling him that the underlying issue is about nourishment (a word that covers a lot of ground). He does not yet "own" the place where he lives, the place where nourishment is produced. Kevin needs to develop more self-acceptance and self-appreciation. For now he is "renting." Nourishment does not mean food in the literal sense. It means spiritual and emotional nourishment, food for the soul.

The place where we live is an expression of our self. It does not mean physical structure, although our house or apartment will reflect our inner attitudes. It means the way we hold the boundaries on our life. It is the place from which we venture out into life. It is our ego's perception of life.

It is also subject to change as new ideas and experiences are presented to us. Kevin is entering a period of change that will lead to the collapse of the old structure of his life and the potential for something new to emerge.

The theme of nourishment appears in the symbol of the hamburgers. Kevin is preparing food but then goes for a ride somewhere with a woman. This is a cause for concern in the dream, which turns out to be unfounded when he returns. This part is very revealing, because for Kevin the feminine is something that can interfere with his "nourishment."

Outwardly, Kevin does not trust women and sees them more as taking than giving. This is a major problem for him. He has built up a long personal history of painful relationship and loss, starting with his mother. Like many men, he has an ambivalent and contradictory worldview about women and the feminine. This worldview is part of his structure for dealing with life and may be part of what is on the way to transformation. Because the food is still good after Kevin returns from being with the woman, it suggests his ideas about nourishment and the feminine/women are inaccurate.

This is really going from a second level to a third level interpretation. Sometimes the distinction, a convenience created for the outer mind, becomes blurred. The second level notes that the hamburgers and the woman are in some way related, and that one issue is about nourishment. The third level, which I inadvertently slipped into when I was looking at the dream, reveals the implication of what is on the second level. In this example, it is that Kevin's ideas about women and "nourishment" are inaccurate.

What about the barn?

"In the recent past" Kevin has been shoring up the structure (where he lives) and rearranging the support. Now he can do no more, or the barn will collapse. It is ready to collapse anyway. Light is streaming in, from the East. Third level interpretation notes that the East is the direction of the rising sun. A new energy has dawned in Kevin's psyche, and the light could not enter if the structure were solid.

Kevin has been involved in self-growth and personal exploration for several years now. He has, in the past, taken much of the work and used it to "shore up" his confidence in himself and his way of dealing with life. He is at a point in his personal journey where he is strong enough to take on alternative viewpoints different in many ways from those he held in the past. The barn is a perfect symbol for this process. The dream says he can no longer continue in the same way. The old structure must go.

This is a positive dream in many ways. The dream barn could be collapsing into a dark pit; the light could be absent and chaos could be present. That kind of setting would indicate trouble and confusion and hard times dealing with the change. Instead, the fresh wind is blowing through and light is streaming in, a very different feeling about the change. The dream bodes well for Kevin's future.

We are constantly faced with change. At times of crisis or at critical junctures in our inner development, dreams will help us understand what is happening. Our outer mind may have no idea about what to do or what change is being called for, but there is always an inner guide and advisor that does know what's going on. This advisor is our friend. A good friend does not always tell us what we want to hear, because real friendship demands honesty. If we learn to trust the inner friend who speaks to us through our dreams, we will open a door of transformation that can allow us to access new heights of understanding.

This next dream also deals with the inner balance of masculine and feminine.

## Ellen's Dream

*Bill (my husband) and I had half-buried and half-covered over a dead man in our backyard. He was buried in the driveway going to our garage/shop. For some reason, we had to move him to the other side. We got him partially uncovered. The dead man really stunk and Bill was gagging from the smell. I couldn't smell him that much.*

*Then the dead man's arm shot up in the air because of rigor mortis. Outside the fence, a van with Auto-Electric painted on the side pulled up and a man got out. A friend of ours pulled up next. They both wanted to use the wood shop in the garage. Somehow, we had to get rid of them.*

*Bill went out to tell our friend. I kept the gate closed. Our friend knew about the dead man. He would help get rid of the other guy with the van. As I held the gate it blew open partially, but I caught it and got it closed.*

It would seem something smells here! That symbol tells Ellen to pay attention. Notice that the masculine partner, her husband, is gagging because of the stench but she cannot really smell it at all. This indicates she is quite detached from whatever it is she has buried in the "back yard." She does not know consciously what she has buried. The back yard is behind the house where she lives, a symbol for unconsciously hiding whatever the dead man represents in her psyche. When there is the smell of death in a dream, it means something has figuratively died and is psychically rotting, part of an alchemical process of ending and renewal. There is no guarantee the death will lead to new possibility. That depends on the dreamer.

The dead man is incompletely buried and she has to dig him up and move him to "the other side." The other side—moving him from an unconscious area to a conscious one. This is a third level interpretation. Does this feel correct to you?

The arm shoots up in the air suddenly. This was a difficult symbol for Ellen—she really could not figure out what this might mean. It is an emphasis, an exclamation point, demanding her attention.

A van arrives with the words "Auto-Electric" painted on the side. This is tricky symbolism. The words tell her an automatic response has been triggered in her psyche. This may have something to do with the dead man's upraised arm (calling for attention) because it comes sequentially in the dream. It is related to the symbol of the arm. Therefore, a third level interpretation says she goes into an unconscious and automatic response pattern when the masculine aspect represented by the dead man wants her attention.

An aspect is only a piece of the whole, a fragment of the totality of who we are. When we speak of aspects of the feminine or masculine we are breaking down the whole into manageable pieces for our understanding. Ellen relates in many different ways to the masculine. This dream is trying to give her information about one piece of what she sees as masculine.

We still do not know exactly what the dead man represents except in general terms. We only know he symbolizes something needing attention, something she has buried and now has to bring into consciousness.

New figures enter, two men, one a friend. They want to use the workshop but that would mean discovering the dead man. One already knows about him. Ellen does not want them to see the man—she blocks the gate, blocks the access. This represents an inner conflict. Part of the conflict has to do with work. This is true in her outer life, since she and her husband own their own business and create a product in the workshop. They are successful and overworked.

Her allies in the dream are Bill and the friend. They symbolize internal masculine thought patterns that co-operate in keeping the secret of the dead man. The man driving the Auto-Electric van represents the part of her trying to bring the whole situation to light. He is the one bringing the message to Ellen that she is caught in an automatic pattern of response. Ellen does not want to hear this and she does not want to open the gate to discovery of what has been buried.

Something tries to open the gate—the wind almost blows it open, but she manages to shut the gate anyway. The wind is symbolic of something that wants to reveal the meaning of the symbol of the dead man. She is not yet ready for the revelation, and that is why she gets the gate shut in the dream.

The dream is telling Ellen something is going on in her psyche and that she is not noticing it or paying attention. Moreover, she is in the grip of an unconscious and automatic patterning about the issue, whatever it is. She is not yet ready to take on the discovery of the problem or its solution. Do you see how I got to this? If not, go back and follow it through again.

How do you feel about this dream? A dream like this is a little confusing on the surface, as most dreams are. A first level interpretation would give valuable information if it simply noted that something was buried and stinking. If Ellen thinks about it and looks for some correlation in her outer life, something may emerge that makes sense. There is also a clue on the first level suggesting the dream is about her work.

Her work is very masculine. She manufactures a product with tools, according to schedules and linear procedures. The reference to work is found in the symbol of the garage/workshop. Perhaps a conflict is growing about expressing herself in this way, through this work. That is a second level of interpretation. She confirmed that she was becoming very bored and unsatisfied with her work when I talked with her.

All dreams picturing death and symbols of death, such as skulls or coffins, refer to the end of something or to suppressing and "killing off" something in the dreamer's psyche. Sometimes these dreams signal engagement with ancient, archetypal processes that can strike such a blow to the ego that feels much like death to the dreamer. Sometimes a dream of death actually foreshadows the real thing, but not usually. In cases of terminal illness, a dream of death may or may not portend the actual event. When it does, physical death is usually symbolized in some other way.

I will never forget the dream of a young woman with cancer (I will call her Jennifer) with whom I worked some years ago. She dreamed of a huge, dark and abandoned house. The house was Victorian, dilapidated, and Gothic in feeling. The setting was dark and oppressive. The halls and rooms of the house were strewn with garbage. Outside, a high fence surrounded the house. The yard was unkempt and cluttered with trash. Beyond the fence lay a beautiful, lush, green field. Jennifer yearned to enter the field, but in the dream was confined to the house and the yard.

This is a dream of physical death. A healthy person might have a dream like this and it could warn of a disease process under way or about to erupt. In Jennifer's situation, with advanced stages of cancer already present, I knew she would die unless something shifted radically in her consciousness.

The most important image in this dream is not so much the house or the yard, littered with garbage. The house is a symbol of the body and psyche ravaged by the disease and the psychological patterns that contributed to the cancer. The image that indicates death is the green, beautiful pasture, but initially I interpreted it in another way. I saw the pasture as a sign of life that could not be reached because of the barrier symbolized by the fence. I was wrong, but more about this later.

I worked with Jennifer intensely during a two-week residential conference. During the conference, focused on experiencing nourishing and healing energies, she improved. She had a second dream that seemed to offer hope. In the second dream, a gate appeared in the fence and the garbage was placed in bags stacked up by the gate, ready to be removed. Because I saw the green field as a symbol of life, I felt she might be able to reverse the disease process. I have seen the reversal of advanced, terminal cancer, so I know this is possible.

Jennifer was psychologically trapped in long-standing family patterns of dependence and frustration. During the conference, her energy and vitality visibly improved and she felt well again for the first time in many months. When she left the conference and returned to her outside life, she was unable to sustain the progress she had made. She was not able to change the routines, situations and relationships in her life that were making her intensely unhappy and contributing to her disease process. The noticeable improvements in her health vanished, and a few months later, she was gone. The dream had indeed prophesied her physical death.

This conference took place in 1986. Since then I have worked with thousands of dreams, and my understanding has grown. I want to share my observations with you because my mistakes in interpreting Jennifer's dreams exemplify one of the core difficulties with successful dream interpretation. That is the overlay of personal, unconscious material onto someone else's dream.

Initially when viewing Jennifer's dream, I locked onto an interpretation of the green, lush field as a symbol of life she could not yet access. It seemed to me that if she could reach the field in a dream there was a good chance for remission of the disease. From this point of view, the second dream indicated progress. Access was now possible, symbolized by the gate in the fence. The stacked up "garbage" I saw as ordering and cleansing of the internal disorder caused by the cancer.

My initial interpretation was correct in part. The disease process was clearly symbolized, as stated above, and it was clear that the first dream indicated a situation of physical death. Where I went off, because of my own unconscious agenda, was with the symbol of the green field. Later I realized the field did not represent life but was a clear symbol for the release from life she unconsciously desired. Seen in this light, the second dream clearly foretells her imminent death. Far from a "hopeful" sign of possible remission, the dream states she is preparing to leave her physical body after first getting things in order and "cleaned up." This is what she actually did do, consciously tying up loose ends and completing arrangements for her death. When this was done, she died.

What prevented me from seeing this right away? The answer, in hindsight and with the benefit of a better understanding of my own psyche, rests with my desire for her to get better. The real hook for me was that I wanted to be instrumental in her healing. I had had some success in bringing through healing energies in the past, and my ego was invested in dramatic and tangible results. Because I liked Jennifer and wanted her to get better, I made the mistake of reading her dream in a way that held out an illusion of physical healing. This was satisfying to the piece of my psyche that knows it can be of service in healing, but which confuses healing with curing. It would have served Jennifer better to recognize that death was truly approaching. Then I could have offered a different kind of assistance and helped her consciously prepare for the transition.

It has been an ongoing lesson over the years to see the traps my psyche can spring when interpreting dreams. This is particularly true when it comes to working with healing energetics. It has been humbling to see my unconscious ego involvement when taking on the role of teacher or guide to others. It has also been empowering, because seeing my unconscious agendas has allowed me to work more effectively and honestly with others and with myself. If you take on the work of interpreting dreams, you too will see how your unconscious presents its illusions for consideration. Dream interpretation has taught me more about the mystery and richness of the human psyche than any other aspect of my work. Perhaps it will seem so to you as well.

# CHAPTER 14

# INTERLUDE— LIFE AS A DREAM

About 300 B.C. a Chinese philosopher named Zhuang Zhu had a dream. He dreamed he was a butterfly, soaring free on the wind. When he awoke, he made the observation that he had dreamed he was a butterfly, but was not sure if Zhuang Zhu had dreamed he was a butterfly or if the butterfly had dreamed he was Zhuang Zhu.

I would like to take a break from inner dreams and offer you a different perspective to consider. I have said that our inner world is reflected onto our outer reality. It also works the other way. If there is a correlation between what goes on inside and what goes on outside, it must be a two-way street. By this, I do not mean that we create the totality of our external reality. I do mean we create our perception of that reality and influence it in some way. If it is true we unconsciously influence external events in a creative sense, then we could look at real events in our external reality and see those events as if they were a dream. This might tell us something we need to know.

This is not a new idea on my part and you may already be familiar with it. The idea that life can be seen as a dream is a key concept of Eastern religious thinking. The idea is simple; take the daily events of your life and look at them as if they were a dream. The approach for interpretation of real life or a dream is exactly the same: you apply all the steps you have learned so far for recording and interpreting dreams to actual events of your life that you are considering.

This can be an interesting experience and provide true insight about your life at any given time. I usually work with this approach when something disturbing or unusual happens to me, or when I feel I really need to know more about whatever happened during the particular day or days I am looking at.

This is another way to take the information presented in this book and use it as a tool for self-discovery and self-awareness in a very practical sense.

Here is an example from my own experience. The event was a car accident that could easily have resulted in serious injury or death. I have written it down as if it was a dream and then applied the principles we are studying to see if I could learn something about it.

## The Crash on the Highway

*I am going to Denver on the Interstate to look at an old vehicle. The car is running well and I'm feeling good. The air conditioner begins to work well, which is unusual. I am going the speed limit, 65 miles an hour. The car I am driving is my 1974 Olds station wagon, and I feel safe in this big, powerful and solid car.*

*As I am driving, I see an entry ramp on the right. Ahead of me, a truck slows down to let someone in. It is a moving van kind of truck, not a big semi but a large truck nonetheless. I pull into the passing lane and start to pass the truck. Just as I come alongside, the truck suddenly veers off to the right. It strikes a large pole and sign, and then veers back to the left towards my lane. This happens very quickly; I start to brake but I know it is too late to avoid an accident.*

*I try to avoid the truck but it slams into the side of my car. There is a loud explosion as all the glass along the side of the car blows in. There is a loud crunch of metal and I am rocked by the blow. I am still going at least 60 miles an hour. The impact of the truck hitting my car drives me completely off the highway and onto the median, which is flat and grassy. There is a huge cloud of dust behind me. I manage to stop the car and turn off the engine. The truck that hit me drives on and disappears over the next rise.*

So far, if this were a dream, we would have plenty to look at. The truck and the car become powerful symbols. The way the driver feels, the air conditioning, the speed, the accident itself and finally the disappearance of the truck all take on significant meaning. But there's more. Let me give you the rest of the "dream" before we interpret it.

*Immediately a young woman pulls up and stops. I get out of the car. She is concerned, helpful. Then an assistant District Attorney stops. I sit in his car and he calls the police. Then a major in the State Patrol pulls up in an unmarked car. All of this happens in a few brief minutes. I look at my car, which is totally smashed in along the side. I sit in the police major's car. The major is saying on the radio that he has the "victim" in his car. I think it is weird to be called a victim.*

*Then another car pulls up behind us. It is driven by an older woman, very angry. She has been chasing the truck that hit me at 80 miles per hour. She is very indignant and gives her report to the police. Then the truck that hit me pulls up behind, and then a patrol car pulls up also. After talking to the major, the trooper is clearly on my side. The trooper is polite, friendly and efficient.*

*The driver of the truck is sitting in the trooper's car with us. He doesn't seem to know what happened. He reminds me of a big, scared child. He is about fifty-five or so. He said he was afraid he had killed me. The trooper gives him a citation for careless driving.*

*The trooper handles all the details and helps me get my car to the other side of the road. It is still drivable although badly damaged. I go home.*

*Two days later I realize I have not yet given thanks for surviving the accident. It has taken me two days to return to my usual way of being and to calm down internally.*

Please take a few moments and review the images of the "dream." Let your mind play freely and feel into the symbolic meaning of the event. What is the message? What are the internal dynamics operating here? What can the "dreamer" learn from the "dream" of life?

Here is my interpretation, as given by the Dreamer Within. Interestingly, the Dreamer Within does not distinguish between inner and outer realities or dream events. This is like the comment by Zhuang Zhu. To the Dreamer Within any event experienced by the psyche, whatever its origin, can be viewed and interpreted. This is characteristic of an impersonal energy. It is not concerned with how the ego personality perceives the event under consideration.

---

## KEY POINT
**The Dreamer Within is an impersonal energy. It does not distinguish the source of any event the consciousness experiences. To the Dreamer Within all experience is real, whether from dreaming experience or from waking consciousness. This means that the intuitive powers of the Dreamer Within can be applied to any situation we experience.**

---

If you work with the Dreamer Within, you will develop intuitive perception that carries over from dreams to waking reality. Once you realize this, your perception of life may change. You will have to discover for yourself exactly what I mean. Here is my interpretation, from the Dreamer Within.

*The dreamer is at the effect of unconscious patterns of behavior established early in life. He is often deceived by the comfort these familiar patterns offer. This is symbolized by the purpose of the trip; to look at an old vehicle. These patterns are seductive and deceptive and will lull the dreamer into complacency if he does not pay attention.*

*The truck represents forces, apparently random, beyond the dreamer's control. He is shown that nothing can be taken for granted. The dream carries a warning message alerting him to his pattern of complacency.*

*There is much resolution in the dreamer's psyche about issues of authority*

*and support. He can now relate to authority as supportive instead of antago-*
*nistic, and can quickly rally support of the collective authority if it is needed.*
*He has also resolved many issues regarding the feminine, shown to be in good*
*relationship with him. A strong feminine energy resides that will go out of its*
*way to help him. This represents an integration of energies of anger with the*
*feminine that presented a problem in the past.*

*The aspect dangerous to the dreamer is clarified by the symbol of the truck*
*driver. He represents an unconscious and immature aspect, childish in origin,*
*which creates harm through its unawareness and inattention to the conse-*
*quences of its actions. Although not consciously destructive, it is careless and*
*dangerous in this sense. This aspect, originating at an earlier stage of con-*
*sciousness, is well developed. The dreamer must pay attention to this force and*
*be on guard for its appearance. Otherwise, severe consequences may result.*

*The dreamer needs to remind himself that his life is an occasion for gratitude.*

When this came through I was not comfortable with what I saw about myself, but I could not deny the feeling of "rightness" about the interpretation. There is also much positive symbolism for me in this event. It is true that in the past I viewed authority, such as the police, in a wary and antagonistic light. I have had many conflicts with authority in my life, beginning with my parents and moving on from there. To experience the authoritative support that instantly appeared after the accident was literally shocking.

I disagree with the police major's assessment of me as victim. I understand the kind of thinking that places this label upon someone in my situation. From my point of view, I am only a victim if I cannot see how I am responsible in some way for my involvement and my feelings about whatever has happened. Because I have taught myself to look for my involvement, I can usually find it. At that point, victim becomes an inaccurate description. I admit this is sometimes very, very difficult. From the point of view of the interpretation, my contribution is clear; not paying attention has consequences. I was paying attention when I was actually driving, but not in the larger, metaphysical sense that the interpretation is addressing.

Any judgment I might make on myself because of the interpretation of the event by the Dreamer Within would be a mistake. What is important is to notice what happened and move on, paying attention in the future.

If I forget to pay attention, as I almost certainly will from time to time, then my task is to pick up the thread of attention when it again becomes apparent. I sincerely hope another close call like this one will not be necessary! It won't be, if I remember the lesson.

You also can pick up the thread of attention by looking at your experience of life as if it were a dream.

# CHAPTER 15

# DREAMS OF BIRTH AND PREGNANCY

I hope that by now you are getting a better sense of the themes dreams present to us. In the specific theme, you can see the general thrust and meaning of the dream. Knowing the theme may not be enough to give you the interpretation, but knowing the theme will point you in the general direction.

This chapter looks at the theme of birth and pregnancy. What is the essence of birth and pregnancy? Once we put aside our usual ideas about it, we see that it is a process of gestation and the bringing forth of something new that did not exist before. As a dream symbol, pregnancy can indicate changes we are nurturing (gestating) internally. It follows that if we dream of being pregnant or giving birth, we are looking at an internal process under development. The development is either not complete or is new for us.

It does not matter if you are male or female in regards to this image. Men and women do relate differently to birth and pregnancy, and that is a factor in the dream. What is important is the fact that birth and pregnancy are part of a universal human experience, whether one is male or female. As a dream image, pregnancy is part of the collective, symbolic pool.

In our physical bodies, pregnancy and birth is the first initiation. The womb experience is embedded so strongly in our psyche that it is impossible to discount it as an unconscious factor. Since dreams access the unconscious, it stands to reason that the symbol of birth/pregnancy will occur in relationship to internal, initiatory processes.

To *initiate* something is to begin a process that may or may not lead to a specific result. There is never a guarantee that initiation will succeed or be brought to fruition. This was well known in earlier societies that practiced initiatory rites. The whole point of many initiations was to confront the individual with severe challenges that might lead to physical hardship or death. The confrontation with death was more than a test of physical abilities and skills; it was the spiritual challenge that had to be met.

Initiatory rites that do not provide the real possibility of failure or death fall into a slightly different category that I consider to be *rites of passage*. A rite of passage might or might not have the possibility of failure built in. A rite of passage, like an initiation, also leads to a different state of being.

I make the distinction because I see rites of passage as ceremonial acknowledgments of a new phase of natural development, states of development that come if one lives long enough. An example might be ceremonies performed to acknowledge the passage from girl to woman with the onset of menstruation, or the recognition of eldership at a certain advanced age. It is also true that a rite of passage might entail meeting conditions beyond just the natural physical progression. If the ceremony contained the possibility of failure, it would then blend into the initiation category. Rites of passage are initiatory and initiations are rites of passage, but for me the determining factor that determines the subtle difference is the danger of failure and death. The stress brought on by danger can lead to transformation.

Dreams can produce images that deal with either initiation or rites of passage, and these factors may overlap. A man or a woman may dream of a ceremony representing a passage into another stage of inner development. Weddings in dreams can be like this. Birth and pregnancy dreams are initiatory in nature, since it is not automatic that the pregnancy will be brought to term or that the new issuance will survive.

It is well to remember that our dreaming consciousness makes free use of imagery and events that actually exist in our waking life, such as work or family situations. A pregnant woman may dream of pregnancy and birth and on the first level, this will refer to the actual physical process.

The larger meaning of the dream will be only partially associated with the actual pregnancy/birth.

Here is a dream that occurred to a woman who, at the time of the dream, was going through a major inner transition. She was forced by external events to re-consider strongly held beliefs about her life. She could no longer ignore the conflict between what her experience was telling her and what her belief system told her ought to be experienced. Part of her conflict centered on developing an inner sense of direction she could maintain in the face of criticism from authoritative, masculine forces that were consistently invalidating her.

# Helen's Dream

*I was in an apartment, dimly lit, by myself. I gave birth to a baby boy. I couldn't deliver the afterbirth. I kept worrying through the whole dream about the afterbirth. I was planning to go with the baby to the doctor the next day, and I was worried the afterbirth would get infected.*

*Sometimes the baby would turn into a kitten that I had to restrain—it would walk out onto the window ledge and I'd have to get it. Someone in the apartment disapproved of the kitten. Then I went somewhere to the front of a movie theater. I saw Susan and some of my friends. I was hesitant about telling them I had a baby, but I did.*

*I was afraid to call my parents and tell them I had a baby—I was afraid of rejection and disapproval. Eventually I called my father and told him he'd had his first grandson. I realized I had delivered before my sister. I thought about putting the baby up for adoption. I didn't know how I would take care of him.*

This dream is very revealing of the emotions Helen was experiencing at this time in her life. Let's use the worksheet to look at the dream. You may already have a feeling about it.

Ask the Dreamer Within to help you as you work. What would you say to Helen if she asked you to help her understand the dream? How well could you feel into the vulnerable emotions shown in the dream? Would you be able to support her in understanding the dream without telling her what it is she is supposed to understand?

# DREAM WORKSHEET

**1. Write down and review the dream (see previous page).**

**2. The images and events in the dream that I feel are the most powerful are:**

- giving birth to baby boy
- problems with the afterbirth
- baby turns into kitten
- someone disapproves
- afraid to tell friends and parents
- considering adoption

**3. I feel that the most important image is:**

- giving birth to baby boy

**4. The way I feel about this image is:**

- worried/she is worried
- something new about masculine forces/energies/aspects in her
- important for her

**5. This image reminds me of: (put down anything, no matter how unrelated it seems, that comes to mind)**

- birth is hard
- no fun
- dangerous

**6. The next image or event I feel is important in the dream is:**

- problems with the afterbirth

## 7. The way I feel about this is:

- something that follows birth
- has to come out for success
- she will have trouble following through with this new energy

## 8. This image reminds me of:

- animals—something primal and basic
- stories about birth
- myths about birth
- blood

## The next image or event that I feel is important is:

- someone disapproves

## The way I feel about this is:

- people are like that
- she has something in her that disapproves of the whole thing

## This image reminds me of:

- parents' disapproval and non-support

## The next image or event I feel is important is:

- baby turns into kitten

**The way I feel about this is:**

• kittens are innocent
• kittens need protection from themselves
• she's worried about the safety of the kitten/baby
• the kitten/baby is in danger
• domesticated natural force

**This image reminds me of:**

• life is dangerous
• have to watch out for children and protect them

**The next image or event I feel is important is:**

• afraid to tell friends and parents

**The way I feel about this is:**

• she is very insecure
• too bad she has to worry about them
• are the friends like the parents?
• she doesn't approve/something in her doesn't approve

**The next image or event I feel is important is:**

• she's considering adoption
• The way I feel about this is:
• she shouldn't do that
• she's afraid she can't handle it/support it
• the baby is difficult for her
• she's not sure she can follow through
• important for her to understand

### 9. Any other details I now remember are:

- none

### 10. I feel that the dream is about:

- creating her own self/piece of self; her uncertainty about this in the face of disapproval from others, especially authority; something about the masculine; uncertainty about self-support

### 11. Another thing the dream is about is:

- she is very uncertain if she can follow through on this without threat to herself

### 12. The way I feel about this dream is:

- important dream for her

### 13. Some other thoughts that occur when I review the images of the dream are:

- she's got a lot going on about people rejecting/disapproving ofher; developing something new in herself confronts this

### 14. Review what you have written.

### 15. When I ask for help from within about this dream, I sense that the dream is about:

Birthing something new about herself that has to do with the masculine areas of herself; the reasons why this is difficult and dangerous for her; her relationship with authority figures; her perception of herself.

## 16. My interpretation of the dream is:

The dreamer is attempting to establish new areas of self-expression that are as yet undeveloped and in danger. This requires the emergence of new ideas about what she sees as masculine forces, inner and outer. The dreamer sees people as disapproving of her. She needs to consider carefully the idea that her thoughts of disapproval are seeded only in her experience of parental dynamics. Her thoughts that people disapprove of her result in disapproval of self; it is difficult for the dreamer to distinguish between self-rejection and rejection by others.

The dreamer is not confident this energy of self can be safely delivered, due to the dynamics of disapproval already stated. She is, however, able to recognize this danger and is able to confront it to some degree. She has courage that can take her through to completion. This is seen in her willingness to confront her friends and tell her father about the birth. The new commitment to self is symbolized in the dream when she tells her father.

The father is a symbol of parental energies and disapproval. He is also the prime symbol of the masculine and how it is configured in the dreamer's psyche. By telling him about the birth of a baby boy, she begins to confront the old pattern symbolized by the father and affirm the new, undeveloped, masculine possibilities symbolized by the baby. These represent an ability to shape her world and structure it in new ways, a function of the masculine.

However, exploration and development of this new area is not yet anchored in the dreamer's psyche. This is the meaning of the thought in the dream that the baby may be given up for adoption. The dreamer's uncertainty about self undercuts her intention. The result is a lack of confidence about her ability to follow through. The issue is still in doubt. This is further symbolized by her concern about the afterbirth, which represents actions that need to be taken to follow up on the new possibilities.

Did the worksheet help with this? The dream is fairly obvious and straightforward in its images. Some details have not been explored, such as the sister or the projected visit to the doctor. Perhaps you have some ideas about these. The dream clearly reveals Helen's insecurity about presenting her true self in the face of feared disapproval and rejection by others. It also shows she has come far enough in her personal development to begin doing this in spite of the obstacles. It would be natural for her to feel doubtful about the outcome.

Helen told me the strongest feeling in the dream was the fear of death and loss of safety, coupled with a fear she would not be able to support herself and the new baby. She felt the baby was a threat to her survival and her old belief structure. This is consistent with the interpretation given above.

Here is another short dream about pregnancy we can look at.

## Marion's Dream

*I am standing behind a shadowy figure who is me and looking at another, pregnant woman who is also me, stretched out on a table. I am observing her. The pregnant woman seems complacent and unconcerned but in the dream, I am concerned because the labor has not taken place.*

This dream is typically confusing because it tells the dreamer something is going on but does not tell her exactly what it is. Many dreams are like this. It does show her a particular inner relationship with the event of the "pregnancy." Without knowing what is ready to be born, there is still a lot of information given in just a few images.

First of all, it is clear to Marion in the dream that all the characters are her. This is often not very evident: in this dream there is no doubt about it, even to her dreaming mind. Whatever the dream is about, in waking life Marion knows she is looking at herself playing out different internal roles and viewpoints. There is Marion the Observer, Marion the Shadowy Figure, and Marion the Pregnant Woman.

We can find the meaning of the dream by looking at the relationship of these three figures. We see two opposites here; Marion the Observer is concerned because the labor that will bring on the birth has not yet occurred.

Marion the Pregnant Woman is not concerned at all. What can we see from this? In addition, between the two is a third: Marion the Shadowy Figure.

The shadowy Marion represents something not seen clearly by Marion the Observer. This figure symbolizes some part of Marion's psyche that stands between her and the process of birthing something new, a birth not yet initiated in the dream. One side of Marion wants this process to hurry up. One side does not care at all about this—it is involved in its own rhythm and timing for the birth, which has nothing to do with what the concerned Marion thinks ought to be going on. This is a split in Marion's psyche, a way of relating to events that should be apparent in her external life, if we are interpreting the image correctly.

Marion in real life does have a pattern of impatience and a tendency to try to push things to completion before they are ready. This results in frustration and confrontation for her and a smoldering, inner resentment. She feels powerless to affect events in the way she would like and her frustration takes covert forms of expression with her co-workers and friends.

What Marion does not see is why she is not willing to let things take their natural course of events and progress in their own timing. She carries unconscious patterns that split her off from herself, literally standing between parts of herself. This is the essential symbolic meaning of the shadowy figure

What is the split about? What is the difference between the two main figures? One is an observer and acts out of judgment about the situation; one is simply involved with the process without concern for the timing. One is mental and concerned; one is feeling and unconcerned. One is detached, one is fully participating. One has ideas about the birth; one is in the process that will actually lead to birth. The split is between feeling and mental functions.

The pregnant figure also represents something developing, near term. Marion is impatient for this to emerge so that she may get on with it. She senses change and thinks it all should have become clear to her by now. That feeling is a reflection of her mental override of the internal, developing and experiential process. The lesson here is one of patience and timing, allowing things to emerge in their own way. By implication, the dream says it is necessary for Marion to let go of her desire to control things and let her feelings have more say. It's a difficult task for her, as for many of us.

Marion was disturbed by this dream so she asked herself for another dream to give her more information. This can be an effective way to get to a better understanding. She got a dream that further developed the theme of a split between mind and emotion.

---

### KEY POINT
You can ask for another dream about a dream you have already had in order to obtain more information. This is frequently an effective way to see more about a specific issue.

---

## Marion's Follow-Up Dream

*I am standing in a large, paved area, like a shopping center or mall. There is a stucco wall along one side of it, and in front of the wall I see myself running across there. I know that it's me and it looks like me but it's a horse. It is a wild, dark, shiny horse, but it looks like me. I am very surprised, but I know that it's me, I know that it's a horse even though it looks like me.*

*There are some other people in the dream. I do not know who they are, but they also know that even though this woman looks like me it's a horse. They want to capture her and they do that somehow. They are chasing her and they want to do some kind of surgical procedure to find out how I can look like a woman and yet be a horse.*

*Then I am me, in the body of the woman. I'm stretched out on this table and all these people are standing around above and looking down at me and that's when I wake up.*

This dream again points out the difference in Marion's consciousness between feeling responses and mental, analytical functions. Part of her is free and natural, like a horse. This is a surprise for her, because in waking life Marion has shut down many strong feelings and ordered her life towards safety, security and staid ways of expression. It has been a long time since Marion felt wild and free. However, this aspect wants expression. The dream portrays this aspect of her as a horse.

The people who want to capture the horse/woman are unknown to her; they want to perform some surgical procedure to find out how a horse can be a woman and vice versa. These are the analytical parts of her psyche, which are not concerned with feelings except as a subject for dissection and study. Once something is dissected it becomes lifeless, at least when we are talking about horses and women.

As in the previous dream, Marion is aware that she is more than one energy at the same time. She is observing, she is a horse, she is a woman who is a horse. She finds herself on the table where the others want to dissect her. This is similar to the image of the pregnant woman on the table in the earlier dream.

From this dream and the first one, it would be safe to conclude some part of Marion wants a less restricted, freer expression in life. Because of the negative ideas she has about the appropriateness of free expression, Marion is presently caught in an unresolvable conflict between feeling and control of feeling. This conflict has been present for her entire life and is now coming to the surface as she makes the effort to discover more of who she is. The pregnancy may result in the birth of a new idea of herself, or aborted through her desire to "dissect" this feeling. Only time will tell.

These dreams occurred on consecutive nights and are an example of how our dreaming consciousness will give us plenty of information if we are open to it. Marion was able to arrive at a fairly complete interpretation of her dreams without my input by using the worksheet approach. It is always much more meaningful if we arrive at our own sense of a correct interpretation. When you work with someone else's dream, always allow the dreamer to try to reach an interpretation before you offer your own conclusions.

By watching the action in your dream about birth or pregnancy, you can accurately determine your real relationship to whatever is symbolically being birthed. Use the information to help you with this new and vulnerable part of yourself. New life is tenuous. Make sure you pay attention to whatever new energy is coming forward.

# CHAPTER 16

# NIGHTMARES

Everyone has had a nightmare at some time or other. One of the interesting things about nightmares is that we usually remember them, sometimes months or years after they occurred. Occasionally we don't remember the dream. We only know something has taken place because we wake up startled, heart pounding and, perhaps, sweating or shaking. All these symptoms are natural physiological responses to terrifying stimuli.

Recently I saw an interesting television program on dream and sleep research, produced by the University of Florida. During the program, the observation was made that the body seems unable to distinguish the difference between the experience of sleeping or waking reality. In other words, what is experienced in the dreaming state is just as real to our perception as what we experience when awake. If you think about your own dreaming experience, you will probably arrive at the same conclusion. This was not news to me, but it is always good to have one's anecdotal experience verified by science.

Since our body doesn't know the difference between what we are experiencing in a dream and what we are experiencing when awake, it stands to reason that a terrifying dream will wake us up.

Why would our unconscious present terrifying images to us? One reason is to get us to pay attention. A nightmare, particularly one that repeats over time, contains psychic material important to see, acknowledge and work with. I am convinced that dreams are in many ways a self-learning process. We may or may not get the lessons and we may or may not pay attention. If the lesson is important and we need to pay attention, a nightmare will at least cause us to take notice.

It's good to look at nightmares, even though our natural inclination is to try and forget them as quickly as possible. The material presented in a nightmare is by its nature so charged that it challenges our objectivity. It is impossible to be objective unless we learn to cultivate a state of observation that is non-judgmental and impersonal. It is the state we are in when we are tap into the Dreamer Within.

The kind of psychological material that shows up in nightmares is of a primal and fundamental nature. It is always part of the deep psyche. I can not emphasize too strongly that you need to go slowly with this kind of material. It may not be something you want to take on at all, and real understanding may take months or years to appear. I mention this because it can be difficult to get to the meaning of such a dream. Go easy on yourself, don't make yourself wrong for how you feel about it, and above all don't worry if you can't figure it out. In time, it may become clear.

There is plenty of reflection in outer society of the inner dream world of nightmares. I find it interesting that so many popular films are filled with nightmarish sequences. The classic example is the series of *Nightmare on Elm Street* movies. Whether the movies are good or bad is irrelevant. A large percentage of our society finds the imagery fascinating and seductive. This is because such films reflect back to us images and cues from our own unconscious that trigger the terrified response. They mirror our disowned shadow material. We are looking here at a subject of endless psychological study. That is not my purpose in this chapter.

If you are a person who experiences repeated and terrifying nightmares, you may wish to consider getting professional advice about the dreams. I say this even though this book is dedicated to the task of learning how to do it oneself. I know well that there is a limit at any given time to what we are able to discover without assistance. There are many dedicated and competent professionals available to help if needed. Dreams of this nature reflect an inner turmoil that holds potential for disrupting one's outer life; they must be handled if you want to achieve calm and harmony. There is a reward available if you succeed in unraveling the meaning of a nightmarish dream. You won't have to have it again!

If I am correct when I say nightmares are about fundamental and important issues, those same issues will be presented more than once over time in an attempt by the psyche to get the message across. This could mean a series of nightmares showing the same material. For the sake of rest and quiet sleep, if nothing else, it is worth the effort to look at the unpleasant dream.

Nightmares signal that inner pressures demanding attention are reaching a peak of intensity. This state of affairs may continue for years unless resolution is achieved. There are many examples recorded of people with recurrent nightmares. Veterans returning from combat or people affected by traumatic events in their lives often have such dreams. The nightmare is the psyche's call for help and healing.

I recall a man, whom I will call Bill, who came to me with such a dream. Bill is a Vietnam veteran who saw extensive combat during his tour of duty. He had not slept for more than one hour at a time for over twenty years. Whenever he began to slip into a doze the same vivid and terrifying dream would wake him up. This was a terrible and destructive burden, affecting his ability to hold a job, maintain relationships and live a normal and productive life.

He was at first reluctant to share his experience with me. This is common when talking with men who have served in Vietnam. People who have suffered enormously traumatic events have no faith that anyone without the same experience can understand their situation. There is a lot of truth in this. It must be recognized and honored, if you want to get to the meaning of a dream someone brings to you. This is particularly true of those initiated in the experience of war. I was in the U.S. Marines, but I never saw combat and was discharged in 1964, just as Vietnam was heating up. I had some common ground with Bill because of my military experience, but it was minimal. I am not one of the initiated.

Bill was desperate. He was ready to listen to anyone who might help him find a solution. He told me his dream.

The dream was always exactly the same. Bill would find himself back in Vietnam, aware he could be attacked and killed at any moment. A fierce firefight would erupt, as real to his dreaming consciousness as the actual events he experienced in the war. Shells would explode all around him, and right next to him his friend would be blown to bits by a shell, covering Bill with bloody body parts and pieces.

Bill would awaken in fear, drenched in sweat. He had been having this dream every day, every time he went to sleep, for twenty years! I would not have lasted as long. He had contemplated suicide many times, and only some very strong inner sense of self had pulled him through to this point.

As we talked, Bill relaxed somewhat and began to tell me his story. It took about an hour, but what emerged as a result of our conversation was a startling realization, not just in his mind but as a powerful sensation in his body.

It is hard to tell this here, because words do not convey the impact of recognition for Bill; the words seem so meaningless compared to the event. This dream took Bill back to the time in his life when he first genuinely realized he was a mortal being and that he could die at any time, in some horrible way. He had actually been standing next to a friend killed in the way described in the dream. He had absolutely no control over this, nothing to say about it, nothing he could do about it, and no way to know that it was going to happen.

Bill had never come to terms with this experience. He was nineteen years old when he served his time in Vietnam. He was an immature teenager, not prepared for an undeniable and uncontrollable confrontation with death and his own vulnerability. Something froze in his psyche right then, stuck in terror as it recognized the real possibility of extinction.

When Bill made the connection with the cause of his problem, he also connected with the resolution: acceptance. He burst into tears. With acceptance of his vulnerability and human mortality came peace. It was a revelation of profound import for him. He went home and slept for eight hours, without a dream.

All of us think we are immortal, when we are young. Although we know better intellectually, life has not yet taught us the truth of our mortality. Vietnam stripped away the illusion of immortality for Bill and many thousands of others. The dream was a symptom of his psyche's shock and fear, and of the consequent denial of the reality of personal death. Seeing the truth consciously and accepting the reality alleviated the need for Bill's psyche to express the fear and shock through the dream, so the dream went away.

Many things other than external events (such as war or accident) can wound the inner being. Psychological abuse, a lack of love and nourishment, uncaring parents or simply a perception by the dreamer that his or her life is not valuable can lead to psychological wounding not easily tracked to external events. Such wounding is real nonetheless, and to the inner self terribly traumatic. It is the inner self expressing and communicating in dreams.

When the inner self is calling for healing and attention, and if the issue is basic enough, a nightmare may be the result. As with all dreams, the nightmare presents information the dreamer needs to understand. There is always an implication that information given to us by a dream is somehow useful. If we can accurately interpret the informationit can be a catalyst for change.

With nightmares, integration and recognition of the underlying psychic material can lead to psychological healing the inner self is requesting. This in turn can lead to transformation of the way we experience life, the way we view life and the way we interact with others. If we change the way we perceive or interact with self, through the work with dreams, it follows that our external relationship with life must change also. We are no longer exactly the same person we were before we integrated the recognition encouraged by the dream. We see things in a different way, feel them in a different way and therefore have a new experience of a life now perceived differently. Our perception determines the quality of our experience and our participation with it.

The following dream presents basic inner issues for the dreamer, who was very disturbed by the dream. You always know something is really important by the sensation you feel in your body. Your body cannot deceive you, although your mind often will. This dream felt so powerful to the dreamer that there was no way for him to ignore the images.

This dream has to do with early, childhood material. I am telling you this in advance so that you may have an idea as you go through the dream about its meaning. It is also about the dreamer's relationship with his mother. Because "Mother" is the basic patterning of feminine relationship and perception of woman by the child, the relationship with the mother will unconsciously affect all relationships with women. Understanding the dream could eventually lead to a shift in the dreamer's outer relationships with women. His mother does not appear in the dream, and the association with her is a third level interpretation. See if you can feel into the various possibilities as you go through the dream.

The first section is not especially terrifying but contains clear symbols amplified later in the dream. The entire dream takes place in a house that the dreamer is renovating. Does that tell you something?

## Erik's Dream: Section One

*I am renovating a house, my house, with some others. There is a workshop going on in the family room.*

We can stop right here and determine the main theme of the dream. Erik's house is where he lives, a symbol of his life structure. He is renovating the house, meaning he is making major changes and is updating the structure of his life. This is not necessarily a conscious process, but it has clearly begun in the dream. The family room setting indicates the renovation is about something in Erik's consciousness centered upon family dynamics, emphasized by the workshop that takes place there. "Work" is being done on basic psychological patterns configured in Erik's experience of family. In real life, family experience was traumatic for Erik. OK so far? Let's go on.

## Erik's Dream: Section Two

*Two naked women are posed as if for a dance. This upsets me; I want nudity to be voluntary. The workshop is about some kind of bodywork or massage. I am going to start the workshop but then an ugly, fat woman begins to lead.*

*She knows what she's doing. She tells the people in the workshop to take their clothes off. They start to undress—there are six couples.*

*As she is pulling off her dress, I see she is menstruating. That's when I tell people that nudity is optional. Then I realize someone not in the workshop is in the basement. A young blond in a red dress. I bring her up and tell her not to look. I am annoyed that she is there.*

We are approaching the nightmare stage, which comes next. Already, though, things are getting out of hand. Erik is trying to control events in the workshop but is not succeeding. The nudity upsets him; nudity represents exposure, something Erik would like to cover up. What is being exposed remains to be seen, but we can get some ideas.

The nudity involves women, so there is something Erik does not want to see about the feminine/woman. This is symbolized by the ugly woman who is menstruating. Menstruation is an essential statement of woman. It can symbolize life and the potential of life. The blood is a visible sign of the woman's power and role as bearer of life. It is a mystery; something Erik does not want exposed. The ugliness emphasizes his inner resistance and unclear perception.

There are six couples. Remember what six can be about? Six and sex are similar to the unconscious and sex is about relationship. This dream is about Erik's basic relationship with the feminine—how he feels about it, how he relates to it unconsciously.

In the "basement" is another important figure. The basement can represent a darker tier of the psyche. Why do you think so many terrible and horrifying movie scenes take place in the basement? Ever notice that? The second most favorite place for horrifying events in horror films is the attic. The movies *Psycho* and *Burnt Offerings* provide good examples. To our minds, basements and attics are where things are stored and hidden away, often unpleasant places of dirt, spiders and crawling creatures. It makes no difference that modern homes may not be like this. The images are burned into the collective psyche, which is why horror films use them so frequently. As we shall see, the core of Erik's nightmare will take place in the attic.

The blond woman in the red dress appears from time to time in various forms in Erik's dreams. In this dream, he is unpleasantly surprised to find her at the workshop. She is in the basement, in the depths of Erik's unconscious. He brings her up into the light, but he is not happy about it. He does not want her to see what's going on. She is part of his inner feminine self, but Erik doesn't want to have much to do with her. This is dream emphasis to show how strongly Erik wants to avoid whatever the dream is trying to tell him about his relationship to the feminine. His inner relationship with feminine forces will reflect outward and influence his relationships with women. That is true for all of us.

One of the things Erik does not want to see is an empowered, mature feminine (symbolized by the ugly, menstruating woman). "Ugly" is a comment on how Erik sometimes looks at the feminine in its empowered aspect. He does not like it. The dream is beginning to reveal a very strong conflict in Erik's psyche about the feminine, inner and outer, a conflict spiraling out of control. The red dress is a way the dream images connect the blood color of the menstruation and its mysterious connection with life.

## Erik's Dream: Section Three

*Now I am working on this house, a large house, on the top floor. Others work below. I tell one of them to get me a different ladder, one light and strong, instead of the old, heavy wooden one—a stepladder. The scene is one of repair and dust. The dust is being blown about by two windows that have been left open.*

*I am painting the room. Suddenly what looks like blood begins to pour from a spot in the ceiling, slowly at first. I see it is really orange paint. I am afraid, uneasy. Then red blood begins to pour from other spots—it is from the attic.*

The dream is deepening. The call for a new, lighter ladder says that a new way of access, a new approach, is being called for. A stepladder has steps. The old steps won't do any more—too heavy. New steps are necessary for Erik. Do you follow? The two windows and the orange paint are symbolic markers in Erik's psyche of feelings regarding sexuality and the expression of sexuality. Remember, he did not like the nudity and menstruation at the beginning of the dream.

This is an oblique reference by the psyche to the second chakra. Chakras are subtle energy centers in the human body. They are associated with different physical, emotional, mental and spiritual functions. They are real (not simply symbolic, a popular psychological opinion) and can be directly experienced, but that is material for another book. There is more information about chakras in Chapter 22.

The second chakra is associated with the integration of sexual and creative energies, and orange is a color often associated with this energy center. It is a color of vital forces, vitality. It is the second chakra—two. Two windows open—letting something "blow through" this area. It is a good sign the windows are open, because windows can symbolize a barrier or separation from something. In this case, it is something about Erik's thoughts and expression of sexuality.

Painting the room is the same as covering something over in the attempt to renovate. This isn't going to work, though. Can you imagine blood pouring through the ceiling from the attic? No wonder Erik is becoming uneasy and afraid! The dream gets worse, as if that were not enough.

## Erik's dream: Section Four

*The blood horrifies me and I am afraid to look in the attic, but I know I have to. I am drawn by fear and morbid curiosity. I open the attic door, or am somehow in the attic. It is dark and hellish, confused, a maelstrom of blood and screams. I see an infant's arm, or perhaps a young child's. Just the arm. I am afraid that I will see a slaughtered child, and that I will have to face it and eat it. Then I surrender and turn to face the murdered child, knowing I have to go through this.*

*There is a confused and horrible impression of scattered pieces of the child. There is lots of blood. I start screaming, a thin, childish cry. No one can hear! Then I wake up shouting.*

Erik's comment about this dream was that it was difficult to convey the sense of horror.

When Erik enters the attic, he enters hell. This sequence is the heart of the dream. Inside Erik is a murdered and dismembered "child." In his psyche, a crucial aspect was slaughtered, butchered, dismembered. The child is Erik; it is a symbolic representation of how he felt during his childhood (and how he still feels inside). He doesn't want to look at this and we can easily understand why.

He thinks he may have to "eat" it. This means taking it in, nourishing himself somehow with it, digesting it. Something inside is ready to take this on, though. He knows in the dream that he must face this terrifying energy, whatever it is, and he does actually surrender to the confrontation.

Throughout the dream Erik is repeatedly reminded he does not want to face whatever is going on. Gradually stronger images lead him to the confrontation. Because of the earlier sequences, he can assume that part of the problem has to do with the feminine. The root cause lies in his relationship with his mother.

Erik's experience of his mother is not positive. He felt manipulated, unloved and controlled as a child. He did not get the emotional and nurturing support he needed and wanted as a child and he felt disempowered by his mother. The symbol in the dream of disempowerment and helplessness is the image of the dismembered child. When he screams in the dream it is the cry of an abandoned child, not the scream of a man. Just as in his childhood, no one can "hear" him. To "hear" Erik would be to recognize and validate him.

Whatever the source of the psychological and traumatic wounding of Erik's inner child, it is time to do something about it. It is time to do something to initiate integration of the traumatic, emotional events represented. More importantly, the dream says he is ready to do this now— this is the meaning of surrendering to the sight of the terrifying images.

What Erik can or will do with this information is up to him. The dream is so disturbing that it may well require professional help to get to healing and integration. If he does not act on the dream, he is sure to have more nightmares in the future about this painful area. If he succeeds in coming to terms with the traumatic psychic material, genuine inner nourishment and security may be established. This can only have positive and far reaching ramifications for his life.

I mentioned above that the image of the woman in the red dress has appeared more than once in Erik's dreams. She appears as nurturing and destructive, young and old, indifferent and involved. Erik is much interested in dreams and has kept records of his dreams for years. He told me that even if he did not keep records he would remember the dreams in which this figure appears. For him this figure always symbolizes something very essential. By looking at the way he interacts with her in the dream, Erik understands something about his inner relationship with the primal feminine.

You may also have a dream figure, male or female, like this. You will recognize it because it will always appear in the same general way, although it may take on many faces and activities not consistent from dream to dream. For Erik the figure is always blond, always beautiful (even in a distorted or destructive aspect) and always in a red dress. She is an archetypal symbol of the Feminine for Erik. If you have such a figure in your dreams, it will also represent an archetypal energy for you and it will show you your relationship with that energy at any given moment.

Over time we can see the progress (or lack of it) we are making on the inner planes in regards to these energies. Dreams tend to present an ongoing commentary on themes or images important to the dreamer. That is why a journal is so valuable as a tool for dreamers. When you look back over your entries, you can see images and themes appear and watch the story unfold. Dreams with evolving information about a particular theme may be of any kind, nightmare or not. I classify these as progressive dreams, and they are the subject of Chapter 20.

Here is a nightmare so loaded with personal, first level material for the dreamer that it has taken her many years to look at the content. She used this dream as an excuse to begin drinking destructively. Maria told me she went over the edge in drinking because alcohol helped her sleep without dreams. Unfortunately, many alcoholics get started like this.

This dream is one of three she had in a period of about a week. After these dreams, Maria began drinking excessively before going to sleep so she would not have to deal with the images. This is what her outer mind told her. In reality, the dream reflects painful inner material she was not then capable of resolving. The dream was a symptom of her inner distress, not a cause. Her response, as with many people in a similar situation, was to blot it out. An important figure in the dream is Jennifer, Maria's actual daughter.

## Maria's Dream

*Jennifer and I stand up to leave the Sacred Heart Catholic Church in our hometown. We are on the right side of the church as we face the altar. As we are leaving the pew, my father approaches to escort us up the aisle to the main entrance. As we approach the entrance I can see all the people who have left the church before us, waiting for us to come out.*

*As we enter the foyer to the church, I notice a metal pole in the center of the doorway. Jennifer and my father are talking to each other, sort of laughing softly. Jennifer turns towards me and as she does she bumps into the pole. She bounces back but the pole has severed her head somehow. My father turns and looks at me. He looks puzzled. I turn and see Jennifer's head bouncing down the steps of the church. I scream and wake up.*

Because of Maria's real life associations with father, church, and daughter, this dream was difficult for her to understand. She is immediately activated by any one of these subjects and is aware that she is unresolved regarding each of them. Reaching a place of objectivity has been impossible for Maria in all three areas.

Let's look at the first section and see if we can get a feeling for the theme of the dream. Remember that if we get a feeling for the theme we will have a good general sense of what the dream is about.

The dream takes place in the Catholic church of Maria's childhood. She comes from a traditional and strict Catholic background, rooted in the Old World context that goes with her Hispanic heritage. Maria grew up in a small town in the Southwest, in circumstances bordering on poverty. Her father was strict and remote, her mother unsympathetic. Maria was conceived out of wedlock, although her parents married before she was born. Interestingly, Maria's daughter was conceived in similar circumstances. Maria has never gotten through feelings of guilt and sin she has about the conception and birth of Jennifer.

You would not need to know the information given above in order to see that something about the Catholic experience is crucial to understanding the dream. The entire dream takes place in the Catholic setting.

If you are Catholic, you understand something about Maria's childhood that others can only guess at. You will also have difficulty separating your thoughts about Catholicism from the symbol in the dream.

If you are not Catholic, your observations about Catholicism are second hand and liable to be skewed. There is nothing like a religious setting in a dream to activate unconscious material, since all of us have lots of ideas about what is right and wrong about any given religious practice.

For Maria, Catholicism seems repressive and controlling. She has a love/hate relationship with the Church. On the one hand, she loves the ritual and sense of communion with spirit and God that she felt in the past when she attended the Mass. On the other hand, she bitterly resents the rules and dogma. She is angry at the suppression of women that she sees in the teachings of the Church. She feels guilty about some of the things she has done, especially sexually, that are in conflict with those teachings, and angry with herself for feeling guilty.

The same might be said for her relationship with her father, another symbol in the dream. Her father carries all of the Old World attitudes about women, sexuality and the role of women and daughters in society. The love/hate relationship is present here also.

Maria's daughter, Jennifer, triggers all of this complex emotional material in Maria. It is only in the last few years that Maria has begun to resolve some of the ambivalent feelings she has about her daughter. She projects the best and the worst of herself onto Jennifer. She has repeated many of the mistakes her parents made with her, and she feels guilty about that.

When we are in the presence of someone who activates feelings of guilt in us, we tend to react with attack, withdrawal or rationalization. Usually feelings of guilt lead to hurt and anger. We usually think the other person is responsible for how we feel. Maria often feels like this toward Jennifer, but this is intolerable because she loves Jennifer. The result is unresolvable inner conflict.

In the dream, the three symbols of father, church and daughter all come together. The theme of this dream is centered on the common elements all three represent to the dreamer's mind. These are guilt, conflict and suppression of self. The dream is going to get Maria's attention and ask her to do something about it.

If she had been capable at that time of resolving the issues, Maria might never have taken the step into alcoholism: drinking was a way to push the psychic material away. It was not the dream that triggered the descent into alcoholism, although Maria produces this as a rationale. The drinking served to provide an avenue of expression Maria could not get to without alcohol because she could not consciously understand and resolve her own inner conflict.

The father comes to escort Maria and Jennifer to the entrance of the church. This symbolizes the controlling influence of the masculine value systems Maria sees as negative. Catholics refer to the Catholic Church as Mother Church. However, the experience is usually not one of being mothered but rather sternly directed. Strong masculine systems of rule and order, in service to a masculine, Father God, submerge the feminine, nurturing aspect. Between Church and father, Maria does not stand much of a chance for free self-expression.

Outside the church, all those who have left before are waiting for Maria and her family to come out. The people symbolize parts of Maria's consciousness that have already left the structure of belief and authority represented by the childhood church. Now it is Maria's turn to leave, i.e., move into a different area of self-awareness not so firmly identified with the controlling energies church and father represent; she starts towards the entrance.

A metal pole splits the entry down the center. This is a wonderful symbol of the split and conflict in Maria. The split is about the whole issue of church and father, and daughter as well. It is a love/hate relationship with them: it is really a love/hate relationship with herself. This is the third level of interpretation for this symbol. The symbol is also man-made and masculine in nature. It is artificial.

Distracted by the friendly conversation with her father, Jennifer bumps into the pole and is decapitated. This is a scene of incredible horror for Maria when recounting the dream. The father is puzzled—"What happened?" he seems to be saying. This dream figure does not understand. It does not understand in the dream and it does not understand what Maria needs in waking life. It cannot relate to her needs and feelings or to the symbol in the dream in a meaningful way.

We need to look carefully at the symbol of Jennifer, because she is the one who is decapitated. Her head rolls down the steps of the church. What does she represent in Maria's psyche? What do you feel she represents?

Jennifer is a symbolic reflection of Maria (it's Maria's dream, after all). She is a younger, feminine aspect, killed by interaction with the symbol of the father and the symbol of the pole at the church entrance. It is not a mature aspect for Maria.

Jennifer represents the potential Maria feels she misplaced somewhere along the way. Jennifer is "the best" of Maria, her projected hopes and fears, strengths and weaknesses. Maria has tried to shape and control Jennifer, just as her parents did with her. She represents the potential bloom of the feminine in Maria's own life. From this point of view, it is easy to see how devastating the image of decapitation is. It is the death of everything Maria wants for herself.

Decapitation as a symbol shows the split between head (mental/thoughts) and body (feelings). This image is consistent with Maria's outer life at the time of the dreams. Drinking is one of the ways Maria can allow herself to become less mental and more expressive. Alcohol bridges the gap.

The dream tells Maria she is trapped in masculine and un-nurturing perceptions of herself and her world. It says she is literally cutting herself off from her emotions, her feelings and her potential. It points out that her negative perceptions of self are founded in beliefs about herself she learned from church, mother ("Mother" Church) and father. The implication is that she needs to discover why she accepted these beliefs and to take responsibility for them. This is a third level interpretation not directly stated in the dream. The dream simply shows the psychodynamics.

In real life, Maria blames church, father and mother for her unsatisfactory relationship with self and her expression as a woman. The dream shows what happens if she does not take personal responsibility for how she feels. Blame of others will never resolve Maria's bad feelings about herself. With personal responsibility comes the power to institute change.

Maria had three dreams in one week in which Jennifer was killed: this is what the psyche will do when it is trying to get an important message through to the outer mind. It will create a nightmare as a signal of alarm and distress. I feel that nightmares always call for some kind of action by the outer mind. Not all dreams demand action. Some are simply making progress reports, others are helping us solve problems, and others are inspirational and nurturing. The nightmare, though, is a signal to pay attention. It ought not to be ignored.

If you are interested in learning more about nightmares, or if you frequently have nightmares, please see my book, *Nightmares: How to Make Sense of Your Darkest Dreams* (M. Evans, 2000). The book includes many examples and looks at common nightmare themes. It provides practical guidance about how to deal with them.

# CHAPTER 17

# REPETITIVE AND RECURRING DREAMS

Progressive and repetitive dreams deal with the same material over an extended period. These kinds of dreams reveal a pattern in the dreamer's consciousness. Some of the most valuable information we can get from our dreams centers on the discovery of unconscious patterns.

A true repetitive dream is one appearing exactly the same each time. Whatever the message is, it is repeated in exactly the same way with the same emphasis. This kind of dream is especially important for the dreamer. It is quite possible to have such a dream several times and then not experience the dream again. Often the dreamer hasn't any idea what the content of the dream is really about, but remembers the dream because of the frequent repetition.

Repetitive dreams signal basic issues needing resolution in the dreamer's psyche. They are often nightmarish or bordering on terrifying, which helps the dreamer notice and remember them. Children sometimes experience repetitive dreams, but there is little they can do to integrate or understand the experience. If understanding is to come, it will have to wait for a later time in the dreamer's life.

Children do not have the life experience to understand dreams, the analysis of self that dream work requires must wait for adult awareness. It is a good idea to remember this if you are trying to help a child who has had a difficult dream.

The following dream is an example. The dreamer had this dream several times between the ages of five and eight. The dream, nightmarish in quality, always presaged a severe asthma attack that would begin immediately upon awaking.

# John's Dream

*When the dream begins, I am standing on an endless plain. The plain is marked by blue lines, regularly spaced in a square grid pattern. The lines stretch as far as I can see. The sky is dark, gray and featureless. The atmosphere feels oppressive and heavy. I sense that there is some terrifying force behind me and I begin to run across the plain. I run faster and faster but the force is getting closer.*

*Suddenly I reach the edge of the plain, which is like a black, bottomless abyss. From somewhere above a shower of heavy gold coins begins to rain down on my head and the impact of the coins hitting me knocks me over the edge of the plain. I fall into the abyss with the coins raining down upon me. At the same time, I hear a deep and frightening laughter. The laughter is coming from whatever is chasing me. Whatever it is, it is laughing at me as I go over the edge. I wake up screaming.*

Immediately upon waking from this dream, John would be hysterical. He would first vomit and then enter a severe breathing episode as the asthma took hold. How could a five-year old child interpret this dream? In fact, it took John forty years before he felt he had any meaningful understanding of the dream. How would you interpret the dream?

Take out your worksheets and see what you can determine. Here is John's worksheet, so you can see what he discovered. Do yours first and then compare them to find out if you tuned in to the same parts of the dream. Don't be discouraged if it's confusing to you. If it took John forty years, it might take you a while! On the other hand, John is too personally involved; you may get to it quickly because you can be objective.

# DREAM WORKSHEET

**1. Write down and review the dream (see previous page).**

**2. The images or events in the dream I feel are the most powerful are:**

- endless grid-like plain
- unknown, terrifying force chases dreamer
- heavy gold coins
- falling and laughter

**3. I feel that the most important image is:**

- all are important, but most powerful is gold coins knock the dreamer off the edge

**4. The way I feel about this image is:**

- strange image
- gold coins are child's image of wealth
- wealth—nourishment
- something about nourishment threatens child
- key image which precipitates fall into black abyss
- feels like total loss of control
- child cannot control events
- angry and scared

**5. This image reminds me of: (put down anything, no matter how unrelated it seems that comes to mind)**

- attack
- overwhelming force
- comic book images

**6. The next image or event I feel is most important is:**

- grid-like plain

**7. The way I feel about this image is:**

- surreal

- seems very structured, regular
- odd image for a child
- seems like a foundation for the child
- terrifying because endless and inhuman—doesn't feel like a human place

## 8. This image reminds me of:

- art images for strange regularity—like Escher, Dali
- chessboard
- trapped

## The next image I feel is important is:

- terrifying force

## The way I feel about this is:

- was very scary
- relentless force
- not controllable
- wants to destroy me
- feels masculine

## This image reminds me of:

- Nazis
- uncaring authority
- irresistible
- my father

## The next image I feel is important is:

- terrifying laughter as child falls off plain

**The way I feel about this image is:**

- must symbolize whatever attacking force is
- feel like this is a key to dream
- laughing at child must be humiliating
- I felt humiliated as a child if people laughed at me
- I felt humiliated by my parents, especially my father

**This image reminds me of:**

- horror movies
- devouring force
- death

**9. Any other details I now remember are:**

- there was no bottom to the blackness after I went over the edge

**10. I feel that the dream is about:**

- I feel that the dream is about not being loved by my parents; there's something else, too

**11. Another thing about the dream is:**

Something about money—why else the gold coins? The money is about nourishment.

**12. The way I feel about this dream is:**

I hate this dream. I hated it then and I hate it now. It makes me angry and afraid and I feel helpless about it.

### 13. Some other thoughts that occur when I review the images of the dream are:

I have never understood what to do with this dream. If I understood the dream I might be able to understand something about myself as a child and now. My parents never paid any attention to me when I said that the dream came before one of my bad attacks. When I told my mother about the dream and its relationship to the asthma, she dismissed the whole idea as ridiculous.

### 14. Review what you have written.

### 15. When I ask for help from within about this dream, I sense that the dream is about:

• my relationship with love and my parents

### 16. My interpretation of the dream is:

I think the dream is about how I felt as a child and how that affected me. I felt unloved by my parents and remote from the rest of my family. My father and mother were divorced not too long after the dream started, when I was six. My parents were always at odds about money, and my father was very controlling about everything. My mother had been born into money as a child, but that was all taken away in 1929. She never quite seemed to forget that. She always seemed to want something more. I think the dream shows how I felt about all this. I felt completely helpless to make anything happy in our home. It seemed I was in the way and not very good at anything because I was sick. I don't think my father liked me much, although in hindsight I know he had a difficult time. So what! I think the sound of laughter was my father's laugh. He often laughed at me and made fun of me. I think the pressures of all that were too much and my way of dealing with it was to get sick and get attention. I think the dream says something about all of this.

John's honesty with his worksheet tells us a lot. His interpretation is good as far as it goes, which is mostly first level with some hints of the second. What is revealing in his interpretation is that it is apparent he has not yet resolved the feelings the dream brought up, then and now. He is still angry at his parents. There is also some anger and judgment directed at himself.

John sees that the dream was a response to the emotional pressures and conflicts he experienced in his family situation. He also sees that a way to get the attention he needed was to get sick. Asthma is an illness closely tied to emotional stress. In my opinion, there is definitely a correlation between asthma and emotional content. In my practice as a psychotherapist, I see many clients who respond to deep emotional distress with the symptoms of asthma.

John identifies the pursuing force as his father. This is a first level and a half interpretation. The second level broadens the field and looks at external forces, including both parents, that humiliate him and "drive him over the edge." On the second level, John is still a victim of something or someone. The third level of interpretation would be . . . what do you think?

Remember that we tend to project our unconscious material onto the external world. Resolution requires understanding that this is what we do. At the same time, we need to appreciate that what we experience as coming from outside us is also inside us. If this inner work is done, we cannot hold onto the thought of being a helpless victim

We all have thoughts sometimes that we are victims, but it is often difficult to admit it. When we see ourselves in this way, we essentially disempower ourselves. It's a Catch-22: We feel victimized because we feel we are a victim! I call this state of affairs Victim Consciousness. In order to fully empower ourselves as conscious individuals, we have to move out of Victim Consciousness and reclaim the power we give away to others to affect how we feel. Because our outer consciousness is not usually aware of the inner dynamics that create feelings of victimization, we experience great resistance to accepting this kind of personal responsibility. The logical result is assignment of blame and guilt onto others. This same relationship of conscious/unconscious dynamics leads to assignment of guilt and blame onto self as well. It is a vicious circle, never leading to healing or redemption.

A third level interpretation of this dream leads us down into John's psyche, where he disempowers himself by blaming others, particularly his father. The third level reading takes this into account.

---

## KEY POINT
**Resolving feelings of victimization begins with willingness to take responsibility for how one feels. This does not mean we have to take responsibility for the event felt as victimizing. It means that since we are the ones who hold the feelings, we are the only ones who can do anything about them. Because the outer consciousness is usually concerned with assigning blame and guilt, there is great resistance to accepting responsibility for self and for how one feels. This is one of the most difficult challenges for personal growth.**

---

One definition of responsibility is that responsibility means the ability to respond. Personal responsibility in this sense means we can respond to feelings of victimization by realizing we have choice about how we feel. This is a major key to personal empowerment, but it means we have to give up our cherished ideas about blame of others. Responsibility for events can be determined and appropriate action taken in response, but responsibility is not the same as blame. There are many ways to begin this inner work. It is not easy work, but it must be done.

John still sees himself as a victim of his parents' uncaring and unloving actions. In this case, a third level of interpretation goes beyond blaming the father and makes the leap to self-responsibility for the feelings of victimization he experiences. This is the crucial juncture for an internal healing process to take hold. John does see that his illness was a way for him to get attention, so he sees that in some way his illness served him. He does not yet see that in serving himself in this way he took on an active participation in the process of his "victimization." Even if the father was uncaring and unloving, John bought into this internally, thinking that his father's actions meant something about him. In actuality, those actions say a lot more about the father than they do about John.

It would not be possible for John to see and understand this as a child. What about John now, as an adult? He is still angry and upset about his childhood experience as "victim" and carries this mostly unconscious perception with him all the time. It is predictable, since this is a pattern of perception in his psyche, that he will see other situations as victimizing him in present time. The unconscious psyche does not distinguish time and place in the linear sense.

---

## KEY POINT
The unconscious psyche does not view time and place in the same way as our outer consciousness. To the deeper awareness, all time and experience is simultaneous. What the outer mind sees as present time is only another simultaneous event to our inner vision. We see this in dream images, where events and places of different life periods often occur simultaneously.

---

This is why a pattern of perception in our consciousness established at an earlier time in our lives may affect us in present time. The inner psyche does not know the difference. Our experiences in childhood, for example, shape our particular perception of the world. We unconsciously create patterns of outward behavior based on our perceived experiences, on what we think happened and on how we adapted to the events. We make powerful, unconscious decisions about life and "how it is." Patterns of perception and response are established that become automatic. We project these perceptions onto present and future situations that appear to be similar. The result is confusion and inappropriate behavior, because we cannot see the situation in present time for what it really is.

We can verify this easily in our relationships if we have learned to look for it. A good example is unconsciously responding to your mate or partner as if they were your mother or father.

When an unconscious pattern of perception is triggered, it determines our emotional and mental response to our present experience. That perception may or may not be accurate.

What can John do with this dream, so many years later? First, he must arrive at an accurate interpretation. He will know when he has gotten it because he will feel it. There will be a sense of certainty about the meaning of the dream he does not yet have.

Here is my interpretation, courtesy of the Dreamer Within:

*The dreamer is experiencing internal conflict between what is required of him externally and his own inner needs. He attempts to establish a regular and orderly basis for his life but this is sterile and inadequate. This is the meaning of the grid-like plain.*

*The dreamer feels threatened and pursued because his inability to control the situation has once more become apparent. Since he is cannot face this unresolvable conflict, he flees to escape it. Since he does not understand the nature of the conflict, the pursuing force becomes depersonalized, faceless and masculine. It is masculine in feeling because the dreamer is masculine and is, in essence, attacking himself.*

*The gold coins represent another facet of the inner conflict. The dreamer's consciousness thinks of riches and wealth as a source of danger. Because he feels responsible for the lack of wealth in his family situation, he equates lack of riches with lack of nourishment and love he wants and needs. Since he feels responsible for this situation, he has come to see wealth and riches as inextricably tied to punishment.*

*The child thinks he is a financial and emotional burden to the family. He feels things would be better for them if he were not here. He thinks resolution of the family financial problems can only be achieved at the expense of his existence. This is not an acceptable solution and leads to a crisis of emotion that produces the asthma attacks. The fall into the abyss symbolizes the annihilation of the child's being.*

What can John can do with this in present time? Does his present life in some way reflect these dynamics? One area to look at would be money and finances. If the interpretation is correct, and if what I have said about unconscious projection onto external reality is true, predictably John would have trouble with money.

In reality, this has always been so. John is quite capable of making large amounts of money and has done so in the past, but he is always in debt and is always worried about money. It is also predictable John would be suspicious and wary of men, not quite knowing how to safely relate to them. This is also true, although work John has done to resolve feelings about his father resulted in many changes in this area.

John does try to establish orderly and limited boundaries in order to control his life and maintain his safety, just like the grid-like plain in the dream. This is changing, as he opens to more fluid and feminine influences. He has often created upheaval of the order in his life in an attempt to bring about change. Intuitively he has tried to escape the symbolic, structured plain of his dream by initiating chaos.

If John wants to change the effects of this pattern, he has to accept that he actively (if unconsciously) participated in his childhood victimization and appreciate the dynamics involved. He needs to see that he carries these same dynamics himself, with humor, love and appreciation of himself as the source of his experience. This will lead to acceptance and forgiveness, both of himself and of his parents. That will de-energize the pattern, which in turn will have practical effects in his life.

This dream is an example of true repetition. The dream was the same each time over a period of several years. The dreams stopped a few years after his parents' divorce, after some stability had been restored to his home situation. Even after so many years, John still feels the impact of the dream and it has periodically surfaced in his memory. Something in John is still trying to resolve the meaning of the dream, though he no longer has asthma and is now an adult. The material was important to him then and it is important now.

If you have a pattern of repetitive dreaming, there is an important message for you contained in the dream. Even if you have not had the dream for years, the material is still important because such a dream always represents an unresolved area of conflict. Outer situations may change and alleviate the stressful stimuli that triggered the dream, then you may no longer have it. The inner situation may remain the same. If the psyche perceives a different, new, external stimulus as similar in some way, the old pattern will activate and the dream may return. The pattern will be the same and the results are liable to be just as unsatisfactory. By understanding the dream it is possible to de-energize the pattern and achieve a different result.

# CHAPTER 18

# UNCONSCIOUS PATTERNS

The power of dreams as inner teachings for personal development lies in the way they reveal unconscious patterns of perception and behavior. An unconscious pattern by definition always operates in the same predictable way with a predictable result, without conscious knowledge. This is one way dreams can be truly prophetic, because once a pattern is identified the result can be accurately predicted. A pattern, if followed, always produces the same result.

Earlier in the book, I used the analogy of a shirt pattern. A pattern for a shirt always produces a shirt. The shirt may have variations in color, size and material, but it will always be a shirt. Another pattern produces a suit or a pair of pants, and so on. Any pattern, once energized, always produces the same result with variations. You cannot get a different, real world result, without changing the underlying and unconscious pattern producing the result. That is why so many of us find ourselves in unproductive and emotionally distressing situations. We are using the equivalent of a shirt pattern to try and create the equivalent of a suit or a pair of pants.

If we unknowingly act out patterns based on unconscious perceptions and unconscious decisions about reality, as I am suggesting, then it follows we must often operate automatically in a way leading to predictable results. The catch is that we cannot appreciate that predictability until we manage to bring the unconscious material into the light of conscious understanding.

Although our ego may not like this much, what I am saying is that we effectively act out all sorts of unconscious patterns in daily life. Because they are unconscious, we don't know the patterns are there. This means we often don't know what we are doing! Of course, we think we know what we are doing most of the time, and that can lead to a lot of difficulties and undesired results.

If you or I are unconsciously acting out a pattern, we will always get a similar result when the pattern is run through to completion. We are not consciously in charge of starting the pattern: it is triggered by the random and uncontrollable stimuli of life as we go about the business of living. If we are unaware of the pattern, we cannot make any changes that might be desirable. This can effectively hamper our health, quality of life and general well being if the pattern is not supportive.

---

## KEY POINT
**Unconscious patterns of perception shape and alter our life experience. They operate below the threshold of conscious choice and influence our behavior. The only way to regain choice is to make the unconscious patterns conscious. Dreams are one of the ways we can see and identify the patterns.**

---

There are some clues you can notice in your life that indicate a pattern of unconscious behavior is active. If you find yourself saying "Why does this always happen to me . . ." or, "It always turns out this way . . ." or, "No matter what I do . . ." chances are a pattern is running in your unconscious.

Patterns don't care about anything. They are not intelligent. A pattern is simply a pattern, finding its pattern fulfillment through whatever action constitutes progression of the pattern to completion. Just like a shirt factory that produces shirts until the machinery shuts down, our consciousness will keep running the same patterns repeatedly unless we act.

Over time dreams can reveal primary patterns active in our psyche. The dynamics of the patterns are displayed by the dream images. One dream can do it, but usually we need to see several examples before we catch on.

Dreams are an effective tool for revealing patterns that unconsciously influence our behavior. Initiating change and shifting these patterns is not easy. Just seeing a pattern will not change anything, but seeing it is the first and most necessary step towards change, if change is desired. What do you want to change in your life? If you ask yourself that question, you will probably come up with something you would like to be different.

John's dream in the last chapter about the pursuing force and the shower of coins reflects a deep sense of uncertainty that demands a response. John, as a child, did not have the necessary adult tools of self-understanding, experience and techniques of self-analysis and self-inquiry that might have alleviated the problem. The result was a skewed emotional response leading to illness, emotional withdrawal and problems with money as an adult in later years. The underlying psychological pattern shown by the dream was observable in the circumstances of John's outer life.

Some of the destructive patterns we can get involved with include drug and alcohol addiction, sexual inadequacies, awful relationships, destructive work habits and any other observable, repetitive and unsatisfying circumstance in our lives. I am assuming here that patterns supporting us in pleasant circumstances and constructive results will not be considered subject to change by our outer mind.

Unfortunately for simplicity's sake, some of the patterns that result in our perceived comfort are two-edged and carry a destructive quality as well. This is one of the reasons addictions of any kind are so difficult to release. An addiction serves one part of the psyche while destroying another. Addiction to alcohol or drugs is a good example of this double-edged result.

Dreams can reveal the heart of the dynamics involved with the pattern we desire to change. In dreams, we can see the essence of the pattern. Once revealed, we can focus our awareness on the pattern involved and work to change it through whatever approach we favor. If the change is accomplished the pattern is in effect de-energized and disempowered.

The shirt-making factory shuts down. This is true whether we are dealing with patterns revealing themselves as psychological problems that affect some aspect of our lives, or psychological patterns that lead to physiological involvement resulting in disease and death.

I realize many will not agree with this statement or its implications. I simply present this to you for your consideration. If you take this as a working hypothesis and set aside belief or disbelief, perhaps you will be able to verify through your own experience the truth of what I have said. I say it because it has proven true in my own experience and I have observed it to be true for others.

Dream work is detective work. Success in solving the case depends on intuitive as well as logical approaches. As the clues are pieced together, the pattern of the mystery is unveiled. Dream work teaches us to balance intuitive and linear approaches: it is a path to integration of self.

Patterns are usually only seen in dreams over time. The clue we might be looking at a pattern is in repetition of the material. This is true, for example, in the case of a repetitive dream that always repeats in exactly the same way. We are more likely to see a pattern in a series of dreams with symbolic images similar in meaning but not exactly the same in appearance. The dreams may or may not show progress about a given situation. That will depend on what the dreamer is doing with the information, consciously and unconsciously.

Dreams indicating patterns often show the same issue in a different light or context. Over days, months, or years a certain theme may repeat itself in our dreams. At first, we have nothing to compare it with. Usually a pattern will go unnoticed unless we have trained ourselves to pay attention to our dreams and to the correlation between our inner and outer lives. After a few dreams in which similar events occur we may notice the similarity. This can be the signal of a pattern in operation.

To analyze a pattern you have to watch carefully to see how the results always come out the same way or nearly the same way. What are the similarities in the dream? What is the dream result of the dream action? How did you feel in the dream? What does this remind you of in your outer, waking life?

Once you suspect your dreams are revealing a pattern, see if you can ask questions of yourself that will give you the shape of it. If you can see the shape, the structure and the components of the pattern, you can unravel your desire for the result that the pattern always brings to you. It is worth the trouble. Think of yourself as a detective with an interesting case. Solving the case brings reward and recognition and leaves you free for other pursuits.

I am not going to give examples of dreams in this chapter. You can see patterns revealed in several dreams discussed in other chapters. Usually there will be a comment about the pattern seen in the dream. You now have enough information to recognize the presence of patterns in dreams without much help from me. Pretend you are Sherlock Holmes and see what you can deduce. Like the intrepid Mr. Holmes, you may ultimately arrive at the observation that the deduction is "elementary."

# CHAPTER 19

# DRUGS, ALCOHOL, AND ADDICTION IN DREAMS

Addiction of any kind cannot be resolved through a dream. What dreams can do is provide clues to the underlying psychological dynamics that result in addiction. I do not limit the definition of addiction to physiological response to physical substances such as drugs or alcohol. We are addicted, every one of us, to patterns of perception and behavior that sometimes have destructive results. This seemed like a good place to talk about this kind of dream. Addiction is a pattern of behavior, and we have just looked at the idea that unconscious patterns reveal themselves in our dreams.

Looking at patterns in dreams can prove to be extremely valuable in cases of addictive behavior. There is a catch, though. There are several prerequisites for using the patterns shown in dreams as an effective tool to address addictive behavior and initiate personal change. These are:

○ **Commitment by the dreamer to accepting the forces of change.** This has to come from within and often requires skilled assistance from without. The assistance can take many forms, such as group work or interaction with a skilled therapist or facilitator who is experienced in working with their own dreams and the dreams of others. I cannot emphasize this too strongly. It always depends on the experience and intuitive abilities of the guide. Trust your intuition when choosing someone to assist you, but base your decision for ongoing work on results.

○ **Commitment by the dreamer to self-examination and to implacable honesty about what is discovered.** You must tell the truth to yourself about how you really feel and what you really think. This is difficult, and often requires support to get through the feelings that surface.

○ **Experience in getting past emotional and reactive responses triggered when we look seriously at dreams.** The seeker must reach for an impersonal, objective and appreciative point of view that sees the symbolic images of dreams for what they are. This is necessary for accurate interpretation, and requires practice.

○ **Lots of patience.**

○ **Acceptance of oneself fully, just as one is.** This is a foundational concept. One never changes a destructive pattern by refusing to accept its reality. At best an uneasy truce is established, an internal standoff always at risk of collapse. Acceptance does not merely mean acknowledgment of the problem, although that is a first step. Acceptance means recognition of how the problem serves the individual, coupled with heartfelt appreciation for service that the problem has provided in the past. If that sounds as though it might be difficult, it is! I didn't say this would be easy.

True release and healing do not take place without self-love and acceptance, although some destructive and addictive patterns can be short-circuited by clear intention and significant inner motivation. We have to want to stop the behavior badly enough to do whatever it takes. Unfortunately, addictive behaviors severely undermine the inner, mental strength necessary to provide the intention and motivation. Drug and alcohol addictions are a good example.

It is possible for addicts of any kind to discipline themselves into avoidance of the addictive component. Twelve-step programs such as

Alcoholics Anonymous, which work well for many people, are an example of this approach. These programs succeed because they provide peer support, understanding and love for the person struggling with the addiction. They call upon spiritual forces for assistance, a "higher power." A sort of demilitarized zone is established in the psyche between the forces of addiction and the forces that do not wish to be addicted.

The inherent flaw in all approaches that treat addiction as an enemy to be defeated or held at bay is that the cease-fire can break down. As long as an adversarial relationship is maintained, the danger of renewed fighting is always present.

○ **A sense of humor.** Laughter is a great healer.

If the above conditions are met, there is an excellent chance that transforming and healing energies will come forward. As with any kind of psychological work that addresses a complex issue like addiction, progress may be slow and difficult. Using dream material can dramatically speed up the process, because it can reveal the underlying dynamics driving the addictive behavior.

The first key to releasing addiction is to see how the addiction serves. Addictions always serve the addicted in some way; the trick to releasing addiction is to build a new, non-addictive alternative to resolve the underlying psychological issues. There is always an option available that will provide the benefits of the addiction without the trauma of destructive addictive behavior, but it can take some work to discover what the option is and how to put it into effect.

If there is physiological addiction, appropriate medical treatment is the first step toward freedom. In dream work what concerns us is something far subtler, the unconscious patterns of perception which led to physical addiction in the first place.

If I had a simple solution to the problem of addiction, I would probably become wealthy overnight, hailed as the savior of many unhappy lives. Unfortunately, I do not have a simple answer available! I offer my observations in the hope they may prove useful to anyone working with addiction.

In a general sense it is well to remember that symbols of addiction appearing in dreams, such as bottles of alcohol or drugs, are first and foremost symbols. Therefore, these things are not just mere representations of an addictive substance. They represent the essence of all such substances. They represent what the substance does for the dreamer, or might do. This is also true for those who do not take drugs, etc. but who dream of these things. The dream can shed new light on how the inner psyche uses the substance or addictive pattern and reveal the root psychological dynamics of the addiction.

Addicts often have some insight about the causes of the addictive process, related to external events and personal history. This may present as almost anything. Some examples are alcoholic parents, peer group pressure, desperate living conditions, abusive circumstances, physical illness, work conditions, stress, and so on. Do you notice what all of these have in common?

The common thread is that all the supposed reasons for being addicted are seen as external. The addict (or the therapist!) points to something and says, "It's because of them, or this, or the situation or the friends . . . " The addict making such a statement disempowers self. The cause of the addiction is unconsciously projected outward and responsibility is shifted. Cause and source become confused, even though the addict may recognize that he or she is the only one who can ultimately change the destructive patterning.

The statement made earlier in the book about feelings of victimization applies most strongly here. As long as a person believes (and thus experiences) that someone or something did it to them, they will never release the addiction. They may handle the symptoms by avoiding the substance. Although the addictive fires may be quelled for a while, whatever psychic energy led to the addiction will not be defused or integrated. Just like a fire left smoldering, flames may burst out in the future at unexpected times and places.

To get to the useful information about addiction found in our dreams requires some practice. First level interpretations will not do the trick. The tendency is to see the dream simply as a dream about the real, physical problem. An alcoholic dreams of drinking and thinks the dream is about the drinking problem. That may be true, but so what? We have to get farther into the dream to derive genuinely useful information.

The following dream comes from a woman who is an alcoholic. She has been sober for many years and successful in establishing herself as a therapist. She works with battered and abused women and with alcoholic women. She has a lot of insight about her addictive behavior. At the same time, she has never really discovered why she began drinking. She is now beginning to learn more about the roots of her alcoholism as she makes new discoveries about herself, revealed in her dreams.

# Allyson's Dream

*I am at a very nice restaurant having lunch and I'm getting ready to leave. As I pay the bill, I ask for a bottle of wine. A waiter brings me a large glass of wine and a small bottle of wine. I drink the glass of wine, open the bottle, and pour another glass. As I drink it, I think to myself that I can't go back to work because my secretary would know/smell. I can't see clients if I've been drinking. I put the glass down and leave the restaurant. I start to walk through a parking lot and I can't find my car. I walk behind a Cadillac that's backing out and it nearly runs me down. I move away from it and cross the street into a park.*

*I am still looking around for my car when I stop dead in my tracks and listen. I say, "I hear you back there." Then two men and a woman come around and stand in front of me. They ask me what I'm doing and I tell them I'm on my way to my car—that I'm out looking for an apartment. We start to cross the street, heading back to the restaurant.*

This is a tricky dream and its meaning is well-hidden. Allyson could not make much out of the dream. She had another dream about a month later related to the first. In the second dream, alcohol does not appear, but she receives more information. The second dream is an example of how information about a similar theme presents itself over time. I will give you this dream now and then we can look at both to see what they reveal.

# Allyson's Dream: One Month Later

*I remember being with a very handsome man who I sensed as someone dangerous. We go to a country cottage/restaurant where I witness a man being taken away by thugs. There is an older, rich looking man there who tells me the man being taken away is going to be killed. He seems to assume that I know why the man is going to be killed.*

*The scene changes and I am in the dining room. The handsome man comes to get me and tells me "the Boss" wants us to see the car that is taking the dead man away. We stand in the driveway as a big white limo drives slowly past us. "The Boss" is looking out the window at me—it seems like a warning. After they are out of the driveway and down the road, the handsome man takes me back inside the restaurant.*

At first glance, you may not think these two dreams are related. Allyson knew somehow that they were, although she had not gotten far with the interpretation when she told me the dreams. It is always valuable when a dreamer reports that different dreams are somehow related. Chances are, they are about the same subject.

The first thing to look for is similarities when comparing dreams that could be about the same issue for the dreamer. We can assume, with reservations, that similar symbols may stand for similar things in that particular dreamer's consciousness. Here are the things that are similar in the two dreams.

○ Cadillac—big, powerful, dangerous car (first dream)

○ White limo—big, powerful, dangerous car (second dream)

○ Restaurant setting—both dreams

○ Return to restaurant—at end of both dreams

○ Companion or companions appear in both dreams

These are clues telling us that in some way the two dreams are related. If we could determine something about these similarities, we might be able to piece together the rest of it. It's like a jigsaw puzzle—we connect the pieces we can quickly fit together, then we move on to the more difficult areas.

A car is a universal symbol that means many different things to people. In this case the car is large, powerful and in some way dangerous. In the first dream, a Cadillac nearly runs Allyson over. It is "backing out" at her, i.e., emerging from her unconscious. What does this feel like as an image? If something is "backing out" in a dream it often stands for material hidden in the unconscious. It is literally in back of or behind the dreamer, not seen, and unknown. OK?

Presumably the unseen driver of the car either doesn't see her or ignores her. This is a statement of the unconscious. Allyson is the one who doesn't see what's happening here—remember, it's her dream. The car represents something dangerous, because it could run over her. The danger of something is determined by one's relationship to it.

If we are in harmony with something, it is not threatening to us. If we are not, it is. Protection means *to be in harmony with*. Whatever the car symbolizes, Allyson is not comfortable about it. This should reflect into her outer life, and we should be able to see it.

In the second dream, the car is a big white limo. The danger comes from the sinister figure of "The Boss" who rides inside. He is a killer. Who usually gets to ride in big limousines? The answer is people who are powerful and wealthy. People who ride in limos are successful, but they may or may not be nice people. The popular image regarding limousines is one of wealth and power. Like the limousine, a Cadillac can also be a symbol of wealth and power, success and prestige.

The key word here is "power." Power is the common element of both images. What kind of power? In Allyson's case, the power feels dangerous. We now know that one of the common elements in the two dreams is a fear of power. The theme is reinforced by the handsome but dangerous man who accompanies her in the second dream. This suggests that the underlying pattern centers on a theme of power as manifested in its masculine attributes.

This slant toward the masculine and negative is symbolized by the rich, older man (wealth and power again) who assumes Allyson knows why a man is to be killed. The same theme is emphasized by the figure of "The Boss." "The Boss" represents the ultimate in dangerous, uncontrollable masculine authority.

In the first dream, Allyson stops dead in her tracks because she senses the presence of someone "behind her." This is like "backing out." The two men and a woman who appear are more of the unseen actors in Allyson's inner play.

In the first dream, Allyson can not find her own car. Do you think there might be something going on here with these two dream actions involving a car? Are the images related? If cars represent "power" perceived as dangerous by the psyche and Allyson cannot find her own car, the message is that Allyson can not allow herself to be powerful. Therefore, by definition, she must feel disempowered. Now we are getting closer to the roots of her alcohol addiction.

What about the wine and the restaurant? We go to a restaurant to be nurtured and to eat, to take in something. In a restaurant, one is served. The food is brought to the diner, there is no work, and it is all about service and nourishment. In both dreams, she goes to a restaurant. In the first she drinks wine and worries about it being noticed; in the second she sees someone being taken away to be killed. The first restaurant is very nice—Allyson likes it there, it is comforting to her.

In the first sequence, she orders the wine just before leaving, when the bill is presented. There is some association here between paying and drinking. In some way, being at the nice restaurant where she is nourished must be paid for and at the same time she orders a drink. One of the ways Allyson felt good in the past was by drinking. A third level interpretation of this short section associates nourishment, payment and drinking. In Allyson's mind, the three are mixed up together. This offers a clue to pursue with ongoing work.

Allyson was raised as a Catholic. When we go for the third level interpretation in a dream, we make use intuitively of all information about the dream and dreamer available to us. Knowing Allyson was a Catholic is important information. The heart of the Catholic and Christian mystery is Sacred Communion, the offering of the Mass. Partaking of the wine and bread symbolizes the redemptive promise of Christ and the taking in of Spirit. Celebrants of the Mass are nurtured and redeemed, mysteriously made one with God.

In Allyson's mind, there is a piece that associates wine and Spirit, wine and redemption, wine and nourishment. To the psyche there is little distinction between the word *Spirit*, meaning a numinous mystery, and spirit, the word that applies to alcoholic beverages. Dissolving oneself in a bottle of alcohol is like the ultimate dissolution into Spirit with a capital "S."

I do not mean to suggest that Allyson's alcoholism is a result of her Catholic upbringing! That is exactly the kind of mistake often made on the second level of interpretation. If Allyson decided the Church was to blame for things she did not like in her life, she would simply be finding another scapegoat and avoiding recognition that she created the problem. What I am saying is that there is fundamental confusion in Allyson's mind between nurturing, spiritual energies and alcoholic spirits. This confusion is configured unconsciously and shows up in her addiction to alcohol.

Let's go a little further with this. The ritual of the Mass makes good on the promise of redemption offered in Christian theology. The redemption is necessary because of a foundational supposition of human guilt as stated in the Doctrine of Original Sin. The condition of being human, from this point of view, is by definition a condition of sin. Therefore, by definition Allyson (and everyone else) is guilty. Her guilt is part of the payment she makes to God for being human. To redeem herself she must take in the figurative wine of Spirit.

To the outer, logical, conscious mind it makes no sense that someone would confuse alcohol and the connection to God, except in approved rituals like the Mass. The reason the ritual of the Mass can be moving and effective is that the unconscious does not make the distinction. This is the experience of the Mystery. All effective rituals allow possible surrender to unconscious forces that transform ordinary awareness into exalted states. In these states, transpersonal energies are experienced. Once activated by the power of ritual, the unconscious sweeps away ordinary perceptions and judgments as it reaches for experience.

Does this sound like what happens when someone has been drinking too much? I am not the first to make an association between alcohol and Spirit, nor to suggest there is a connection between drinking and the thirst for connection to God. As far as I know, the first to suggest this was Carl Jung. I feel that Jung was right. In Allyson's dream, the third level of interpretation takes all of this into consideration.

In the second dream, Allyson is with a very attractive but dangerous man. He symbolizes something about her inner relationship with power and the masculine. Can you see that this is similar to the symbols of the cars, the "Boss" and the older man?

A killing is initiated in the restaurant. The man who is to be "killed" is a piece of Allyson that expresses itself in masculine ways but which is overshadowed by a fear of power. If Allyson chose to express this piece in waking life, she might meet with resistance and figurative killing in the outer, competitive world where she works. Any woman who has run up against the negative face of the masculine power structure knows exactly what I mean.

Here is a trap opening before us in our interpretation. The second level of interpretation sees the external masculine as the enemy and blames its feelings of disempowerment and fear on this convenient target. If we stop here, we will not get to the real message the dream contains. The third level of interpretation assumes Allyson has personal responsibility for feeling disempowered, regardless of externals, and looks for information about that. This is difficult!

One of the reasons Allyson drank was for the sense of power she experienced. If any of you have been serious drinkers, you know what I mean. As the inhibitions drop away, new and sometimes very assertive or aggressive behaviors appear. The psyche enters an unlayering process that quickly slips out of conscious control. One of the reasons people drink excessively is to be out of control. Different parts of the personality are demanding expression and alcohol or drugs can allow this to happen. When Allyson was drunk she could do and say things she would never permit herself when sober.

At this point in our interpretation of the two dreams we can say that the theme is about disempowerment and a threatening and ambiguous relationship with the masculine and men (whatever that means to

Allyson). It is about the fear of power, the desire to conceal this fear from others and a desire for connection to spiritual nourishment and source. This is quite a lot. Now we can see why Allyson has reasons to drink, although it remains to be seen what she will do with the information.

More details are revealed in the first dream by her thought about the secretary and the clients. They must not know Allyson has been drinking. First level interpretation looks at Allyson's self-judgment about having been a drunk and fear of exposure. The second level of interpretation recognizes she now takes appropriate behavior in her life by not getting drunk. The third level sees there is still something internally that "drinks" and that the other interpretations are secondary to this essential recognition.

In both dreams, Allyson heads back for the restaurant at the end. This is a crucial common component. It means Allyson has not handled the basic issue; she will return and does return to the previous pattern. This is where she is stuck symbolically. She needs to see what the "restaurant" is really about and to understand the symbolic meaning of what takes place there. Understanding could eliminate the necessity to return. Implied by the images of restaurants is that one of the underlying themes she must deal with is the need for nourishment, nourishment of the soul and the emotional self.

Allyson is looking for an apartment in the first dream, meaning something in her is trying to energize a new way of living in the world. Reaching further, the third level of interpretation looks at the word apartment and sees it as a statement of wanting to be "apart" from the pattern. She is not able to achieve this, shown by the image of heading back to the restaurant with the people who came up behind her. She is still under the dominance of her unconscious forces, i.e., forces "behind" her.

In summation, the two dreams show basic issues driving self-abusive and addictive behavior for the dreamer. It could take years of therapy and self-work to resolve these issues, and even then they might never reach a stage of resolution. That will depend on Allyson. In the meantime, she has had the strength to stop drinking and short circuit the destructive behavior brought on through the symptoms of the addiction.

In a broad sense, symbols of drugs, alcohol and other addictive substances or behaviors in dreams emphasize unconsciousness or a lack of awareness. Drugs suppress conscious awareness, in most cases. The addictive symbols represent something unconscious, not understood. This is true even if there is no physical addiction. If a physical addiction is present, then the dream will reveal some of the underlying psychological dynamics of the addiction.

A smoker might dream of smoking a cigarette and acknowledge addiction, but not understand why the cigarette was smoked. The first step in dealing with addiction is acknowledgment of the addiction itself. The second step is the activation of a strong desire for change of the addictive behavior. The third step is recognition and acceptance of the purpose of the addiction, whatever it might be. The purpose is the service that the addiction performs for the addict. The fourth step is growth into a new possibility of behavior that can provide the same service in non-destructive ways. Once the last step has been achieved addiction ceases to be a problem.

## Jack's Dream

*I inject myself with a syringe, twice, two ampoules. It is a clear drug, like morphine. There is litter all over the floor from doing this, from taking the drug. I hurry to clean it up so my brother won't see it. There is some difficulty doing that.*

Jack was at one time addicted to drugs but has been "clean" for many years. This dream shows something still active in his psyche keyed to the experience of drugs. Please remember that when the psyche is dreaming it is experiencing the dream as if it were reality. Taking a drug in a dream is the same for the psyche as actually taking it in waking life, and it will be taken for the same reason. The underlying motivation is the same.

There are two big advantages to acting out addiction in a dream not available in waking life. For one thing, there are no physiological side effects of the addictive action. More importantly, the dream may give information from the unconscious about why the addictive substance is required. This is what we were looking at with Allyson's dream above. The same is true for Jack, although much less information is given.

In your mind's eye, see if you can picture jack injecting the drug into

himself. See Jack inject not one, but two ampoules. The image of a nee-
dle penetrating the body is just that—-an image of penetration. This is a
good example of how we need to look closely at the actions and images
in dreams. Most of us would see the image of the addict injecting himself
and not reach for the meaning the image contains as a symbol. As a symbol, this is an act of penetration. In this sense, it is a sexual act.

Now we also have to remember that sex in dreams is mostly about relationship. Injecting oneself with a drug is, on this level of interpretation,
an act of relationship with the self. What kind of relationship? We don't
really know yet but there are several clues. Those clues are:

O **two ampoules**

O **clear liquid like morphine**

O **litter on the floor**

O **afraid the brother will find out**

O **difficulty cleaning up the mess**

Two ampoules could just be taking more of the drug, but that is a first
level interpretation and inaccurate. *Two* is the key here. Two is "more than
one." Two is a number that does not stand alone. Two is a number of balance. Two ones balance each other and make two. Are you with me so far?
Two ampoules means the act of taking the drug is an act of balance. This
is difficult to see because it requires a third level look at the image. The
dream reveals that the symbolic and addictive pattern is an attempt to
achieve internal balance. This fits with the idea that taking the drug says
something about Jack's relationship with himself.

The balancing element of the drug is clear in color. Clarity is like purity in this case. It is like a representation of clear energy, not unlike the idea
of alcohol as a symbol for Spirit. Of course, morphine also dulls and alters
the awareness. It is, after all, a poor substitute for Spirit.

The litter on the floor is the result of taking the drug. The image means that succumbing to the addictive way of trying to achieve balance results in trash and clutter, debris and litter in the psyche. It is difficult to pick up the litter, a warning to Jack that the pattern has physical and mental consequences.

The thought in the dream that the litter must be cleaned up or his brother will find out reflects Jack's relationship with his real brother. In waking life, Jack tends to see his brother as authoritative and judgmental.

Jack's brother is older and in many ways took on the role of an absent father. The dream says the addictive behavior is tied to Jack's feelings about authority in his life, especially masculine authority. A good second level interpretation at this point would focus on those feelings and relate them to the real addictive behavior Jack once showed when he took drugs. What is the third level of interpretation?

The third level is not dissimilar to Allyson's dream given earlier. In her dream, the issue was one of disempowerment. This is also true for Jack when it comes to masculine power figures, starting with his father and later with his brother and other authorities. The third level demands Jack pull back the blame he assigns outside of himself and look for the reasons why he negates his own power. You do not have to know about Jack's personal history to derive this from the dream.

Injecting oneself with drugs is a distorted expression of power. It is also an intimate expression of relationship with self. It is an expression against the authority of others over self, a rebellious act. It serves as a substitute for true empowerment. Jack's dream, although he has long been "clean," tells him he has not resolved this issue of self-expression and relationship to self in a nurturing and constructive way.

Since the dream has presented the images to him, it is safe to assume the pattern of self-destructive behavior and disempowerment of self has been activated. This does not necessarily mean Jack will return to drugs. There are many other ways he could act out the pattern and achieve the same result. That is the importance of the dream. It is a message to pay attention and notice how he is reacting in his waking life. Sometimes self-defeat is the most addictive pattern of all.

You may dream of taking drugs even if you have never had the actual experience. You may dream that you are addicted, caught in a disempowering loop of repetitive behavior no longer under your control. If such a dream appears, pay attention. Whatever the symbol may specifically be for you, in general it will represent a way by which you substitute unconscious action and behavior for a more aware state of being. The service provided by the addiction will inevitably do something for you that you have been unable to do consciously for yourself. Jack's use of drugs to overcome feelings of disempowerment is a good example. The addictive pattern is a result of not handling the real, underlying issue. One reason to take dreams seriously as practical advice for life is to see the real issue and take appropriate action if necessary.

# CHAPTER 20

# PROGRESSIVE DREAMS

Progressive dreams differ from repetitive and serial dreams because they are neither directly sequential nor exactly the same. They are similar to the other types in that they present images centered on the same issue in the dreamer's consciousness. Something is under consideration by the psyche and over time, several dreams show the dreamer just how things stand. New information may show what inner progress, if any, has been made.

Like repetitive and serial dreams, progressive dreams are valuable for revealing underlying, unconscious patterns. They also show how the dreamer feels about the effects of the pattern. The pattern may not be so dramatic as, for example, a physical addiction. But just like a physical addiction, a pattern effectively takes over control once activated. Whether the pattern has to do with drugs or one's relationship to authority makes little difference. Free will and choice in a conscious sense are unavailable if we don't know the pattern is running.

When we look through our dream journals and records, we may see several dreams portraying similar, although not identical, images and events. These are often not remembered until we go back over them. The outer mind quickly forgets past dreams unless there is some particularly good reason to remember them. Dreams are usually stored in short-term memory, which is why they vanish so quickly when we wake.

When you see a series of common images and/or themes, you know you are looking at a pattern. You also know you are looking at something in your consciousness calling for attention and perhaps change. If you can decipher the clues, you will achieve a much clearer insight or understanding about who you are and why you act the way that you do in certain situations. At that point, choice again becomes available to you.

For example, I had a series of dreams over about a year that consistently involved cars (vehicles) that were overheating or sliding backwards, out of control. Sometimes the brakes didn't work, sometimes I was in the car or not, sometimes someone else was driving. Often it was winter in the dreams. Always there was a female companion with me. All of this told me some consistent pattern was demanding attention. In the dreams, I could see repetition but also a progression. You can be sure I was relieved when the brakes began working in the dreams, even imperfectly! At that point in the progression I could repair or restart the cars. It was good to notice that the dreams began to have a summer setting, and that my female companions were less upset, happier and friendlier.

At that time in my life, I was experiencing serious second thoughts about the work I was doing. I was struggling financially and attempting to understand what exactly it is that I do now. I made several false starts. Part of my work involves opening to what I call feminine energies—energies of inspiration and intuition, energies more concerned with the flow of the moment rather than the logical goal of the future.

The winter scenes of my dreams told me something was figuratively frozen inside me. In winter, things are slowed down and in a contracted state of animation. It is not a time for forcing growth. One must be patient when winter has set in. I was being asked by the dreams to feel into disowned, emotional areas. I needed to see how I was "spinning my wheels" and making ineffective use of the "power" that was available to me. Anger was one of the emotional components, and this was one of the symbolic meanings of the overheating engines.

Over the period in which these dreams occurred I noticed many correlations with my outer life. The dreams reflected my true feelings about how things were and challenged me to reach for a different perception of my situation. The information they provided helped me understand what was happening externally, in my waking life. Gradually that began to shift as I made changes. The dreams changed also until things were running smoothly again.

Interestingly to me, I know many other people who have somewhat similar dreams. The car in our society has become a universal symbol with many meanings. This is easy to verify for yourself—just watch television ads. If you are even moderately observant, you can easily see that cars sell by association with values that have nothing to do with the car as a functional piece of machinery. These associations include power, control, sex, freedom, clean air, mobility, wealth, exotic experience and adventure, the ocean, masculinity, femininity, nourishment, personal security and safety, and frequently, youth. I could go on, but you get the idea.

Television ad people are well aware of the unconscious associations we project onto outer reality. This is one of the foundations of successful advertising. Sometimes the manipulation of the psyche is quite subtle. For example, in one ad a very quick background shot shows a man, sexual, bare-chested and dark-skinned, playing a piano (erotic, mysterious, fun) while a fan is blowing (hot, sexy). The curtains dance over the open windows (free—no boundaries). Meanwhile the voice over drones on, extolling the product. The ad is selling the product with images of exotic sex and romantic involvement, appealing to the unconscious rather than the rational mind. The message is in the images and only secondarily in the words. Just like a dream.

The TV people know images are far more potent than verbal information. Images shape our lives and our thoughts and opinions. Images are often substituted for truth, unlike our dreams, which always present truthful material. Our psyche is happy to acquire and use the collective images that constantly bombard us. Therefore, there may be a Ford in your future, but that future may lie in your dreaming consciousness!

One of the fun benefits from working with dreams is that you will develop an ability to see beyond the images presented by TV ads, programs and movies. Newscasts, for example, will take on a different meaning: the bias that is always there will become more apparent. It will be harder for the deceivers to trick you! You can hopefully appreciate the attempt and bring a new awareness to what you see. You will also start seeing things you never saw before, adding a whole new dimension to the enjoyment of film and visual entertainment.

---

## KEY POINT
**Working with dreams teaches you to feel into the real meaning of unconscious and symbolic images. Learning to attune to this symbolic meaning enriches the experience of all of your life, not just dreaming states of awareness.**

---

What I have written above may seem like a digression from the subject of progressive dreams, and it is! Thinking of the series of dreams I had containing the car images led me to the other material. That is an example of how dream work influences our outer perceptions. We start making associations that are not directly apparent, such as the connection between dreams and TV ads. Dream work encourages intuitive leaps of understanding in life and stimulates new perceptions.

Getting back to progressive dreams, these sometimes show that nothing has really changed, although a significant period of real time has passed. A dream may appear in childhood one or more times and then show up again, with variation, in the adult consciousness. There is once again an opportunity to see just what is going on and perhaps do something with it. The psyche is patient and it will present important themes repeatedly for your consideration. When the adult has the dream, he or she has options that were not available to the child. If the adult has a dream that occurred as a child, this means that the same underlying dynamics are still operating. It is easy to see that this might not be the best thing for the adult. Here is an example.

# Diana's Dream: Childhood

*I am in my mother's bedroom at night. She is asleep in her bed on the left side. I go to her with great fear, trying to wake her up. I am trying desperately to tell her I am dying but I have no voice. I am shaking her and holding my throat. She awakens and looks at me. She keeps saying, "What? I can't hear you." I keep trying to communicate that I am dying. She tells me she can't hear me and to go back to bed. I wake up.*

Diana had this dream, more than once, when she was about six years old. Years later, she had another dream that repeats the same theme with variation. Here it is.

# Diana's Dream: Pubescent

*I am out in my parents' front yard where I live, a well-manicured lawn with landscaping. It is the afternoon. A baby rattler bites me. I know this snake is more poisonous than a grown rattler. I go to my mother and show her my thumb (it's the left thumb) with the bite and try to tell her I've been bitten. I can't be heard. She ignores me. I go to my father and he doesn't pay attention either. I am very frightened because I think I will die. I wake up.*

The first thing we need to do is look at the things that are similar in the dreams. The things that are different in the second dream give us information that applies to Diana's life at the time of the dream, her pubescent life. It makes sense that the dream would do this, since she is no longer a young child. On the other hand, the same dynamics of consciousness present when she was six are present now. This is the similarity and the basis of both dreams.

What is similar? As with other dreams, we can take a worksheet approach and see what comes up. We'll vary it somewhat to take into account the similarities and differences.

# DREAM WORKSHEET

**1. Review and write down the dreams (see previous page).**


**2. The things that are similar in the dreams are:**

- dreamer goes to mother/parent
- can't be heard
- afraid she will die
- can't get any response that she wants
- terrified and very frightened
- something about left side, left thumb, left


**3. The things that are dissimilar are:**

- snake is shown as cause
- time of day—night in first, afternoon in second
- father appears in second
- outside/inside
- manicured lawn

Continue through the worksheet as you have done with the other dreams and see what you can intuit and discover. You already have an idea about what the dreams are about, don't you? Let yourself feel into the similarities, which reveal the basis of the pattern, and the differences, which reflect the later development. Let your mind make any associations it feels, and don't forget to ask the Dreamer Within to help you with the dreams.

These two dreams contain significant information for the dreamer. In a little while I will give you two more dreams that Diana had years later as an adult. These will continue the inner story. Right now, what can we see?

The most apparent thing that leaps out is the relationship Diana had with her parents. Without knowing anything about her personal history, the dream shows strong emotional turmoil and upset about communication with the parents, especially the mother. This is a first level interpretation, but important nonetheless. Diana cannot be heard, she is not validated or acknowledged by her mother and father. This is so important to her that she literally feels she will die from lack of nurturing and support. Remember that she first had this dream when she was only six. She is trying to communicate that she is "dying." If the parents could hear her, this might be averted. OK so far?

The dynamic of wanting and needing external support and thinking she cannot be taken seriously is still operating in her life at the time of the later dream. This could be a real problem in adult relationships and an obstacle to a satisfying life.

The deeper meanings are a little more difficult to see. What exactly is it that needs to be communicated or acknowledged? Where is the difficulty centered? The first clue is in the emphasis on "left." What is our collective association with "left?" For Diana, it could be a play on words—Diana has been "left," left out, left behind, etc.

Another possibility looks at collective associations. In the collective, "left" is not a good thing. Left has associations with the sinister, the dark and is often associated with the feminine, with woman. The reasons for this perception go back many centuries and emerged through different cultures and stories. In Western metaphysical studies, the left-hand path is the path of Satan, the path away from the light. This association has its roots in the Judaic/Christian ethic, which emphasizes masculine and ordered structures over feminine and chaotic, natural forces. The left-hand path is the path of the chaotic, the feminine, nature, sexuality and the pre-Judaic Earth Mother and all her representations. It is anathema to the right-hand path of the masculine, God the Father, restraint of sexuality, and control of human nature.

How could a little girl of six or a pubescent girl of eleven have any knowledge of these connotations of "left?"

The answer to that question is one of the mysteries revealed through the experience of expanded states of consciousness. If we humans are actually in some way connected to a greater consciousness and wisdom, for all purposes infinite and aware, then that is always true regardless of age, sex or conscious appreciation. If that is true, then it must follow that we always have potential access to that wisdom and consciousness. In turn that means all information and all ideas must be in some way available to us. Therefore a child of six or eleven can attune, unconsciously, to any image and idea held by the greater awareness.

The implications of this statement are mind boggling. I do not ask you to accept it, only to consider that it may indeed be so. Carl Jung recognized this possibility when he formed his theory of the Collective Unconscious.

From this perspective, "left" in Diana's dream takes on a new meaning. There is something here about the feminine, and of course, Diana is a girl/young woman. The mother, principle image of the feminine for the child, is indifferent and invalidating. The child's sense of self as feminine is diminished and pushed away. This has important ramifications for Diana's sense of self as a woman.

Is there something in the second dream that may amplify this? I feel that the snake image is the other clue to the real meaning of the dream. The snake is another symbol that generally gets a bad judgment in our culture, for the same reasons as "left." It is also a symbol of claiming the human condition, therefore suspect. This is the heritage of the Garden of Eden allegory, so firmly rooted in the basis of our Western religious traditions.

In the Bible story, the snake is the agent that leads to the human acquisition of the knowledge of Good and Evil, the forbidden fruit. The apple initiates the birth of the human ego. When Eve takes that fatal bite, nothing will ever be the same again: it awakens the conscious knowledge of self that separates human from animal. It is also the knowledge of self (in the story) that separates human from God. The human children defy God the parent and gain knowledge of their separate and human condition. As a result, they become responsible for their own well being. This includes the awareness of sexuality, viewed as a great sin, which produces shame. This shame has to do with the physical body and the human condition. The body now becomes something shameful and unclean. The snake has become associated with evil and sexuality, one and the same in most Western religious thought, except under proscribed conditions.

Although the snake has many other meanings as a symbol, in Diana's case I feel we are looking at an echo of this myth and that the area addressed by the dream is her sexuality. I am talking about sexuality as an expression of relationship, femininity and being in a feminine body, not just the physical act. The snake is immature in the dream, a poisonous snake. This suggests that Diana has an undeveloped sexuality at this stage of her life (when she had the dream) and that the whole idea of sexuality is threatening to her. Of course it is; she is eleven years old.

She has set up an ordered and neat inner existence in relationship to natural forces, including sexuality: she attempts to control them. This is the meaning of the neatly manicured and landscaped lawn. The chaotic energies of the inner feminine threaten this security. This certainly fits with the onset of adolescence and the physical maturation of sexuality.

Diana receives no support or understanding from the parents in her dream, who presumably might guide her or help her with this.; this actually was her experience in real life. On the second level of interpretation she might now, as an adult, see that she blames her parents for her feelings of inadequacy and non-support and work to change this.

The third level of the dream is difficult and subtle, and requires a certain intuitive leap. This is usually the case with any dream; there comes a point where something else has to emerge to get to the real meaning. Since this is not precisely a linear process, it is difficult to express exactly how we arrive at the interpretation. That is the function of the Dreamer Within: to provide understanding of the dream based on more than a direct, linear linking of symbolic evidence.

On the third level, Diana's dream is about her relationship with self. In adult life, she is a woman who experiences fears about her sexuality and femininity. She has struggled to find the internal support that will enable her to validate and express herself from an authentic center. The patterns preventing this development are childish in nature. The child is not comfortable with adult expressions of sexuality or self-support and never will be. Those are not appropriate expressions for a child. The problem is that Diana is still somehow stuck with the child's perceptions and relationship with life and this in turn is not appropriate behavior for an adult. The childish patterns are still operating.

Resolution requires Diana to stop projecting her needs for support and emotional nurturing onto others. This includes her parents but is not limited to them, since she will carry this patterning into all her relationships. This does not mean she should not ask for or look for external support. It only means that her challenge is to find inner resources that give her a sense of self-validation as a woman. The issue of sexuality is a core issue of her self-expression. Whatever she does to increase her sense of inner security will carry over into all parts of her life, including sexual expression.

Sixteen years later Diana had two more dreams, two months apart. These dreams continue the developing theme and comment on the progress made. By now in her late twenties, Diana had been working over some years with self-awareness and self-discovery approaches. She was beginning to focus on women's groups and women's issues as she reached out to explore the meaning of femininity. These dreams indirectly touch the issue of sexuality but mostly relate to Diana's developing sense of self. They presage development and change in Diana's psyche. Here are the dreams.

## Diana's Dream: #1

*I am approaching the door of a big, white house. It is two stories high. I am on the path that leads to the front door. I am about at the street, not close to the door. As I approach, I know that when I reach the door and enter I will die. I also know that it is not yet time to enter. I wake up.*

## Diana's Dream: #2 (two months later)

*I have died. I am not in my body. I am concerned that George, who is in charge of my body, will not wait the required three days before cremating it.*

The central issue for Diana at this time in her life is self-authorization. This may be the central issue for most of us! Out of genuine self-authorization comes authentic expression of self, including sexual expression. Authentic expression means being who one is in a way true to one's inner needs, feelings and uniqueness, without compromising those needs and feelings to standards set by others.

We do not live in a society that readily supports this kind of authenticity. This is becoming more obvious as the society becomes increasingly parental and authoritative about "what's good for you." If you don't think this is true, take a moment to notice how many ideas and rules are floating around these days about what's good for you.

In the first dream, Diana is approaching a transformational period. She knows that to enter the house is to die. She will not be the same after entering. She also knows it is not yet time to enter.

What does the house represent? "Two stories" is an oblique reference to sexuality. Two is the number of the second chakra, which affects the sexual energies. Two is a number of relationship: it is also a number of balance. Entering the house symbolizes something about balance and sexuality, although nothing more is said about this in either dream.

What do you think of when you think of a "white house?" Who lives in a White House? In America, it's the President, father figure of the nation, symbol of high masculine authority. He is the one who is supposed to know what to do in times of crisis and he is the one entrusted with the guidance of the national family. In Diana's dream, the big white house represents something about authority. To enter the house and die means to change something in Diana's consciousness regarding authority and secondarily something about sexuality.

If Diana transforms something internally in the way she views authority, her perception will change and so will her relationship with external authority of any kind. This is an integral and necessary part of any process of self-validation. Please notice that this is an internal process, leading to different relationship externally.

In the second dream, the transformation begins: Diana has died. She is in limbo—not in her body. This is the dangerous part of the initiation. She is concerned about George rushing the process. George is her husband. The cremation scheduled to come after the symbolic three days is the completion of the transformation, a successful conclusion. Cremation—

transformation through fire—new state of being. This cannot be rushed. The figure of George represents the part of Diana committed to masculine perceptions of what is right and wrong. These parts of her psyche base their judgments on masculine value systems.

When I talked with Diana about this figure of George, she said he represents a masculine side of her responsible for carrying through on actions she does not completely trust herself to do. Since Diana does not trust the masculine either, she has a serious problem! In the dream, she was worried because she was dependent on this masculine figure and had no control over the outcome. She is caught in a double bind of mistrust in herself and mistrust in the masculine. Part of the transformation that has begun will center on establishing better self-trust and self-authorization.

Diana is rightly concerned that her older, familiar and well-established ideas about how she is supposed to be, symbolized by George, will interfere and abort the process of transformation. Feminine authenticity is not discovered through expressing masculine values, but she does have to learn to trust the internal masculine to support her self-expression. The dream cautions her to stay alert.

The three day time period is most interesting. Where else do you see a three day period as a crucial element of transformation leading to rebirth and a new state of being? In the West, it is the period between the Crucifixion and the Resurrection. Before the Christian era, the same time period of three days appears in many religious and ceremonial observances. As we go back in history, it appears often as the symbolic transition period between death and rebirth to a new and greater awareness.

For an excellent example, look up the myth of Inanna, Queen of Heaven and Earth. This epic story of the transformation of consciousness dates to early Sumeria. For a modern Jungian interpretation of the myth read the excellent book, *Descent to the Goddess*, by Sylvia Benton Perera.

This sequence of dreams over many years shows progressive development in a long and ongoing process. It makes sense that it would take many years, perhaps an entire lifetime. Future dreams should carry on the theme, keeping Diana abreast of events and developments. In turn, she should be able to notice that her life is changing in ways which reflect the inner progress shown in the dreams. This has proven to be the case. Over the last two years, Diana has developed a different sense of self. She backs herself up more, even when this makes waves in her relationships. She has a different sense of her own ability and authority. When uncertainty arises, she deals with it differently. She is consciously choosing to explore and work with the feminine in a way that goes beyond simplistic assertion of her rights as a woman. Her dreams reflect this changing reality.

# CHAPTER 21

# CHRIST AND THE DEVIL IN DREAMS

Sometimes dreams present us with images of the struggle to understand our relationship with the Sacred. Although dream images of the Divine and the Sacred are always relevant to personal expression and consciousness, such dreams are on the border zone in the psyche between personal and impersonal realms. The dream images will differ by virtue of our culture, heritage and upbringing. Christians, Hindus, Muslims and Jews may have different images, as do all of the ethnic, cultural and tribal societies and traditions of our diverse world.

All cultures have images of the Sacred and spiritual. All of the images stand for numinous and mysterious forces that are transpersonal and beyond human. All of the images in some way suggest or convey the power of the Divine, by whatever name or form it is called or known.

In the West, we have Christ, God the Father, angels and saints. We also have the devil, demons, and images of evil on earth. You can see these negative and positive images on your TV or at your local theater any day of the week.

In Eastern spiritual traditions, God is a universal reality expressing all possibility and form, manifest and unmanifest. In the West, the three great monotheistic religions of Islam, Judaism and Christianity have split the evil, negative aspects off from God, and personified them as Satan. These are seen as separate from and at war with God. In the East, the negative is just a different face of God, part of an eternal cycle of change and transformation. It is much a part of God as anything else.

The spiritual challenge in the Eastern traditions is to recognize and appreciate these different faces of God made manifest in human form. Spiritual understanding and evolution take place through recognition, experience and integration of the many faces of God in one's own being. Success in this task leads to realization of the nature of God, and experience of self as not separate from the Divine.

In the West, the task is seen quite differently. We are taught to deny the negative and focus diligently on the "good". The existence of evil on earth is thought to be a result of man's original sin in achieving the knowledge of good and evil, inspired by the treachery of Satan, the personification of evil. Humanity is considered essentially evil because of this sin and may only redeem itself through particular actions, contrition and submission as defined by each of the three great religions. Failure to do so will lead inevitably to damnation and eternal torment.

In the East, the torment takes place through continued return to the suffering of life on earth. The soul is reincarnated until the spiritual lessons are learned and one is set free from the cycle. In the West, there is only one chance to get it right. If you fail you face an awful punishment; eternity is a long time to suffer.

Leaving aside questions of theology and opinions or beliefs about who is right, it makes sense that our dreaming mind will choose the familiar symbols of its cultural heritage to represent mythic forces of divine and supernatural good and evil. If we are entering a crisis in our spiritual development, these symbols may appear in our dreams. These symbols may also appear during times of fear or inspiration in our inner and outer lives.

This chapter looks at dreams of Christ and the devil, because the dreamers are all Christian in background. Someone from a Judaic background might dream of Moses, or the coming Messiah. Evil might be represented by a figure from the Judaic tradition of demonic form, such as Azazel. Christian and Jew alike might pull in representations from the

Old Testament. Hitler (or another) might substitute for the devil, but not necessarily, as Hitler represents many things to many different people.

In the West, because of our religious traditions, these images are particularly well suited to reflect the inner psychic struggles inherent to human consciousness. Conscious integration of content labeled by the psyche as good and evil is perhaps the most difficult of all psychological work.

Dreams in which images of good and evil appear hold the potential to reveal how we contain both possibilities. This in turn may lead to new options of choice about expressing good and evil in our lives. If we experience fear about something, the dream may shed light on the problem. If we receive inspiration, we may be uplifted and strengthened for whatever task is at hand. The following dreams give examples.

# David's Dream: #1

*Another man and I have taken Christ down from the cross and are attending to Him. We lay him down on the floor. There is a scar, fairly large, reddish and healed, on the area of his left shoulder. It is like a burn and puncture combined. The scar covers the front of the joint where collarbone and arm meet. He seems alert and somewhat tired.*

*The other figure disappears. I want Christ to instruct me, to heal me. I ask Him to shift to the energy that will heal or help me. He does so, and it is quite bizarre. His whole face changes, becoming purple and green. There is a sense of aura and power about Him. His eyes are very strange, three eyes, very weird. He begins to send energy to me. I feel it; at first it is uncomfortable, then painful and makes me nauseous.*

*I say to Him that I feel I am possessed. I ask Him if that is so, and can He drive out the possession. He has given me what He can, and instructs me to look above, where I can see a black shadow, like a nimbus, around my head. In the outline of the shadow, I can see demonic horns, like the devil. By this I know that I am possessed and that Christ can not do anything about it—He has already done what He can. With strong emotion and a painful feeling I say, "I've tried so very hard, can't You help me then?" There is a feeling of frustration and sadness in the dream. I realize that Christ can do no more.*

This is an important dream, showing an inner battle raging in David's consciousness. David has spent considerable time working with different teachers in the pursuit of spiritual knowledge and inner harmony. He has done a lot of psychological work, attempting to understand himself. He knows enough to recognize that he contains many possibilities of self, some of which are destructive and self-serving. He classifies his unconscious material under the general term of "shadow." Shadow is a Jungian term for unconscious content, often viewed as negative, that is not seen or understood for what it is. David fails to recognize that he also carries unconscious areas of service and compassion that balance his shadow. He is hard on himself, thinking he should know more than he does or be farther along the path he has chosen.

Without knowing anything of the background I have just given you about David, you can tell a lot from his dream. What do you think, so far? Is David "possessed" by the devil? If you think so in any literal sense, perhaps you need to look a little more closely at your own psychological material! Here are the critical questions you can ask in order to understand the dream.

○ **Why is it uncomfortable for David when the Christ figure sends energy to him in the dream?**

○ **What is the meaning of the demonic outline in the shadowy cloud above his head?**

○ **Why can't Christ help him any more than He already has?**

○ **Why does the dream begin with taking Christ down from the cross?**

○ **What is the meaning of the scar and the healed wound?**

○ **Why does Christ take on such a bizarre aspect when He shifts to the healing energy?**

○ **Why does David feel so terribly sad and frustrated at the end of the dream?**

Thinking of critical questions is another method you can use to get to the meaning of a dream. Make a list of questions about all the images you do not understand, or that you feel are important. Sometimes just asking the question will trigger the answer. There is always meaning and purpose behind every dream image or event or feeling. If nothing else, the questions will help you focus your attention upon the dream.

---

### KEY POINT
**You can discover the meaning of some dream images/events by phrasing questions about them. Sometimes asking the question will provide the answer.**

---

It might be helpful to know what David thinks the image of Christ symbolizes. There are many meanings that David, you, or I would very likely associate with the Christ image. There may also be personal associations for any one of us. What does Christ represent as a symbol? More importantly, what does Christ as a symbol represent to David? Here is his list:

○ **compassion**

○ **salvation**

○ **forgiveness**

○ **love**

○ **unconditional love**

○ power to heal

○ wisdom

○ connection to God

○ teacher

○ caring

○ help

These attributes are all positive. I asked David if he felt there were any negative qualities, and this is what he wrote down:

○ **commitment**

○ **surrender**

○ **sacrifice**

○ **pain**

○ **suffering**

○ **will change me**

○ **I will fail**

○ **something else but I don't know what**

These lists are very revealing. They tell David how he feels about establishing a genuine relationship with the spiritual teachings symbolized by the Christ figure. The first list shows all the wonderful things that David thinks the Christ energy could do for him: the second, the reasons why he has trouble allowing that to happen.

The theme of the dream is David's struggle to integrate powerful and conflicting feelings about his relationship to Spirit. The dream shows the current status of the struggle. David's psyche is at war with itself.

In the first section David and a helper take Christ down from the cross, a Christ tired from His ordeal, but alert. This signals completion of some inner process. In Christian teaching, the process of the crucifixion is necessary for transformation to take place. Without crucifixion, there is no redemption. The sacrifice is essential for the completion of the pattern. A sacrifice has taken place in David's consciousness, and now the next phase is beginning. Notice that one of David's negative connotations for the Christ symbol is sacrifice.

More than sacrifice is needed, however. This is true in the larger sense of the Christian epic and in the personal sense for David. The key element in both is that the sacrifice must be acknowledged and accepted. Otherwise, it has no personal meaning for the individual. This is the cornerstone of Christianity. Acceptance of Christ's sacrifice results in personal redemption, not the sacrifice itself. The sacrifice of Christ demonstrates the transformation of human form through personal realization, suffering and surrender to the impersonal influence of the Divine. The Crucifixion provides the most visibly important teaching. The taking on of human form by God is one of the core teachings of the Christian mysteries.

In David's dream, frustration and sadness arise because Christ can do no more. He has done all he can, sending healing energy that makes David uncomfortable and sick. This reaction shows David is not yet willing to accept the teaching of the Christ figure, although drawn strongly to it. This does not mean the teaching of the Christian religion! It means the example Christ the Teacher brought to the world as a figure of Unconditional Love, compassion, healing and willingness to surrender to the Divine. These qualities appear on David's positive list.

This part of the dream says David has work to do! He has reached a point in his spiritual development where responsibility for further transformation is clearly his. The transformation requires integrating the teachings symbolized by the Christ. The sacrifice must be accepted, but this is not yet possible for David or he would not be made ill by the energy.

The bizarre appearance of Christ as He shifts to the radiation of healing energy is a symbol of the underlying transformation of consciousness necessary.

The source of frustration is unconscious forces blocking development, symbolized by the black cloud or nimbus around his head. These are "anti-Christ." The wise Christ figure calls his attention to the cloud. The demonic aspect or suggestion of the devil emphasizes contrasting elements in David's psyche that resist the message of love and healing. For David it is like possession, since he constantly runs into inner barriers preventing recognition, experience and conscious union with the Divine. Those barriers exist in every human consciousness. The reason great teachers such as Christ appear is to help us cross those barriers into spiritual awareness and consciousness. The devil is a symbol representing everything opposed to the message of the Christ.

The scar on Christ's shoulder shows a wounding and a healing that has taken place. The left side may suggest the feminine; Christ is a feminine energy of spirit and healing in masculine form. This is one of the Christian mysteries. The location of the wound suggests cutting off or disabling the left arm, a symbol of disempowerment. It seems to have been a bad wound. The hopeful sign in the dream is that it is healed, a symbol of work accomplished in the past as part of David's evolutionary process of spiritual growth and inner healing.

The dream tells David clearly that the work now rests with him. It is time to take integrate the teachings and reach for inner resources that will activate the Christ energy of healing, love and compassion.

David had another, related dream a few months later. He dreamed he had to enter an underground tomb, where he would die. This was inevitable in the dream. He knew he had to enter the underground passageways of the tomb, and in the dream calmly accepted his fate. This is a classic dream image of inner transformation, similar to countless mythic examples, including the three days Christ spent in the tomb. It represents a distinct time of transition from one state to another and surrender to transformation.

A few months after the dream of the tomb, David had another dream in which Christ appeared. Taken overall, these dreams represent both a progressive aspect and a transformational aspect, as discussed in earlier chapters. Here is the second dream of Christ.

# David's Dream: #2

*I am a high school or college coach, coaching a softball or baseball team. They are dropping the ball and I think it is hopeless. Suddenly there is a beam of light from above, and I look up. There is an older wooden building with stairs and a room at the top, on the second story. I climb the stairs and enter the room. Inside the room Christ is standing. I realize that he can solve the problems with the team dropping the ball and other problems as well. He radiates kindness and compassion. I fall to my knees and begin sobbing. I wake up crying.*

What do you feel the dream is about? If you had these dreams over nine months, as David did, what could you discover about your inner journey?

The Christ in this dream has entered the fully transformed state. The time of transition is over. Now we see Christ in His full power, radiating love and compassion, and David reacts in a way much different from the earlier dream. By falling to his knees, David is acknowledging that power. At the same time, he recognizes that the Christ message holds the answers for him. Something has changed in David's psyche.

Being a high school or college coach implies immature development. High school and college students are not adults and they are not mature; they are learning something. The team represents all of the varied parts of David's psyche that are trying to work together and learn about spirit. They are dropping the ball! In spite of the coaching, the team is not performing as well as they could. A baseball team that drops the ball is not going to win many games. Dropping the ball is a collective idiom for failure.

The solution for David requires ascent to a different stage of consciousness, i.e., climbing the stairs to the next level. The message of the dream is that integrating and applying the teachings of Christ can solve David's problems. This is an overwhelming recognition in the dream. In my experience, people who truly open to the heart energies of love and compassion are often overwhelmed by emotion and relief. They cry more often than not. David is no different.

The figures of Christ and the devil are mythic in our collective consciousness. They represent the polarities of good and evil, darkness and light, life and death. They are symbols of issues of power and expression of self in relationship to the Divine. How we view these things will be revealed by the dream symbols. The issue of power is particularly important. Few of us are able to escape the conflicts that arise when we are required to express personal power.

Authentic self-expression of power in our society is a highly charged issue. We are confronted daily with the split between what we are told is good and right and evidence of power expressed in ways exactly opposite to what is taught. Somewhere along the way, each of us makes decisions about what power means. Some of us decide to be powerless, in order not to confront the potential that exercise of power holds for distortion and harm to self and others. In this sense, power is thought of as evil. It often appears as the devil or other demonic images in dreams.

It doesn't really matter what kind of power expression we are talking about. Most of us are not dealing with external power issues of great responsibility such as being President, commanding an army, or directing a large corporation. For most of us, the issues are personal ones involving sexuality, family, work relationships, finances and the like. These are the ordinary things of everyday life. It is here that we fight the battles with ourselves over what is right and wrong.

The heart and soul of the transformational journey is the struggle to express an internal authenticity of extraordinary divine expression in ordinary circumstances. To do that we must face our inner demons and integrate the teachings of human and divine compassion that put them in their proper perspective. To dream of Christ and the devil is to dream of our human potential and our struggle to be conscious.

Here is an interesting dream of the devil.

## Moira's Dream

*The devil is after me. He wears a long, black robe. A necklace with round silver pieces is around his neck. He is VERY tall and his head is small in proportion to his body. I can't see his feet. He just floats along. His face is always dark. I can see slender horns, perhaps 6 inches long, on his head. I think, "You can't have me." I remember his fingers come around my ribs from behind me. His fingers penetrate my body on the right side and go into my ribs.* Pain! No, resist, survive, survive! *I feel a shock to my body. I wake up instantly, very alert.*

The first thing that stands out in this dream is that Moira cannot see the devil's feet or face. The feet usually connect us to ground, to earth. In the dream, the devil floats along. This is a symbol of detachment: the devil represents something Moira has detached herself from, some inner, psychic reality. When I see symbols of detachment, I know that the dreamer has cut him/herself off from some difficult emotional area. She cannot see whatever this is about, cannot see the "face" of it, i.e., what it looks like.

The distorted aspect of the small head and tall body is also a clue, telling us that perhaps the issue symbolized by the devil, whatever it is, is not as serious as Moira thinks. It suggests she has blown the whole thing out of proportion. It may also re-emphasize that she is not seeing things clearly.

We still don't know what the problem is, but we do know three things about it so far. Moira is detached from the issue in some way; she does not see it clearly and cannot recognize it for what it is; and it is something that has become distorted or blown out of proportion in her psyche. The small horns, symbols of the devil's power and sexual nature, also emphasize that the problem is smaller than it looks.

The image of the devil familiar to us in the West is derived from the image of Pan, the Greek god who ruled the Dionysian forces of nature. Pan was a horned god with the lower body and hooves of a goat, noted for wild displays of drinking, fertility and sexuality. Pan is the master of the flute or panpipe, and his music seduces one into the sensual realms, away from the cares and responsibilities of logical and orderly life. One of the principle associations with the devil in the West is unrestrained sexuality.

In the dream, the devil penetrates Moira with his fingers, a sexual metaphor. This dream symbol is about expressions of sexuality with which Moira is struggling. She is not comfortable with sexuality, which challenges an undeveloped area of her psyche. Part of the problem is that

Moira was sexually abused as a child. This gives you background information that helps to confirm the interpretation, but it is not necessary to know this in order to see the sexual content and the fear of it symbolized in the dream.

The penetration causes pain; Moira resists and wakes instantly, alert and ready to act. This shows well-developed defensive modalities that protected her in the past. Alertness was her best protection as a child. Resisting and alertness was equivalent to surviving. Moira's survival was often threatened during her childhood.

The problem is that she is now an adult, married, and no longer subject externally to the abuse she suffered as a child. However, the issue is unresolved. That is understandable if we know her background. If we did not know something of her history, we could still see from the dream that she resists surrender to dark and threatening energies she associates with sexuality. We could also see that she does not understand exactly what the problem is and that it has become distorted and over-emphasized in her thinking.

External circumstances have triggered something for Moira and it is time for her to take a look at the problem. This is why she has the dream. The necklace of round silver pieces suggests the thirty pieces of silver paid to Judas (Moira is a Christian). In this case, the necklace is a symbol of betrayal, associated with the devil. It means that what the dream devil represents is equal to betrayal of something in her mind. Could it be the expression of sexuality and "Dionysian" activities is seen as inner betrayal? Round is also a symbol of something feminine. This is a third level association.

The same night that she had the dream above, Moira dreamed of a beautiful and radiant woman holding a budding wand, accompanied by a magnificent lion. There was a second lion nearby with a man cowering next to it. This dream was showing her an entirely different possibility of expressing strong feminine energies of life and sexuality. In both dreams, the relationship with the masculine is skewed, shown in the second dream by the image of the cowering man. Moira lacks balance, but balance is possible. That is the meaning of the budding wand (a symbol of positive, life giving masculinity) and of the first lion.

Moira finds herself in a time when the feminine can be developed and emphasized, but this requires submission and serious reassessment of her thoughts about the masculine. There is often a period of adjustment when we try to move into a larger sense of self, when it becomes necessary to emphasize one aspect at the expense of another. If all goes well, eventually a balance is struck. This is especially noticeable if we are attempting to energize a sense of our authentic self as man or woman.

Christ and the devil in dreams represent two sides of the same coin. Achieving psychic balance of these energies is a principle task for spiritual growth and awareness.

# CHAPTER 22

# MYTHIC DREAMS AND FIGURES OF POWER

The works of Carl Jung often trigger recognition and validation of my own experiences. I did not read Jung until after I had already discovered some of the complex deceptions my mind had created to mask my unconscious psychic material. Jung worked extensively with dreams. One of his most controversial and important ideas was the concept of what he called the collective unconscious. The idea has staggering implications. In essence, the concept is simple although difficult to integrate meaningfully.

As individuals we have a unique expression of self, in large part an expression of our unconscious thinking and perception. According to Jung's theory, our unconscious is shaped by personal experience and history and by a much larger, collective human experience. If true, the implication is that we are directly connected (through our unconscious) to the entire history and experience of the human race, since the time humans emerged as distinct life forms. It follows that any form of consciousness, human or otherwise, could be part of this great, collective mix. We may also be connected through the collective unconscious to the future experience of the race as well. This idea seems to find confirmation in the strange world of quantum physics, where time and space interact in ways unfamiliar to our normal, conscious experience.

Conscious expression then becomes largely a manifestation of personal unconscious dynamics influenced by the larger, collective pool of human experience and unconsciousness. One implication is that we must become aware of those impersonal and unconscious elements if we want to express our maximum potential. Another implication is that these elements affect us whether we are conscious of them or not.

Put more simply, we are beings of a collective nature attempting to express ourselves individually. Jung called the struggle to become aware of these inner relationships the path of individuation. It is possible that Jungians may see this somewhat differently, but this is my interpretation.

What does this have to do with dreams? Our dreams show us images based both on personal history and unconscious, collective experience. These are the great themes of myth and story, universal themes occurring repeatedly in every culture. These images weave their magic through all of us in some way or another. They are intimately connected with the experience of God and Spirit, and with being human. This great pool of collective experience represents a universal and invaluable teaching for those who care to pay attention. It is accessed directly through our dreams.

In earlier times, societies of the world recognized the importance of the myths and stories of their culture for what they were and used them as an anchoring point. The stories provided stability and continuity in a dangerous and mysterious world. Today things are different. We have not succeeded in creating a new and unifying cultural myth to live by that might provide stability, although there have been many attempts to do so. On the contrary, cultural myths and traditions are repeatedly attacked and revised, in an attempt to appease emerging power groupings and special interests. Revisionism in many forms is destroying myths everywhere, in every modern society. This is part of a painful, global process of social dissolution and personal and collective evolution. It is an alchemical and complex process of total change.

The result is that true teachings must now be sought on the inner planes, since there is no outward and accepted agreement. But there is a ready tool of discovery waiting for our attention, the inner doorway to universal wisdom that opens in our dreams.

The great themes are themes of transformation, reclamation, the quest for communion with God and the evolution of the human spirit. These are seen in such stories as the Sumerian myth of Inanna, the Arthurian legends, the Hopi and Sufi teaching stories, to mention only a few. These stories are roadmaps of consciousness, laid out by spiritual travelers who attuned to the essential mystery of human experience in ways reaching beyond their creators' time and place.

Our dreams take up the mantle of storyteller and teacher, casting us in some role in the greater human epic. Ability to understand the role we are playing can reveal valuable truths about who we are. We always have the choice to continue playing the role in the same way, change the way we play the part or take on a new part altogether.

One of Jung's key ideas is the concept of archetypes. For me an archetype represents a great, collective patterning of human energy. All archetypes have a transpersonal quality in common. They go beyond individual human experience to mythic proportions. They appear as gods and goddesses, divine and semi-divine heroes and heroines. They are symbolic and mysterious realities that exhibit qualities of universal human patternings, distinguished by their numinous and trans-human aspect. *Numinous* means that something carries the quality of the Divine, the Central Consciousness. We can give these numinous, universal attributes descriptive names to help anchor our human understanding. Some examples are The Nurturing Mother, The Fool, The Wise Old Man, The Crone, The Devouring Mother, The Sun God, and the Maiden. They appear in myth, in legend, in dreams, in great art. If you would like to see some examples, look at the engravings of William Blake, read the Odyssey, or look at the Major Arcana found in the Tarot.

These archetypes do not always represent positive energies. The Devouring Mother is an excellent example, as is The Devil.

Our dreams will sometimes present these figures. Because we are dreaming about them, we must have some personal relationship with the larger, impersonal energy they represent.

A dream that presents an archetypal figure of great power may take a long time to understand. One barrier to understanding will be the dreamer's inner issues about personal power. The dreamer's dreams will faithfully reflect the truth about those issues, but the unseen inner agendas of the ego's self-expression often seduce the dreamer into an inaccurate interpretation.

Archetypal dreams are especially important for understanding our inner conflicts and strengths, and the behaviors we demonstrate in our outer lives. For example, a person who resonates with the pattern of the Messiah will demonstrate this pattern externally, whether realized consciously or not.

Many of the archetypal patterns contain essentially positive and negative components at the same time. That is appropriate, since they are impersonal in their configuration and thus not subject to human ideas of good and evil or right and wrong. Archetypes simply are what they are. It requires the addition of conscious understanding and observation on the part of someone caught up in one of these patterns to tip the process one way or another.

For example, The Messiah, as an archetypal pattern, is a configuration of energies that can save or destroy. It is a pattern of enormous power, and if constellated in an individual capable of carrying the pattern to full expression there can be far-reaching consequences. An example of someone who carried this pattern in recent times is Adolf Hitler. Another negative example of this expression is Jim Jones. Both of these men manifested the pattern destructively. Destruction is a component of the messiah pattern, since transformation requires the death and collapse of an earlier perception. When combined with personal charisma, a powerful and immature ego and a lack of awareness, the results can be devastating.

By paying attention to these archetypal figures when they appear in our dreams, we gain two great benefits. First, we may see that the power of what is vibrating in our consciousness is pushing us towards some distortion. The nature of the impersonal is indifference to personal concerns about life. This can lead to expressions that are in essence anti-life, as was seen in Nazi Germany or the compound in Guyana. Dreams revealing these dynamics can warn us. We can choose to apply our conscious and individual free will and avoid expressing this kind of distorted behavior.

The second benefit is that doing such work allows us to see these patterns operating in others. If enough people were aware of how these archetypal patterns affect us, perhaps the individuals who carry the destructive manifestations would not rise to positions of such great power in the collective as they have in the past.

Here is a dream of The Messiah that demonstrates how an appreciation of the impersonal, archetypal image offers a possibility for personal understanding.

## Kurt's Dream

*I dreamed I was with a crowd of people. There was a hill and a paved street. It was daylight. We are waiting for something. Then Christ comes over the hill. I am surprised to see Him, and glad. I think He has been in prison. He has black hair, blue eyes, black beard, and a white robe. He looks a little fanatical. I know this is the Fuhrer.*

*I say to Him, "Has anyone ever been so loved as you, mein Fuhrer?" I open my arms to Him. There is excitement among the crowd. He embraces me, my heart is beating fast. Then He steps back, waiting. I realize I am supposed to lead the people or speak to them, but I am not sure what to say or do. I am His representative to the people, to lead for Him.*

Kurt is not German and is not a Nazi. The association in the dream linking Christ and "the Fuhrer" is a perfect example of the dark and light side of the Messiah pattern. There can only be one messiah, only one true messenger of God. The messiah brings this true word to his followers, who then act as his emissaries in the world. This part of the pattern demands submission to certainty that the messiah brings absolute truth in his message.

Followers of any messiah bring their own interpretation to the "truth" and distortion sets in. This leads to fanaticism on the part of the followers, usually manifested through unconsciously driven, destructive actions. In Christian history, for example, one only needs to consider the horrors of the Inquisition. The Nazi example is well known.

As the dream opens, Kurt waits expectantly with a crowd of people. The "people" are Kurt: this is Kurt's inner, collective expression. Over the hill comes Christ, a figure of power, carrying what Kurt describes as a slightly fanatical look. The dream is beginning to show the shadow material. That suggestion of fanaticism is what Kurt needs to look out for in his personal development. It is the look of the true believer who knows he has found truth and right.

Kurt is surprised to see Christ because He has been in prison. This is a wonderfully straightforward and clear piece of information. The energy of the messiah figure, whatever that means for Kurt, has been imprisoned, locked away in his psyche. Now it is free. This portends change for Kurt. What the change will be is unclear, but this energy has now become active. Kurt is making progress in his spiritual and inner growth, and is now ready to interact in a conscious manner with this psychic area. He is beginning to integrate what the figure represents. The dream provides information about this inner relationship.

The quotation, "Has anyone ever been so loved as you, mein Fuhrer," was spoken by the Nazi leader Hermann Goering. It turns up in the news-reels and endless documentaries of Hitler and the Third Reich often found on your TV. It is the statement of a believer and flatterer, who gains status and power by association with the messiah. At the time those words were spoken Hitler was indeed loved by millions who saw him as their literal savior. This piece of the dream is like the Christ/devil split we looked at in the last chapter. The association with Hitler, the Fuhrer, is like the association with the devil.

Kurt opens his arms to receive the embrace, and the crowd stirs. Kurt's heart is beating fast as he moves towards union with the Divine figure. They embrace and Christ steps back, waiting. Now what? With the bless-ing bestowed, Kurt is supposed to take up the banner and lead but he doesn't know what to do.

This section shows how much Kurt wants this union with the Divine. It also says he does not know yet how to communicate the message to the crowd: how does he get the message of the Christ across to himself? He is uncertain. That uncertainty reflects Kurt's true ambiguous relationship to this patterning of forces.

When you ask for knowledge about this dream, what do you get? Can you see the inner relationships Kurt is working with?

In real life, Kurt actively influences others, who sometimes assume he has an inside line to the Divine. He has been tempted to take on the mantle of teacher of Divine truth, because it is easy to believe in what you say if it has some element of truth and power to it. Kurt would like to be loved by millions, and this aspect is not far from the surface.

The dream is cautioning him to pay attention to this tendency towards fanaticism, certainty of absolute truth, and the divine right to lead others. This applies to his "conscious" mind (where he has a tendency to deny anything that conflicts with what he believes to be true) and to behaviors acted out in the real world. Kurt must watch for the emergence of the "messiah" pattern he carries in himself and for the distortion that accompanies it. The dream reveals the archetypal patterning.

The dream also shows considerable potential. If Kurt can constructively integrate the pattern, he will gain success in his work as a teacher. It is not yet time for this to happen, though. Kurt has things to learn before he will "know what to do."

The next dream is so full of classic archetypal images that I would suspect it was fabricated if I did not personally know the dreamer. I have seldom seen a dream so mythic in nature. This is a dream of the initiatory transformation of the inner feminine as it takes on a more active role for the dreamer. The integration of what this dream portends will certainly take years. The dream is long, so I will present it to you in sections.

Please get comfortable and take your time with each section. See if you can resonate with the images. Let your mind freely associate from your own experience. If you are well versed in myth and psychology you will easily recognize the collective images. If you are not, you will still be able to feel into the images and sense their significance. Knowledge of symbols and myth can make it easier to interpret dreams, but is not necessary for understanding. You have an innate ability to tune into the accurate meaning of the dream. You have been exposed at one time or another to everything seen in the dream, although you may not remember it.

## Sandra's Dream: Section One

*I find myself crawling down a long, dark tunnel. The tunnel is round and the earth walls touch my body. I come out into a circular opening in the earth.*

This opening sequence is a classic image of entering a place of transformation and change, right out of the shamanic traditions. The image is womb-like. We usually think of the earth as feminine—"Mother Earth." The tunnel is like a birth canal, but at this point the journey is in reverse. Sandra emerges in a circular space, back in the womb. This dream will be about core perceptions and experience of the feminine for the dreamer. This is clearly apparent in the next sequence.

## Sandra's Dream: Section Two

*At the far side of this circular chamber a woman is seated on a golden throne. She is black and is dressed in a black robe. A circular golden pin of a snake devouring its tail is in the center of her breast. On her head is a golden crown, with a motif of skulls and crescent moons. Her hair is long and hangs in tangled ropes. Her eyes are closed but I don't believe she is asleep—merely waiting.*

If I were trying to find an image of the archetypal feminine, I could not do better than this. The Black Queen is an ancient figure, and her decorations appear throughout history in mystical images of death, transformation and wisdom. The snake that devours its tail is very old and symbolizes the circular existence of all life. It stands for wisdom, rebirth, transformation and the renewal of the spirit. It is a symbol of knowledge.

The crown of skulls and crescent moons is found in many ancient cultures. These symbols first appeared in Asia and the Middle East. For millennia, the crescent moon has been a symbol of rebirth and the beginning of all things. The skulls bring in the aspect of transformation. Transformation requires the death of something so that the new may appear. Skulls and crescent moons together present a clear message that the figure on the throne represents initiation and transformation. For Sandra, the image suggests potential transformation of her view and experience of self as a woman.

The Black Queen is an archetypal representation of the hidden, primal side of the feminine, dangerous to those who will not acknowledge her. This awesome figure sits, waiting, on her throne of gold. The gold represents purity, power and the connection of Spirit with the world. Gold represents rule and authority. Gold is the pure refinement of the raw material of the earth. Gold represents the transformation of the mundane through Spirit.

## Sandra's Dream: Section Three

*I begin to dance before her. This is a passionate dance and yet it is a dance of submission. I am clothed in veils of seven colors. The outermost is amethyst, then indigo, blue, green, yellow, orange and the one closest to my body is red. As I dance I remove the veils one by one. Each one is harder to remove than the last but at last I stand naked before her. I am very hot and out of breath.*

You have probably heard of the dance of the seven veils. It is unlikely you have seen it! The association most of us have with the dance of seven veils is one of eroticism, sexuality, femininity, beauty and surrender. It is supposed to be a dance of passion and submission, just as in Sandra's dream. You probably don't know that there is a hidden meaning to those veils. Why seven? Why is seven a number associated with magic and luck and superstition?

In metaphysical literature and in the great religious teachings of the East there is frequent reference to seven major energy centers in the body called chakras. The word chakra is Sanskrit and means wheel or disk, because to expanded vision a chakra may appear as a spinning wheel of color. In psychology, chakras are considered to be strictly symbolic representations, but believe me when I say they can be tangibly experienced even if they are not seen. Chakras are real.

Chakras are a connecting link with the transpersonal and spiritual. In illustrations, they often appear as a system of seven body centers, located at different points and rising in a vertical line from the base of the spine to the top of the head. These major chakras (there are others) are shown in the colors of the rainbow, beginning with red at the bottom and ending with violet or amethyst at the top. Work with the chakras, as presented in ancient yogic teachings and in other traditions, may lead to transformation of the human experience and union with the Divine.

I am telling you all of this because it is helpful in understanding the seven veils of the dream. Removing the seven veils is an act of submission, preparing for transformation to come. This same symbolism shows up as seven gates in the myth of Inanna. Inanna descends to the underworld (ruled by her black and terrible sister, Ereshkigal) through seven gates, shedding articles of clothing as she goes until she stands naked before her sister. This dream is picking up the same mythic thread.

How are you doing so far? If this story looked like a movie instead of a dream, what would you think the movie was about? Can you feel the part of you that responds to such images?

## Sandra's Dream: Section Four

*I look up and the woman has now opened her eyes and is looking directly at me. She has terrible eyes—they hold the knowledge of all things. I am afraid of her and at the same time feel she is sacred. She rises and comes forward and stands in front of me. At this time she is also naked. She reaches out with her right hand and begins to touch my body. At the same time, she touches her own body in the same way.*

*She starts by pressing her palm flat on my forehead. I feel the hot blood well up under her hand and begin to drip down my face. She has done the same to herself and as she removes her hand I see the bloody handprint on her face. She touches me in this way all over my body, at the same time touching herself. She looks horrible, the blood is welling up and dripping down her body into the earth. I know that I must look the same. We stand face to face and our hands are raised with her hands touching mine. I look into her eyes and feel that we are sisters.*

The Dark Queen begins the initiation, the transfer of energy. The terrible eyes are a feature of this dark side aspect, and convey the essence of her nature. She is a Shadow figure, not usually consciously appreciated or even recognized. She is an aspect all men unconsciously fear for her destructive powers. Her usual manifestation in the outer personality is unconscious and destructive.

If you would like to see an example of this energy at work, watch the movie *Fatal Attraction*. Glenn Close gives an amazing performance that includes this dark side aspect as one of the prime components. The more the feminine and its needs are unrecognized and pushed away, as exemplified in the character played by Close, the more this aspect comes forth in the picture. The dark side of the feminine does not require trappings of mythic symbolism to show us her face. She exists in all of us, men and women alike, and may emerge at any time if sufficiently provoked.

The blood is another symbol of life forces and primal energies, an essential part of the ceremony and passage to a new state of being. Sandra's recognition of herself in the other ends this section. She feels her kinship: it is herself she is looking at.

## Sandra's Dream: Section Five

*And then I start to swallow her. I do this in the way of a snake; opening my jaws wide and swallowing her whole, head first. This takes a long time and when I have fully ingested her I feel that my body is very large and swollen. Then I look down and see that I am pregnant. I crawl, sweaty and bloody and pregnant, back up the earth tunnel. At this point, I wake up.*

There is an obvious, strong sexual component here. The expression of sexuality has an essentially dark side to because it is primal and ancient, impersonal and amoral. Full expression of sexuality is not a feature of our culture. No one escapes conflict between what society says is allowable and what the primal psyche can demand.

Union with the Black Queen takes place. The devouring aspect of the queen is mirrored in Sandra's act of swallowing her whole. She devours and nurtures herself (swallow=food=nurture). Then she returns to the surface, pregnant and bloody. The birthing of what this dream is symbolizing has not yet occurred.

This dream is about something Sandra wants very badly, a sense of power as a woman and as a sexual being. It is a deep dream of the deep psyche. The terrible, bloody-handed figure of the Black Queen represents something feared and long repressed, but things are changing. The potential for expression is now gestating inside her.

In the past, Sandra was attracted to the New Age philosophy of "Love and Light." She carries energies not consistent with that philosophy. She lacks inner balance and understanding of these forces. True manifestation of expanded love and a positive experience of life may depend on recognition that she contains in her psyche dark side aspects like the Black Queen.

Deeper understanding of self lays the groundwork for tolerance and understanding of others. Sandra's challenge is to find a way to integrate and birth the Black Queen. The dream holds this promise out to her.

There is another consideration, related to suppression of her dark side. The dream reflects her desire to be special and to have special knowledge. Sandra has an inkling of this. The desire to be special is something we all bring to self-discovery, although sometimes we don't know it!

One of the functions of dreams is to provide a sense of compensation for lack or excess in outer life. A wealthy man may dream of being poor. A woman who feels powerless or suppressed may dream of having great power and expression. This dream can be seen as compensatory, but the deeper interpretation honors the symbols for what they are and what they portend.

This next dream is one I had a few years ago.

# The Crystal Woman

*I am in a room somewhere. A powerful, tall woman, blond, wearing a long dress or gown of lavender/white is standing before me. She says, "Tell me how to energize a crystal." She has a large, amethyst crystal, roughly diamond shape. I also have an amethyst crystal, more columnar in shape than hers. I tell her lots of things about working with crystals and she goes away to work with it.*

*When she comes back, she has mastered it. She says to me, "The most valuable thing you told me was to focus the mind on the crystal and then bring the energy through from the bottom." In the dream I am startled by the simplicity of this as compared to all the information I had given her. Then there is a section of the dream I don't remember.*

*She comes again and asks me the same question. This time I reply, "You focus your mind on the crystal and bring the energy through from the bottom." She nods, pleased, and goes away. She comes back as before, having mastered it, very pleased. In the dream I remember what she said the first time, which is why I tell her what I did. She has a very commanding presence.*

This is certainly a dream of power. I have a sense in the dream of energizing the crystal in order to use it for some powerful purpose. The woman is mythic, commanding, archetypal. She is not an ordinary woman!

There is a strong clue here in the color of her dress, similar to the crystals she and I are both holding. The correlation of colors suggests that she and the crystal symbolize something in common. There is an association between the images emphasized by the common colors. A third level reading says that energizing the crystal and energizing what the woman symbolizes are the same thing. Whatever she represents will be empowered by the process of "bringing the energy through from the bottom."

It is also the woman who tells me this in the dream. Originally I tell her many things—I have figured it out, so to speak. This is a masculine process, a linear, informational process. From all I have told her she comes back with information, simple in its essence, that goes straight to the heart of the matter. This is the advice about bringing the energy through, twice repeated in the dream.

When something is repeated twice, particularly a clear and well-remembered statement such as appears in this dream, you are looking at an important message. You must make a connection between the message and the other symbols contained in the dream. In this case, the message is not so much about crystals (although that is a way to do it) but about my inner relationship with feminine forces.

In the dream, the Crystal Woman is pleased with the teaching and is pleased even more when I repeat her teaching back to her. It is a loop; it appears that I gave her the information, but she is the one who communicates it clearly to me.

This is a positive dream, as it tells me there is an open channel of communication with the transpersonal and that something in me is willing to listen to the message.

It is easy to see from comments throughout the book that I place a lot of attention on our inner relationship of masculine and feminine. Archetypal and impersonal feminine energies are critically important. The dream is telling me to empower the feminine, to balance mind (focus your mind) and feeling (bring it up from the bottom). The Crystal Woman is telling me that I can do this. Do you see how I arrived at this interpretation?

I have had other dreams where a feminine figure acts in a teaching capacity. The figure is always numinous and mysterious. She always radiates an aura of power and wisdom. I have also had dreams of the terrifying and destructive aspect of the feminine. This figure is so clearly beyond human that archetypal seems like too mild a word for her. I have seen the Crone and the Nurturing Mother appear in my dreams. Each of these dreams of the transpersonal feminine has remained in my mind and each has felt important to me in ways most other dreams do not.

These archetypal images always herald something moving at the deepest levels of the psyche. If and when they come to you, you will recognize them by their presence and mysterious aura. They stand out in our dreams. When we meet these figures in our dreams we are touching upon one of the great mysteries of human experience. They reaffirm our common humanity and touch it with the breath of something beyond human at the same time.

# CHAPTER 23

# LUCID DREAMING

The idea of lucid (conscious) dreaming has become very popular recently, and a book about dreams needs to talk about it. If you have read this book with moderate attention, you know that I feel the dreaming state is a wonderful tool for self-discovery and information. My experience is that our dreaming consciousness connects directly to wisdom far surpassing the knowledge usually available to our waking minds. This means I have some considerations about recommending lucid dreaming practices, unless and until the dreamer is well experienced in working with normal dream states.

I see the dreaming consciousness as an interface, a connection to a wealth of resource and information not normally available to the conscious mind. It might not be in our best interest to impose our less aware and less developed outer awareness upon this enormous resource. That is what many people tend to do when they take up lucid dreaming practice. Lucid dreaming is usually an attempt to control, change or direct the information received from the unconscious in dream states. It is an attempt initiated by the ego to maintain or develop personal power. We want to control something because we think that we will obtain some advantage, or because we fear it and feel threatened by it.

From my perspective, there are two immediate problems with lucid dreaming. First, the motivations for establishing power and control are usually unconscious and therefore not consciously understood. Remember, if something is unconscious, by definition we do not know it exists. Second, if the dreamer succeeds in inserting conscious participation or control into the dream, the dream information is changed to suit the dreamer's idea of what is wanted. The underlying message is lost. The dreaming state is taken prisoner by the ego's overriding desire to make the dream be the way it wants it to be.

However there is a genuine, spiritual use for conscious dreaming techniques. They can teach us lessons about reality and alternate states of experience and existence. It is no accident that ancient traditions recognize a magical and mystical component to conscious dreaming. Many tribal societies use dreams as a tool of great shamanistic power. In these societies, the shaman has learned to seek information through dreaming, using the context unique to his or her tradition. This may or may not involve the use of hallucinogenic drugs. It will always involve ritual and highly focused intention.

Sometimes the purpose for entering an altered state of dreaming awareness is to connect with a spirit guide, often a force of nature like a bird or animal. The guide in turn provides information. Sometimes the purpose is to search for healing information or locate something specific in the "real" world, such as an herb or power object. You can see a good presentation of this in the film *The Emerald Forest*.

Sometimes dreaming is used as a tool for white or black sorcery, to help, instruct or manipulate others. In societies that have such a tradition, this magical dreaming leads to tangible results. Practicing shamans who follow traditions of dreaming are able to enter many progressive stages in their dreams. They consistently warn of the potential dangers in doing so. The shaman goes deeper and deeper into the dream reality, waking on each new level. After the fourth level, we are told, things start to get dangerous.

One of the best examples of lucid or conscious dreaming in contemporary literature is found in the books written by Carlos Castaneda. For example, Don Juan's directive to Carlos to look for his hands in his dreams is a classic and effective instruction. When the dreamer finds his hands in the dream it is a cue to the dreaming consciousness, causing it to "wake up" in the dream and pay attention in a different way. Looking for a visual cue in your dream is one of the techniques you can use to become lucid.

In a few tribal societies, lucid dreaming is a tool for confronting inner fears that appear in dreams. The dreamer can handle the troubling material by changing the way in which the threat is perceived (changing ideas and attitudes about it) or can gain mastery over it in the dream by transforming it into something else. That certainly can be a valuable therapeutic aid in some situations. For the most part, I prefer to seek an understanding of the underlying psychological dynamics that drive the imagery in unpleasant dreams. You do that by looking at the dream in the ways we have been practicing throughout this book.

We have much work to do before we clearly understand our unconscious motivations. When we take on a new technique of inner exploration, such as lucid dreaming, there is a real risk of aborting stages of development in our expanding awareness. The pursuit of expanded consciousness always carries with it the risk of distortion, never seen for what it is at the time because that is part of the distortion! Lucid dreaming can support or hinder the process, depending on purpose, preparation and intention.

In the tribal societies with a tradition of conscious dreaming there is a lot of training and preparation for the task. Not everyone does it or is encouraged to do it. The shaman or medicine man/woman undergoes difficult and extensive training, designed to stabilize consciousness while in the altered dreaming state and create harmony with the powerful forces accessed through the unconscious. Few of us are trained in this way. It requires much more than technique to work safely and successfully with all of the experiences that can be reached through conscious dreaming.

There isn't any question lucid dreaming can open windows that are exciting and provocative of growth. However, it also seems clear to me there is much work to be done in looking at the self through normal dreaming states before lucid dreaming should be attempted. That work may take many years. Please consider these remarks if you are interested in lucid dreaming or have already begun to explore practical techniques for conscious dreaming. Taking time to discover and integrate the psychic material presented in regular dream states is a necessary step on the path to reaching understanding of self.

Having said this, if you are determined to experiment, here is a simple technique for inducing lucid dream states. I did not invent it, nor do I recall where I learned it, but it works. If you are disciplined and alert, you may get some interesting results. You are responsible for what you get.

Just as it is necessary to record your dreams and teach yourself how to remember them, it is necessary to support lucid dreaming with outer preparation. This is consistent with the shamanistic traditions, which have the benefit of ancient and proven ritual practices and a spiritual context for the process. Anything you can do that will provide a similar context is desirable, especially the focus on spiritual content and purpose. Prepare yourself for lucid dreams with meditation and contemplation; consider your motivations.

During the day, whenever you remember to do so and as part of any preparatory ritual you create, trace the letter "C" on the palms of your hands. Do this with one of your fingers. I have known people who actually wrote the letter "C" on their palms with a pen. The "C" stands for "Consciousness." Do this every day, with intention. The intention is that you will use this visual and tactile tool to trigger a lucid dream. By pressing the letter onto your palms, you anchor the mental intention in the physical plane. This is very effective. It may take some time, but eventually you will have a dream, and in that dream you will notice the letter "C" on one or both of your hands. Seeing your hands is a signal in the dream to become lucid, i.e., to realize that you are dreaming and that you are aware in the dream. Then you can start to look around in the dream with conscious attention.

It also helps to write down your intention for lucid dreaming. A shaman might spend hours or days preparing a painting or a design that represented his or her intention for the conscious dream. You can do the same by being clear about what you wish to accomplish. I suggest that you focus at first on simply becoming lucid in your dreams, not on a specific problem or desire you might have that could be a subject for lucid dreaming. As you become more proficient in achieving and maintaining lucidity, you can then experiment with specific areas of interest.

When you go to bed, relax and turn your attention to your desire for establishing a lucid state. Keep yourself easily centered on your wish to become conscious during your dreams. At the same time, tell yourself you will remember and record your dreams. Remind yourself of the cue or trigger that will signal to you that you are dreaming. It could be to look at your hands in the dream, to see the "C" on your hands, or some other visual clue. Mechanical devices, lights or sounds may also provide cues. Whatever it is, remind yourself as you are drifting off that the cue will trigger a conscious state inside your dream.

Once you have established lucidity in the dream, take your time and try to notice everything you can about the dreamscape you are experiencing. If you wish, you can change the dream at this point. I would recommend that you not do this, but rather allow the experience to guide you. When I achieve the lucid state, I always experience a distinct and physical electric feeling in the dream. Usually the colors of the dream intensify, and I become aware that I am now dreaming and "awake" in the dream. Often there is a brief period of greenish tint to everything. Your experiences will probably be different.

Some people use lucid dreaming to create fantastic sex, gratify their most expansive wishes, or otherwise indulge all of the ego's desires. It's your decision. If you really want to enter the mysterious world and alternate dimensions dreams can access, then you will be patient and allow the dreams to instruct you. These dreams can be an entry into a dimension where genuine spiritual instruction is available.

I recommend you also learn to provide a symbolic trigger that allows you to awaken from the lucid dream. It can be anything you choose; the important thing is to know you can awaken when you want to. After all, the world of dreams is a mysterious and sometimes frightening place, and when we add in the factor of consciousness, the rules change. The societies that still practice dreaming in this way know it is not something to take lightly. Treat lucid dreaming with respect, or you may get more than you bargained for.

If this sounds like a warning, it is meant to be. Most discussions of lucid dreaming I have seen tend to dismiss considerations of possible negative results from the practice. However, centuries of shamanistic tradition and informed common sense suggest otherwise. The personal unconscious alone contains material not always pleasant to confront, as anyone who has had a nightmare knows well. How much more mysterious, then, is the realm of the greater, collective unconscious we access through dreams, with infinite potential beyond our personal experience?

I speak from experience when I say it is clear that the borders of the known can be crossed quite unexpectedly when we explore genuine techniques for altering consciousness. Lucid dreaming can be applied in this way. Beyond those borders, the normal rules do not apply and safety is not assured.

Dreams have always been gateways to the unknown and the mysterious for those who sought to understand and use them in this way. We enter unknown and unexplored territory when we apply lucid consciousness to our dreaming experience. On ancient maps cartographers would often place the phrase, "Here be dragons," when the territory was unexplored and unknown. It is wise for the traveler on the inner journey to pay attention.

# CHAPTER 24

# UFOS AND
# ALIENS IN DREAMS

UFOs have been around for a long time in our dreams and in our human experience. Illustrations dating back to the 15th Century and archeological sites from many different locations depict objects that look like UFOs from a modern perspective. Whether they were objects seen in the sky, pictures of magical dreams or symbolic presentations of religious beliefs, we shall never know—all of these are possible explanations. What is interesting to me is that there is one sure way to gain consistent understanding from the images. We get consistency by looking at the images symbolically, just as if they were part of a dream.

Many times in these pages, I have asked you to set aside your normal perceptions and considerations when looking at a dream. It is not possible to get to the deepest meaning of a dream without doing this. It is only the first level interpretation that comes out of ordinary thinking: that often has little to do with the real message of the dream. There are so many thoughts, theories, images and speculative comments concerning UFOs that it is impossible not to be influenced by what we have heard about the subject. That means we have to be even more alert to the symbolic meaning of such an image when it appears in our dreams.

There are certainly lots of conflicting thoughts about UFOs! What these images meant to ancient peoples and what they mean to us today is both similar and different. Similar, because there is an underlying, archetypal meaning to the shape and sight of the image that resonates in the human psyche, whether modern or ancient. Different, because today's modern communications, media and entertainment technologies have deeply imprinted an awareness of images of aliens and UFOs upon our mass consciousness in a way never before possible.

UFOs as symbols easily take on positive or negative meaning. The current collective preference leans towards the extremely negative and threatening: the film *Independence Day* is a good example. The potential meaning of UFOs as dream symbols is enhanced by the common idea that broad-reaching government conspiracies exist to hide the truth about them. This lends an undertone of paranoia, suspicion, issues with authority and threatening masculine forces to the meaning of the symbol. This kind of psychic material is from the dark side of our unconscious. Something alien to us is disowned by us, is unknown to us, is pushed away from us.

On the other hand, there are also dreams in which UFOs bring helpful, wise, or nurturing aliens. In these kinds of dreams we may board a wonderful spaceship and fly away to some magical galaxy, where we are shown wonders and given wisdom.

These apparently opposite possibilities can be understood symbolically as an expression of the most profound and ancient wisdom teachings. In essence, these teachings tell us there is one, universal, divine intelligence, whole and complete unto itself and containing all possibility. The symbol of this universal force, in its earliest form, is the sphere. The sphere represents undifferentiated wholeness. It is a presentation of perfect union, before our imperfect human thoughts cause the inevitable separation into dualistic perceptions of polarities like dark and light, masculine and feminine, form and not-form, and so on. These are teachings that present the totality and oneness of God, i.e., the mystery of God as all things and possibilities. According to these teachings, if God is light, God is also surely dark; God is all.

The flying disc or flying saucer is like the sphere, an image of this union of all possibility and expression. If we think of the symbol in this way, we can see UFOs in dreams as numinous and archetypal symbols of unity, wholeness and the divine mystery. As such, when they appear in a dream the message is going to be about some aspect of the dreamer's relationship to an inner, psychic condition of union and wholeness. This is how Carl Jung viewed UFOs—in his day, "flying saucers."

This symbolic interpretation has nothing to do with the issue of whether or not flying saucers actually exist. In his book *Flying Saucers* (Princeton University Press, 1976), Jung once said about flying saucers that, "...something is seen, but one does not know what." He was not sure if UFOs were real objects or not. He took the position that since he could not know with scientific certainty what exactly was seen in the skies of his time, he would discuss UFOs in terms of what he actually did know. His expertise lay in the realm of exploring the human mind and the collective unfolding of consciousness in humanity, an area where dreams reveal our inner truths.

Here's a UFO dream.

## Richard's Dream: Buried Saucer

*As the dream opens I find that I am a Marine again, but I know that I am not really back in the military. I am with other Marines, in uniform; we are on some sort of exercise, moving through woods and swampy ground. We begin digging. Then we are digging in a mine (mines) in the ground. The mine starts to flood. We will probably not be able to stop it.*

*The scene changes. I (we) am (are) on a flying saucer. The saucer is completely buried underground, perhaps in a large cavern, and we have partially uncovered it. It's very large; I can see only part of it, the part that's been uncovered. It's circular, with an even row of windows around the top. I am walking in a curved hallway there, inside the saucer. We want to re-power the saucer. We partially succeed. Some lights come on, and there is some machinery functioning, but the saucer is not ready to fly. It's still buried.*

*The scene changes again. I am on the freeway outside the LA airport. The freeway is very crowded. There is a brilliant orange sunset ahead, with lots of clouds. A very intense sunset. I see the shadow/silhouette of a flying saucer, large against the clouds. I can see the whole shape and the silhouette of the windows around the top. There are also shadow people dancing on it. I think this is a very interesting pop art display, how did they do that? Then I see some balloons; at first I mistake one for a saucer, then I realize it is just a big balloon.*

In this dream, the flying saucer is a symbol of some possibility not yet fully emerged into the dreamer's waking consciousness. The opening sequence sets the theme: Richard finds himself back in the military. He is part of an organized military exercise, i.e., part of a structured and organized event. It is a dream comment that he is working in a structured way to discover something. In real life, this is true. What he seeks is a deeper connection to spirit. When the saucer appears, later in the dream, we are seeing a confirmation of that search.

For Richard the military represents an ordered existence. As a symbol, it represents a collective and disciplined approach. It is also a masculine symbol. Masculine and feminine are juxtaposed in the opening setting of swampy ground and woods. The context for the exploration is a natural process that blends masculine and feminine dynamics. Woods—masculine, swampy ground—feminine, unconscious.

The Marines are digging in a mine. "Mines" in the military sense, represent danger. In this dream, I feel that is a secondary meaning for the symbol. It will certainly be dangerous to something in the dreamer's being to take on the exploration, but the principle meaning lies elsewhere.

A mine goes into the earth, goes underground, into the darkness and thus into the unconscious. We mine for something valuable. This particular mine is flooding, and the flooding cannot be stopped. The dream tells Richard an irreversible, internal process has been initiated that will result in dissolution of old ways and perceptions.

Then we see the saucer, buried deep underground, found as a result of digging in the mine. Richard is on the saucer, trying to power it up. He has some success but the saucer isn't ready to go yet. What do you think this means?

If we see the saucer as a symbol of unity and wholeness, then this dream is about Richard's quest for deeper spiritual realization and union with the Divine. It tells him he is making progress, but there is more to do. The saucer represents mysterious power and unknown procedures and processes; it's big, it's got unfamiliar technology. There is an implication that at some point it will be ready to fly. The key to understanding how to use the saucer is "buried" inside the dreamer. His unconscious can provide the vehicle for spiritual exploration he seeks and he is getting closer to making it available. It is being "uncovered" in his psyche.

In the last scene there is some final information and, by implication, a warning. The freeway is crowded; full of cars and people. It is a collective setting, a symbol of collective movement. In this case, it is probably a symbol for all of Richard's inner forces that are moving along towards the sunset. A sunset is an ending; something is ending for the dreamer. This is symbolic of a major change or shift in the dreamer's psyche. By implication, outer change will follow.

Outlined against the clouds he sees the shadow saucer shape, with shadow people dancing on it. It is as if his psyche is saying that he sees the shape of what is hidden but has not realized the substance. Because the image is silhouetted against the sunset, there is a direct association between the ending of one thing (the sunset) and the recognition that something new and unknown is beginning. Dancing is an expression of movement and perhaps, joy. This too is only seen in shape and is still intangible, a shadow image from the shadow side of the psyche.

The dream comment about a pop art display emphasizes that Richard is not only ambiguous about the process but that he is not clear about the authenticity of what is happening. The symbol of mistaking a balloon for a saucer is an implied warning. It is telling Richard to be careful not to confuse appearances for the real thing.

OK? If this seems confusing, go back through the dream and follow the process of association step-by-step. Get a feeling for how the interpretation arises from the initial associations. Remember, we get to genuine understanding by realizing the implication and unstated possibilities derived from associations connected to the images.

Aliens in dreams may be benign or threatening, but in either case they represent something unknown and unfamiliar to us. "Alien" is not understood, not familiar. This makes dream aliens a marvelous symbol for unfamiliar constellations of psychic energy in our unconscious.

In many popular movies, aliens appear as insect-like creatures. Insects are very early life forms, and are very suitable for activating primal feelings of fear. If you want to see a dream about aliens, see any of the *Alien* movie series starring Sigourney Weaver. My personal preference is for the second in the series, but they are all good in the sense I am talking about.

Imagine you had a dream like one of these films. In *Aliens*, the alien being is so far from human it is a nightmare form, right out of the primal psyche. The only similarity between human and alien is hostile, when Sigourney Weaver calls the alien a "bitch." She's a mother alien, after all, but not the kind of nurturing mother we might like to have.

As a symbol in a dream, this alien would definitely get our attention. As an archetype, she falls into the category of "The Devouring Mother," a pattern well known in Jungian psychology. It's a pattern displayed in many ancient myths and stories. Our present society demands a modern myth that mirrors the contemporary culture. Our culture is one where technology plays a dominant role, a technology often frightening to us and fraught with potential for enormous destruction. All of the "Alien" movies feature the trappings and forms of inhuman and powerful technology. They provide a mythic setting for the images of the ancient archetypes, well-attuned to our times.

Films like "Alien" are very successful, although they leave much to be desired in terms of serious intellectual or thoughtful content. They don't need intellectual content or great writing to succeed. The films are targeted at the part of us that reacts with a reptilian and primal response. This is not an intellectual response, and filmmakers know that. Aliens and monsters of all kinds are a powerful reflection of unconscious, dark side, primal content. The images on the movie screen portray our deepest fears, the terrifying psychic content we have disowned from our outer, civilized consciousness.

These films often end with ambiguous victory over the alien threat, after heroic life and death struggles that prove the protagonist worthy. By identification with the hero, we too are redeemed through struggle, defeating the dark forces threatening to overwhelm us. It is an initiatory process, played out in fantasy. It's like a dream, because some part of our psyche does not know the movie or the dream is not reality. The movies, at least the ones that succeed and are remembered, are collective dreams.

The next time you go to a movie that features aliens as a prominent part of the plot, watch it as if it were one of your own dreams. If that seems too difficult while you are watching, caught up in the action and emotion, after the movie think about it as if it were one of your dreams. Just like a dream, all of the techniques we have learned for looking at dreams can be applied with equal success to movies. What would the movie/dream mean? Why did something affect you with fear, anger, horror or some other emotion? If you watch films as if they were your dreams, movies will never be the same again. They will be better!

# CHAPTER 25

# DREAMS AND PROPHECY

Over the years, I have come across many prophetic dreams. Stories of tuning in to the future through dreams are a thread running through human experience. In ancient societies the reality of prophetic dreaming was recognized and honored. In our modern, scientifically-oriented society, reports of such dreams are dismissed as fantasy and mistaken delusion, or at best as anecdotal and unworthy of credibility. That is a mistake.

Prophetic dreams are certainly not explainable by logical means. It is not possible to identify and isolate the specific mechanism in the human mind that can permit an accurate prediction of future events to take place. Perhaps Jung's concept of the collective unconscious could explain it, but that still leaves only speculation and theory rather than proven fact. Nonetheless, such dreams do occur and do foretell real events, as has been seen many times throughout history.

One of the best known historical examples of true prophetic dreaming occurs in the Bible. In Genesis we find the story of Joseph, gifted by God with the ability to interpret dreams. Of course, we need to accept that the story actually took place with historical characters. This is a problem for some. For me, the story seems to have the ring of truth to it. There does seem to be some archeological evidence for some of the circumstances and details of the Genesis account.

In the story, Joseph has two dreams that anger his brothers and stimulate their envy. In the first dream, he and his brothers are binding sheaves of grain in the fields. Joseph's sheaf rises and the sheaves of his brothers bow down to his. When Joseph relates this dream, without commenting on it, the brothers get angry.

As far as the brothers are concerned, they are not about to bow down to Joseph! Then Joseph has another dream and sees the Sun, the Moon and eleven stars bow down to him. This is even more unpopular in the family. His father, Israel, correctly takes this to mean that he (the sun) and his wife (the moon) and eleven sons (the stars) shall bow down to Joseph. He rebukes Joseph for saying such a thing.

Notice that Joseph is simply telling his dreams at this point, and everyone is getting upset! This is a typical response to a prophetic dream, for such a dream often portends change and change is uncomfortable. When people are faced with information threatening the status quo, they tend to react negatively, rather than take in the information and use it wisely.

His brothers treacherously sell Joseph into slavery. In captivity, Potiphar's wife falsely accuses him of sexual approaches. He lands in Pharaoh's jail, where he accurately interprets two more dreams for the Pharaoh's butler and baker. These dreams prophesy the fate of the two men; the butler is restored to power as Joseph said he would be, while the baker is hanged.

Two years pass and then Pharaoh has a most upsetting dream. He dreams of seven fat cattle rising from the river and feeding in a lush meadow. So far so good, but then seven lean cattle emerge from the river and eat up the fat ones. They do not benefit from this large meal.

Pharaoh awakens, very disturbed, and goes back to sleep. He dreams again, that same night, and this time there are seven fat ears of corn on a single stalk. Then seven lean and meager ears spring up right after them, "blasted with the east wind," and devour the fat ears.

Now Pharaoh is a wise ruler, as rulers go in those days, and he knows something is going on with these dreams. He calls together his magicians to find out what the dreams mean, but he gets no satisfaction. Then the butler remembers Joseph, still held in the jail. Pharaoh sends for Joseph, who interprets the dreams. More importantly, he uses the information given in the dreams to advise Pharaoh on what to do. Joseph is able to appreciate how dreams may show, by implication, the wisest course of action. He is one of our best models for working with prophetic dreams.

The dreams refer to seven years of good harvest followed by seven years of devastating famine. It is important to see that the dreams only give information. Most prophetic dreams are like this. It is left to the dreamer to take action, if needed, based on that information. This is what Pharaoh does, appointing Joseph to oversee preparation for the famine to come.

In due course, the famine arrives and because Egypt is prepared, it increases in power while the other countries suffer terribly. Joseph's earlier dreams come true as well. His brothers come seeking food and make obeisance to him, not knowing they are bowing down before the brother whom they believe to be dead. Eventually the father and mother and all the brothers come to Egypt under Joseph's protection. Thereby the second dream is fulfilled also.

The story of Joseph and Pharaoh's dreams presented in Genesis shows that dreams can be an accurate guide in our life. It teaches that the true wisdom of Spirit and the Divine can make itself known to us through our dreams, and that following the wisdom leads to good results.

We can learn to recognize and understand prophetic dreams and act upon the information symbolically presented in the dream images. Because prophetic dreams show either a possible or a coming future reality (given that it is a prophetic dream), we can choose to prepare consciously for the event. We can take whatever measures are necessary or indicated by the dream. This is one reason people occasionally have dreams that foretell the future. Because we have the forewarning, disaster may be softened or averted. Sometimes the events foretold are sweeping and collective in nature, sometimes they are limited to our personal lives and sphere of influence.

Here is a true story of a prophetic dream. The dream came true but not exactly as first interpreted by the dreamer. I will call the dreamer Susanna.

Susanna is a good friend of mine, like a sister to me. I have known her for over thirty years. She has four children, ranging in age from 20 to 29, and is an intelligent and sensitive woman. In the past she has had prophetic dreams, usually of a disturbing nature, often involving the illness or death of someone near to her. Naturally, she has come to dread such dreams because they always portend bad news. That is a common response to prophetic dreams. If any of you has had dreams of this nature, you may have had the same reaction. It is only human to try to avoid unpleasant information. However, prophetic dreams are really a blessing, even when this may not be immediately apparent. They allow us time to adjust and to prepare ourselves for what is coming.

Susanna dreamed that one of her sons was in a bad car accident. She saw the car driven by her son entering an intersection and struck by another car. The collision was very bad, and she knew her son's car was severely damaged. She saw three skulls in her dream, and when she awoke, she took this to mean her son would be killed in the accident.

As you can imagine, given her successful prophetic dreaming history, Susanna was very upset by the dream. What could she do? What would you do?

In a situation like this, it is almost impossible to control events in an effort to avoid the foreseen result. Could Susanna have prevented her son from ever driving again? Could she in some way prevent someone else's careless driving? There did not seem to be a good solution or a concrete action she could take.

Susanna did what many of us might also do, given a situation totally beyond our power to control. She turned to prayer, spending an entire day seeking the intercession of the Divine to try to avert the accident seen in her dream. Remember that Susanna had been right in the past. Her prophetic dreams have always had a distinct "feeling quality" (her words) about them, and she knew this was one of those dreams. She is also a spiritual person, so prayer was a natural response to crisis in her life.

Sure enough, the accident happened just as she had seen in the dream. The amazing thing is that her son escaped without serious injury. I saw the car he was driving, and it was badly damaged, fit only for the junkyard.

What would have happened if Susanna had simply waited to see whether the dream came true? Would there have been death or serious injury to her son? I feel that by doing something in the only way that she could, Susanna may have averted a far more serious consequence, indicated by the death's heads in the dream. Did the power of prayer intervene and protect Susanna's child? I like to think so. We can never know, but I think that if I had such a dream I would take a leaf from Susanna's book and recognize that this was more than I could handle by myself.

The key to taking action because of a prophetic dream, if action is needed, is having the courage to honor the feeling and truth of the dream. This can be difficult. It is understandable we might feel too embarrassed to actually adjust our behavior, based on a dream.

I recall reading about two excellent examples of prophetic dreams. In both cases, the dreamers avoided disaster because they honored the information received in their dreams. In both examples, the dreamers could take definite actions.

In the first case, the dreamer had a recurring dream every night for a week. You will recall that in the earlier chapter on recurring dreams I said that these kinds of dreams are particularly important, because they convey a message from the dreaming consciousness to our waking mind especially needful to know. Such dreams are like an urgent telegram or special delivery letter.

In the dream, the dreamer was on her way to the grocery store and found herself taking a route different from her normal one. To her horror, a child ran in front of her car (in the dream) and was killed. A disturbing dream! In this case, by paying attention, a good result was obtained.

One day not long after the dream, as the dreamer drove away to go shopping she noticed she was wearing the same clothes as in her dream. She drove slowly, finding herself taking a different route than usual because of a detour. Remembering the dream, she constantly kept her foot ready to stop the car. Sure enough, a child, the same child seen in the dream, ran out in front of the car. Because she was ready, the dreamer was able to stop in time and avoided the accident. Acting on the information seen in the dream made the difference

In the second case, a woman purchased tickets for a train journey to visit her dying father. That night she dreamed of a terrible train crash, of the wreckage and destruction, and of searching for her daughter among the injured and dying. In the morning, she decided not to take the train, although the journey was of such importance. Instead, she made other arrangements. The next day's headlines proclaimed the wreck of the train she was to have taken. By acting on the dream information, she missed possible death or injury for herself and her daughter.

Although I do not know these dreamers personally, the stories also have the ring of authenticity and truth to me. These were average people, like you and me, who had prophetic dreams that stood out in their minds so strongly they had to pay attention. They shared their dreams as personal stories and had no agenda to accomplish or profit to gain by doing so. Of course, there is no proof that the dreams were prophetic, since these are anecdotal stories, and therein lies a source of confusion and difficulty.

It is clear to me that no proof that will ever be acceptable to the scientific community regarding prophetic dreaming. You cannot take the dream and put it under a microscope, or quantify its molecular structure or project it as a particle or wave of energy. You cannot repeat the prophetic dream at will and measure it against results. Prophetic dreams are unique and personal events, although they may portend collective events of great magnitude, as in the story of Joseph's Egypt.

The problem with prophecy is that we can never know if it is accurate until after the fact—that is the nature of prophecy, which forecasts events that have not yet taken place. That means we must fall back on our own best judgment and our feeling about the matter when we have an experience of prophetic dreaming. We will probably not find much validation from the external world for our dream until after the fact, and that poses difficulties.

How do we tell the difference between a "regular" dream and a prophetic one? There isn't a simple answer, but there are guidelines we can follow. First, we need to know something about regular dreams, which I will call "psychological" dreams. By this I mean dreams arising entirely from the contents of our personal and unconscious mind, or psyche. Most of this book is about dreams like this. I make a distinction between *personal* areas of consciousness (known and unknown) and *transpersonal* areas that are in touch with some greater wisdom. In my experience, all of us have both kinds of dreams.

It is from the expanded and transpersonal that prophetic dreams arise. A few common indicators often mark these dreams. First, we usually remember such dreams quite easily. As with Pharaoh, they tend to wake us up and disturb us because of the unexpected information. We may also go back to sleep and have the dream repeated in a different way or again in the same way. Remember the ears of corn in Pharaoh's dream? They stood for the same thing as the cattle in the earlier dream, in the same relationship, and the message was repeated in different images for emphasis. In both dreams, the images were symbolic presentations of very specific information.

Sometimes "special effects" in a dream may indicate a prophetic element. We have to be careful here because such effects can also occur in regular dreams. Special effects include things like intense music or sound. There may be specific and clear, spoken sentences that give advice to the dreamer. Writing may appear and be very readable, with an important message. If you dream in color, the colors may be greatly intensified or heightened. If you dream in black and white (many people do) then a section may appear in color. When any of these things happen, *pay attention*. Even if the dream is not prophetic, the effects are there to emphasize information you need to know.

Another indicator of a prophetic dream is a feeling of certainty that this dream is different in some way from a regular dream. Perhaps it has an unbelievably vivid feeling of reality, more so than normal. More likely, it will just *feel* different. This is one reason why science has so much trouble verifying events like prophetic dreams. Feeling is not an acceptable scientific measurement in terms of proof and documentation.

A common problem of interpretation is the tendency to place a literal meaning upon dreams not meant in this way. For example, a woman dreams that her girlfriend is pregnant and gives birth to a little girl. She takes this to be prophetic, since she does have a girlfriend who is expecting a baby, who then does indeed deliver a baby girl.

This kind of dream is much more likely to refer to the inner dynamics of the dreamer rather than the actual event. Pregnancy and birth are significant events, but unless there are complications, one doesn't really need to know if it is a boy or a girl. I have found that genuinely prophetic dreams only foretell external events important for the dreamer to know about. This is different from the inner life "regular" dreams reveal. The prophetic dream forewarns of some difficult or transforming event coming into one's life that manifests itself in real terms in waking reality.

It is also possible to have a dream that appears prophetic at first glance, but is actually based on information already known. If you know someone is ill and the person dies, this is not necessarily prophetic. Your unconscious already had the information it needed to predict the death. In a way the dream is prophetic since the event actually occurred, but this is not unexpected and prophecy is not needed to get the information across. The important point to remember here is that true prophecy, as I define it, means tapping into wisdom and information that could otherwise not be known.

I tend to categorize prophetic dreams into two major and distinct categories. These mirror the difference between the personal and the transpersonal, although the information always comes from an expanded state of dreaming awareness. The first kind are dreams specifically prophetic for us as individuals, such as Susanna's dream of the auto accident. In the second type, we may dream of events affecting large numbers of people such as an earthquake. In either case, we may be forewarned of something that affects us personally. However, we need to be careful or we can easily mistake personal symbolic messages for collective ones.

The problem with dream images suggesting collective events is that they are frequently not prophetic but simply refer symbolically to some event in the dreamer's personal psyche. Misinterpretation can lead to severe over-reaction to what seems to be a prophetic dream. One of our challenges when looking at dreams is to know the difference.

We have all heard predictions of doom and disaster in dreams and from other sources as well. Our natural tendency is to worry about such things or deny them because we desire a different result. I feel that when dreams appear to predict undesirable events we must take them with several grains of salt, but pay attention nonetheless. If I was planning a train trip and had such a vivid dream as in the example given earlier, I would probably cancel the trip also. People might laugh, I might be inconvenienced, but if the "feeling" was there, I'd trust myself and act on the information, even though I am sure I would be uncomfortable in doing so.

On the other hand, suppose I dreamed about the detonation of an atomic bomb? My inclination, based on years of experience, would be to see this as a personal and symbolic message from my self to my self. Perhaps something is "blowing up" inside or I am at war with myself about something. Perhaps I am in a process of radical transformation internally. I would not take this to mean that nuclear war was coming.

Too much emphasis is placed on the negative and doomsaying predictions that abound in our culture. Predictions found in the Bible, in dreams, in the works of psychics like Edgar Cayce, and from other sources of information are easily misinterpreted because of the unconscious material everyone projects onto the dream or prophecy. It is important to realize we may easily misunderstand prophecy and prophetic dreams. Given that a dream really is prophetic, we may unknowingly color our interpretations because of our unconsciously held perceptions.

Once we know this, we can relax and look at the material shown in the dream without feeling helpless about it. As Susanna did, we can always turn our difficulty over to a higher power. We can be aware and watchful, as was the woman who drove with her foot on the brake, waiting for that child to run in front of her. We can prepare for the future, as Joseph did in Egypt, using the wisdom presented in dreams to guide us in our daily affairs and living.

In our most profound dreaming states, we connect to a cosmic source of wisdom that sometimes grants us access to the future. Prophetic dreams jolt us out of the daily and mundane routine of our lives. They remind us of how great a mystery life is and how much we have yet to discover.

In this new millennium. predictions, prophecies, dreams of transformation and dreams of the end of the world as we know it are being reported and experienced everywhere. What does this mean? How can we take what we have learned about dreams and apply it to these disturbing stories and events? The next chapter looks at this intriguing time.

# CHAPTER 26

# THE NEW MILLENNIUM

The New Millennium—just the phrase itself seems to contain power and meaning. The new millennium signals a time of enormous change and unparalleled challenge for the Earth and for all the beings that live upon it. It is not so much that we have passed the marker of a particular year (2000 or 2001, take your pick) but that the progression of human events has reached a critical juncture never before seen, and we know it.

Prophecies of all kinds abound, reaching into the first 20 years or so of the new century. Many of these prophetic warnings tell of great and disastrous changes, upheavals and fearful events. Others balance the theme of destruction with a joyful picture of abundance, peace, harmony and love. What does it all mean? Where do we find the true guidance we seek? How do we make sense of the conflicting stories, legends, predictions and information?

The human race is approaching an inevitable turning point in consciousness. The problem is that we are unable to say with certainty what that will lead to, or exactly when it will take place. Anything can happen, and in that truth lies great potential.

It is always true that great change, whether personal or social, is accompanied by upheaval and destruction of some sort. It is part of the eternal cycle of life and spirit. Creation and destruction go hand in hand and are inseparable from one another. Nothing lasts forever except truth and Spirit. Dreams, prophecies, myths and revelations all underscore the same undying story. We are mysterious beings, multi-dimensional, imperfect in our knowledge and intimately woven into the fabric of the spiritual and physical universe.

When we are stuck in the illusion of our perceptions and bound by the limitations of our massive egos, something has to change if we want to break the strictures and expand into new possibilities. This is true for individuals or for societies. We only need to look at the long pageant of human history to see the pattern emerge: creation, preservation, destruction—and then a new creation.

Each of us has a role to play in this great collective dance, the ongoing evolution of the human race. To play that role with consciousness is the greatest challenge any one of us can face. With increasing awareness comes new recognition, guidance and expression of our innate spirit. Dreams are a gateway to an expanded dimension where we can feel Spirit and self as one.

The New Millennium holds forth the promise of Heaven on Earth, but it equally holds forth the promise of Hell if we do not pay attention. There are global, spiritual forces at work that will not be denied, whether we choose to believe in them or not, forces for energizing change and new creation. We will participate, willingly or not, in those changes. More, we will consciously do our part to affect those changes, or we will simply contribute unconsciously to the process, for good or for ill.

I hope that as you have read this book you have begun to see that we contain all possibilities and potential. We have the ability to bring conscious awareness and discretion to the process of our spiritual evolution. Our dreams show us our real selves, as single souls and as an expression of divine intelligence and will. They show us our relationship to the infinite while at the same time giving us truthful information about our individual part of the dance and the underlying psychological and spiritual motivations for our unique expression. Prophecies can be confusing and contradictory in many ways, but our dreams are an immediate source of guidance and inspiration to move us through the coming times. All we need do is learn to pay attention to them.

As the new millennium begins, there are more and more dreams coming through that deal with both the personal concerns of our single lives and with the common human experience. These dreams offer teachings about the nature of our human condition and will provide, for those who listen, a framework for understanding the change that lies ahead. As always, there is a major pitfall we have to avoid. This is our strong tendency to project our fears and our hopes onto the dreams, thus skewing the meaning to suit our inner desires.

Earlier in the book, in the chapter on catastrophe and war, I mentioned I would share a dream with you about flooding and prophecy. This dream was about a great flood and a new map of the world. Decades later I was startled to see a map of a post-millennium world identical to what I was shown in my dream, created by Gordon-Michael Scallion. He has predicted catastrophic floods and the emergence of a new society in the twenty-first century.

My dream occurred in 1966, long before I ever heard of Scallion and before I had read the works of Edgar Cayce, who also predicted earthquakes and floods. It was a compelling need to understand this dream that led me to read Cayce. Ultimately it caused me to focus on dreams as a master key to spiritual and psychological discovery and exploration. I can say with some accuracy and with the benefit of hindsight that this dream changed the future course of my life.

My dream agrees with many other images and visions from a variety of sources. As such, it qualifies as a collective dream, seeded in the transpersonal, larger human unconscious. However, I have a personal relationship with it.

In my dream, I was aboard a fishing boat during a great and storm-tossed flood. I was alone on the boat, looking out at dark and raging waters through the glass windows of the bridge. At the same time, I was aware of a presence: the "Pilot" was on board as well. He was controlling the ship. On one of the windows was a map of the United States and North America. Written above the map, in large capital letters of bright red, was a message. The message read, "Pay Attention!"

The map showed lands devastated by a great flood that I knew was in the future, even as I rode the stormy sea of the flood in my dream. On the map the ocean reached past the Rocky Mountains; the West Coast was now somewhere near Kansas; only islands marked the place where California once existed. The U.S. was split in two, roughly along the line of the Mississippi, extending from the Great Lakes to the Gulf of Mexico. Probably a third of the present nation was under water. Years later I was amazed when I saw Scallion's map, which appears to my memory to be identical to the map shown to me in my dream, right down to the new coastline.

Although the dream has to do with personal material for me, it also clearly contains images that have appeared to many different people in dreams and visions. Many take such dreams and visions to be prophetic of actual major changes to the physical Earth. Could we be nearing a time of world upheaval and change?

The image of a great flood is deeply ingrained in the human psyche. Just about every culture has a myth or legend of a great flood, and there is archeological support for the occurrence of a deluge in the past. Theories of how such an event could have happened or might yet occur are many. One favorite is a sudden polar shift of the earth's axis. Other explanations include divine wrath, misuse of destructive energies by ancient and undiscovered civilizations, and collision with a huge asteroid or comet.

One of my all-time favorite movies is *The Wave*. It stars Richard Chamberlain and weaves a strange tale of Aboriginal magic, dreams and secret forces at work that affect all of humanity. After a series of premonitory dreams and events, the movie ends with the approach of an enormous wave, which will surely destroy all before it. But is the wave a dream or a reality? One of the things I like about this movie is that it is not possible to tell.

*The Wave* is only one of many movies, good, bad and indifferent, that reveal the primal myths and fears we carry in our reptilian and ancient collective psyche. What all these films have in common is the approach of an enormous, indifferent and unstoppable force that results in widespread devastation. Sometimes the rationale is spiritual or religious, as in the Biblical tale of the great flood. Sometimes the new gods of science are assigned the blame. Sometimes alien and hostile armies approach from beyond the borders of our known reality. Sometimes we glimpse a facet of an ancient, collective dream that cannot be described, where words and description are irrelevant, but feeling is undeniable.

Recently I had a new dream of flooding and prophetic events. I don't think it's an accident this dream occurred while writing this revised edition.

As a prelude, you should know that in recent months I have been undergoing a disturbing and powerful series of dreams. These dreams clearly indicate a major shift in my own, personal reality. The impact of the dreams was so strong that I was unable to write or do much of anything for several months. I was emptied of creative and interactive energies. It has been a time of dissolution for me, a process that continues, but which has stabilized. If it had not, I would not be able to write these words!

The dream I would like to share with you is linked to the earlier dream from 35 years ago, although the association is not apparent in the outer symbolism. However, I can feel the association very strongly, and I always trust my feelings about the meaning and content of dreams. Both dreams are consistent with the many myths, prophecies and predictions of the entry into the new millennium. They have a clear collective implication. Here is the dream I had last week.

# Atlantis Returns

*I don't clearly remember the first part of the dream but the governing structure of society or civilization has somehow broken down or been removed. I know in the dream that I have to improvise. I am in charge, somehow, and I know telepathically what needs to be done. It's a new situation.*

*Then I am at the [Eastern] edge of the [North American] continent; the water [ocean] is rising and people are worried. The ocean is not storm-tossed, just blue, a light chop, a clear, featureless sky. I can see that the edge of the continent is slowly sinking, and water is coming up over the edge of the land. Suddenly there is a shift in the ground and not far off shore I see an entire continent rise out of the water, ancient, with an ancient city on it. Very big city, it all rises up at once and I understand that this is why the flooding had started before. Now that the city and land have emerged, there won't be a problem.*

*The city is stained dark from being underwater for centuries, but it is also complete and undamaged. It seems mostly dry and looks livable, with a little cleaning up, perhaps. It appears deserted, but even so, I can see two or three lights in the city, which amazes me, since the city has been underwater.*

*The city is protected by a wall, about two stories high, not extremely high as in the old fortified cities of history. There is a regular series of open, arched gates in the wall, which stretches on as far as I can see. It will be easy to enter the city. I comment to someone that the design or architecture is not human, whatever it is, not when it looks like that.*

*At some point, a powerful voice tells me that the dream is important because it has a larger, collective meaning.*

Section by section, the dream reveals a lot of information. One of the most important events occurring in the dream is the voice telling me the dream is not just of a personal nature, but has collective meaning as well. I always pay special attention to this kind of message in a dream. You should also, if it occurs for you. These kinds of messages come from some larger and wiser part beyond our normal state of dreaming awareness. The voice is distinctly not my own, nor does it feel like "me" to me.

The feeling of a dream is one of the criteria I use to evaluate its importance and meaning. In this case, the dream falls into the "big dream" category. The voice and the unknown presence I talk to are the same as the unseen presence of the "Pilot" in the earlier dream of a great flood. I can feel the association between the two dreams: this is the voice and presence of the soul.

This dream has both personal and collective meaning. The first section sets the theme, a theme of the breakdown of the governing order. This is entirely consistent with the recent sequence of dreams I have been experiencing. The old way of seeing things has broken down. I am no longer able to rely on the older way of doing things; I have to improvise. However, in the dream I do know what to do in this new situation. The message is that I need to trust my inner wisdom to get me through the difficult period. One of the common threads in prophecies concerning the end of the millennium is the breakdown of existing governing structures. But let's go on through the rest of the dream from a personal viewpoint before we discuss the larger implications.

The next section shows the dissolution of something. It is developing the theme of breakdown of the old order and revealing some of the inner dynamics. The continent is sinking, the water is rising; people are worried. The "people" is a symbol of my diverse inner self, the people who live inside me, if you like. I am uneasy with the change, the dream says, as I watch the inevitable progress of the inundating waters that threaten the status quo. There is a reason for the inundation, as is soon shown.

In waking life, I am quite uneasy with the changes I am currently experiencing. This part of the dream is simply reflecting back to me the truth about how I feel. As if I needed any confirmation!

The ocean represents many things to me. Certainly it is the great and infinite mystery. I often think of it as feminine in nature (but not always), and as a representation of spirit or of the unconscious. It is unplumbed, unknown, vast. My impression regarding the ocean in the dream is one of presence, not threatening in any way, just powerfully present and in a personal sense, indifferent. Personal, in relationship to the ocean, is a projection. The ocean doesn't care what we think about it.

Suddenly the ground shifts (it slopes suddenly towards the shoreline in the dream). The ancient continent arises intact and at once from the depths. In the dream, it is clear this process of emergence is what caused the flooding that people were worried about before. Now that the emergence is complete, this will no longer be a problem. That is good news for me, as it clearly says that something has "emerged" in my psyche and that the "flooding" is now over.

What does the city symbolize? What is the flooding? Flooding is a common image in dreams. In alchemical symbolism, flooding is a sign of dissolution. Dissolution is part of a complex process leading to the transformation of the old into something essentially purer that was hidden and present in the older form. Flooding has many meanings, depending on the images and on the correct interpretation of the meaning of water for the dreamer. In this case, alchemical association for the symbolism feels correct to me.

The ancient city and continent symbolize the rebirth and emergence of something older and hidden within my/our psyche. It is mysterious, it is even inhabitable. It is ancient. It is a surprise, because the outer mind did not know it was there. It is disruptive to the way things have been. It is a symbol of ancient and collective humanity. Cities are structured and ordered societies that contain a full spectrum of humanity's possibilities and experience. Who among us can exhaust the resources of a great city, or experience all it contains? Would we want to?

The lights in the city are truly surprising to me in the dream, because it has been underwater (submerged in the unconscious) for so long. Yet, someone is already living there. Again, good news for me because it shows that I have already begun the exploration of what this represents, even if I am not yet consciously aware of this. It is my dream and I am the one who inhabits. Collectively, there is a somewhat different meaning, and I will get to that in a moment.

The wall is a distinct feature. The arches are rounded at the top and regular in sequence. This suggests a feminine context for exploration of what the city represents, e.g., intuitive and open, based on feeling and intuitive approaches. It will be easy to enter the city, a fact I note in the dream. I am surprised and pleased that the gates are open. One might enter the city at any one of the gates.

I comment to someone, unseen, on the non-human design and architecture. Non-human means alien: alien means unknown, foreign to, and different from. Alienated means separated from, cut off from. What is alien (non-human) is unknown to the psyche. That city is not familiar to me, nor do I know what lies inside it. It is not part of my conscious experience. However, it is about to be, or I would not have had this dream. I am certainly attracted to the exploration, in the dream and in waking life.

If this dream were only about my personal journey, it would still qualify for big dream consideration. However, there is that intriguing and specific message in the dream about the collective implications. In fact, the message emphasizes that the real importance of the dream lies in those implications. What are they?

I am still working with this dream, even as I write, but I have a good sense of the meaning. If the dream is addressing the universal, human situation, then it is showing us something about our current and future situation as a race. It is commenting on the underlying and current condition of the race, the context of human existence.

We can easily confirm the message that governing structures have broken down in our larger, outer reality. Look around you; the process has begun. Would you say things are nicely under control and well ordered? You can easily see the dissolution depicted in the dream reflected in the enormous problems besetting humanity. Things are in a state of disintegration, from the global environment to the rampant moral and ethical absurdities everywhere in evidence in governing structures and world societies.

The message of the dream is clear. An interpretation with an eye to collective meaning implies that humanity does actually know what to do in this situation and has the ability to improvise and respond. We have the technology, knowledge and skills to address the situation, if we can be motivated to do so. We can improvise and get results.

The emergence of the continent and city symbolizes the emergence of an ancient knowledge and wisdom for living together as a human collective. This potential is not yet realized or explored, but there are a few lights in the city, i.e., a few steps have been taken towards the exploration. The wisdom resides in our collective unconscious. We are looking at a representation of an ancient spiritual process.

I called this dream "Atlantis Returns" because of the obvious association with the stories of that lost continent. New millennium stories, myths and prophecies often mention Atlantis. What is the story of Atlantis and how does this fit into the prophecies?

Most contemporary versions say that Atlantis once existed east of the present United States and was home to an unknown (non-human?) wisdom and technology. According to the stories, a cataclysmic inundation destroyed the continent almost overnight (or in separate events over several thousand years). Atlantis sank with its people, cities, wisdom, and technology. The modern story maintains the cataclysm occurred because the inhabitants misused power through corrupt and wrongful application of unknown energies, in ways against the natural order of life. Finally, the predictions say Atlantis will rise again, as part of new cataclysmic earth changes, revealing needed wisdom to guide us into the New Age. Even Scallion's map shows Atlantis off the coast of what is now Florida.

Well! Let's think about this for a moment. The story of Atlantis seems to have started with mention of a land "beyond the Pillars of Hercules" in Plato's *Dialogues*. Much of the current description of the civilization of Atlantis was seeded by a novel published in 1882, *The Antediluvian World* (Donnelly) that described a utopian, harmonious and neo-classical society. This was followed by more revelations of the lost continent from the famous psychic and founder of the Theosophical Society, Madame Blavatsky. Finally, the stories were reinforced by many writings of the prophet Edgar Cayce. This in turn has seeded generations of channeling and psychic experiences further embellishing the Atlantean story.

Whether the stories are true or not, they present us with images that resonate eerily within. Our psyche seeks for meaning of these dramatic events in terms of our present day experience. The story of Atlantis is a teaching story, not least because it is essentially a symbolic and psychological drama of the glory and tragedy of human existence.

In a dream of collective meaning, when Atlantis returns huge changes are in the offing. Everything Atlantis represents in the stories and myths is implied by the dream image. That includes all of the wisdom as well as all of the potential mis-use of energy and power deemed responsible for the disaster. All of the bright and dark content of the human psyche is inherent in the symbol. When Atlantis returns, nothing will ever be the same again. It is a sign, an omen of irresistible change.

I feel strongly that this dream is truly prophetic, but it does not necessarily mean that a physical continent will emerge, or that great floods will sweep over the land. The dream indicates that the time is beginning when the underlying and timeless energies of Spirit, change, creation and destruction will come to the fore. From the dissolution of the old will emerge an underlying, mysterious, timeless presence and potential. This is true for individuals pursuing the path of Spirit. It is also true for societies struggling to find ways to exist in a world out of control, who find themselves at the effect of enormously complex forces for change.

At the end of the First Millennium after Christ, there were sweeping tides of change and dissolution at work. In the West, these were seeded in the mass psyche by the idea of the Second Coming and the New Millennium prophesied in the Bible. In that simpler and barbarous time of the tenth century A.D., you never knew when destruction and change, in

the form of death, fire, plague, famine or war would come riding into your
life. Change was constant; the only certainty was death; and everyone lived
in hope and fear of the coming new order. Does it sound familiar?

We have come full cycle, not so very different from our ancestors of a
thousand years ago. The only real difference is that the advances of science, medicine, and communications technology have taken us from the
dark ages to an age that, if not exactly bright, holds at least the potential
for becoming so. To make that potential real, we will have to call upon the
ancient resources and organizing principles of spirit and wisdom. We need
to have something emerge that offers a new possibility. We need the reap-
pearance of Atlantis, so to speak. We need universal, spiritual renewal.

Atlantis as a collective myth or image represents wholeness, an ideal
place and time, a unified society and a wisdom of spirit supposedly
beyond our own. The yearning for the re-discovery and re-emergence of
Atlantis is the unconscious yearning of humanity for wholeness and re-
connection to Spirit. It is a desire for personal healing and for a greater
healing of the catastrophes and woundings that have already befallen the
earth. This is mostly a Western image, but the flood and destruction
Atlantis represents appear in the myths of many cultures. If Atlantis
returns, it will signal sweeping change in our human experience.

Humankind has always longed for the appearance of some momentous
sign or event to signal change and new possibility, when times are hard
and life is difficult. Many people feel like this now and it is no different
now, in that sense, than it was at the end of the last millennium. What is
different is that today we have the resources available that could allow
genuine transformation to take place. That will happen only if they are
coupled with appreciation of the reality of Spirit and compassion for our
common human condition.

Will our dreams of a new, more nurturing and spiritual society become
reality? My dream indicates the process has started, but that it is still early
days. Those few lights in the risen city are a few points of consciousness
contained in the larger darkness and ancient unconscious rhythms of our
human existence. It is up to us to enter the city and take up residence.
We must light our lamps, illuminating the ancient knowledge, eternal
spirit and human potential of our divine heritage. That is the meaning of

the reemergence of Atlantis, and it is the challenge we face as the twenty-first century begins. When Atlantis returns, the new millennium will have finally arrived.

Spread the wings of your dreams, and let yourself soar into the next thousand years. The dreams we dream now will shape the future of hundreds of generations to come. Choose to dream of a new millennium bright with promise, and the promise may be fulfilled. From our dreams arise the foundations underlying the reality of our waking world. Let that world be one of beauty and spirit, given over to energizing the true expression of Divine will and abundance.

May the door of the Temple of Dreams be open to you.

# Summary

I have tried to show in these pages how our dreams can be a powerful and accurate tool for self-discovery. The techniques I have introduced will work for you if you give them a fair trial. Some may feel better to you than others. You may also develop your own unique method for remembering and interpreting your dreams.

Inaccuracies of interpretation come from the outer mind. Throughout the book, I have said that we project our unconscious material onto our dreams. The unconscious mind imposes a filter upon our conscious perception. It doesn't really matter if we understand this fully or not. What matters is that we remember our minds will do this without our knowing it. We have to make a basic assumption: nothing is as it appears and we must look more carefully to get to the real meaning of what we are looking at. This becomes very apparent when looking at dreams. A great benefit of dream work is that this new way of looking for meaning spills over into other parts of our life: we get a little closer to whatever "reality" is.

The concept of three "levels" of dream interpretation has been helpful to me and to others. There is always a first level interpretation based on what is familiar and known to the outer mind of the dreamer. This is almost never what the dream is really about. It is one of the reasons for so much confusion about dreams.

The second level will reveal useful information and insight on the dreamer's relationship with life. It is reached by feeling into the symbolic language of the dream and letting spontaneous associations with the symbols make themselves known. It requires developing the beginning of an intuitive grasp of the meaning, coupled with a process of logical association and deduction.

The third level holds the key to resolution and action, if action or resolution is required. The third level is the most difficult to reach, because it requires an intuitive and non-linear leap of understanding. On this level we make associations and draw conclusions not at all evident during an earlier stage of interpretation. We know the interpretation is correct when we feel a sense of correctness, of being right, in our body. It is a tangible sensation.

Once we tap into third level understanding of dreams, we have a new resource available for significant change in our lives. In itself, the third level recognition does not bring resolution of any issues contained in the psyche. What it does do is help us realize that solutions are possible and that we can take steps to energize them. Third level recognition reveals that we are the source of our confusion and that we are the source of our empowerment or our lack of it.

The third level is reached by accessing the Dreamer Within. This energy is impersonal and objective, and it is not concerned with the issues that trouble or confuse our outer consciousness. It communes with a pool of wisdom that is part of our personal life experience and our collective human reality. On the third level, we find the genuine meaning of the dream and the full and truthful interpretation. With practice, you will be able to reach this level and understand your dream.

The techniques given are frameworks for exploration. The meditation to attune to the Dreamer Within, for example, can be altered in any way you see fit. Adapt it to suit your personal preference and needs. The important thing to remember is your intention when preparing to meditate. It is necessary to ask for cooperation from inside yourself. You are attempting to evoke something in your psyche that knows how to interpret dreams, which is qualitatively different from invoking assistance from without.

The worksheet is effective for working with your dreams. Repeated use of this tool will teach you how to approach your dream in a way that encourages intuitive and non-linear states to emerge.

You can see from the dreams I have chosen as examples that there is a lot to learn about the mystery of our human consciousness! It is not necessary to know a lot about psychology or myth or symbology, although such information may enrich your understanding. Your dreams are personal and unique and their meaning is known to your deeper consciousness.

The great themes of human experience appear in your dreams because you are part of that experience. All of us are trying to express ourselves as individual parts of the larger human collective. We are not independent of the collective, but do have a unique relationship with it. Once our ego accepts that, new possibilities become available to us.

All of the polarities of life occur in our dreams. Triumph and defeat, good and evil, right and wrong, black and white, feminine and masculine, nurturing and devouring, humiliation and exaltation will present themselves. We can learn to see our personal relationship to these forces. If action and change are called for, our dreams will point the way. By taking the time to understand dreams, we can empower ourselves through the information given. We can attune to a greater consciousness and a sense of spirit and wholeness.

This book is based on experience and practical usage. Dream interpretation is an art, and like any other art requires practice over time to reach its potential and flowering. You have to be willing to not take yourself too seriously. Don't be discouraged if it seems overwhelming or difficult at first. It took me many years to feel reasonably comfortable with my own ability to accurately read dreams, even after I knew I could do it. I'm stubborn—perhaps it won't take you as long.

It is best to go slowly when interpreting dreams for others. As you work on your own dreams and put into practice the information in this book, your capacity to see into the dreams of others will improve. I have found it is necessary to watch carefully for my own unconscious material when I am working with another. You will need to do the same.

The secret of interpreting dreams is to recognize that we have an innate ability to connect with a vast store of wisdom and perception. If we learn to use this ability, we quickly gain understanding that might otherwise seem impossible. True understanding of dreams comes from an honest attunement to the feeling of the images, and this requires inspiration and guidance. It cannot be done solely by the outer mind, or by consulting a list of symbols with possible meanings.

Each of us has a unique language of dreams. Each of us may discover the meaning of our own symbolic language and the language of others. If you are willing to be guided by the inspirational forces within and without you, you can reap a harvest of wisdom and self-discovery from your dreams.

ALEX LUKEMAN

# Online References

The Internet provides a new, fascinating resource for dream learning opportunities. If you have a computer and access, you can spend as many hours as you like looking at dreams, learning about dream analysis and techniques, and sharing your thoughts about dreams with others.

Any good search engine will take you to some initial pages about dreams, and from there you need only follow the links. Inside of an hour, you will have found more than you can absorb in days.

Because web addresses tend to change rapidly, I am not going to list more than a few specific references. These are stable and professional, and should be there when you go to look for them. If they are gone, well, there is a lot of material out there—just follow the links.

Some recommended web pages and their addresses:

http://onlinepsych.com/jungweb
http://www.dreamgate.com/asd-13/4r00.htm
http://www.icemall.com/allabout/newagedre.html
http://www.sufism.org/threshld/society/articles/dreams.html
http://www.outreach.org/gmcc/asd/
http://cybertowers.com/selfhelp/
http://www.phys.unsw.edu.au/~mettw/edreams/home.html

# Bibliography

Capra, Fritof. *The Turning Point*. New York: Simon and Schuster, 1981.

Carus, Paul. *The History of the Devil and the Idea of Evil*. New York: Land's End Press, 1969.

Castaneda, Carlos. *A Seperate Reality*. New York: Simon and Schuster, 1971.

————. *The Art of Dreaming*. New York: HarperCollins Publishers, Inc., 1993.

————. *The Power of Silence*. New York: Simon and Schuster, 1987.

————. *Journey To Ixtlan*. New York: Simon and Schuster, 1972

de Castillejo, Irene Claremont. *Knowing Woman*. New York: Harper & Row, Publishers, 1974.

Edinger, Edward F. *Anatomy of the Psyche*. La Salle, Illinois: Open Court, 1985.

————. *The Mystery of The Coniunctio*. Toronto: Inner City Books, 1994.

Erdoes, Richard and Ortiz Alfonso. *American Indian Myths and Legends*. New York: Pantheon Books, 1984.

Ferguson, Marilyn. *The Aquarian Conspiracy*. Los Angeles: J. P. Tarcher, Inc., 1980.

Field, Reshad. *The Last Barrier*. New York: Harper & Row, Publishers, Inc., 1976.

Joy, W. Brugh. *Joy's Way*. Los Angeles: J. P. Tarcher,Inc., 1978.

Jung, C,G. *Alchemical Studies*. (Translated by R.F.C. Hull.) Princeton, New Jersey: Princeton University Press, 1967.

————. *Dreams*. (Translated by R.F.C. Hull.) Princeton, New Jersey: Princeton University Press, 1974.

————. *Mysterium Coniunctionis*. (Translated by R.F.C. Hull.) Princeton, New Jersey: Princeton University Press, 1963.

————. *Flying Saucers*. (Translated by R.F.C. Hull.) Princeton, New Jersey: Princeton University Press, 1978.

Miller, Robert J. and Robert W. Funk. *The Complete Gospels*. Sonoma, California: Polebridge Press, 1992.

Ouspensky, P.P. *A New Model of the Universe*. (Translated from the Russian under the supervision of the author.) New York: First Vintage Books Edition, 1971.

Pagels, Elaine. *The Gnostic Gospels*. Toronto: Vintage Books Edition, 1979.

————. *The Origin of Satan*. New York: Random House, 1995.

Perera, Sylvia Benton. *The Scapegoat Complex*. Toronto: Inner City Books, 1986.

Shah, Idries. *Caravan of Dreams*. New York: Penguin Books, 1968.

Steiner, Rudolf. *Cosmic Memory*. New York: Harper & Row Publishers, 1959.

Wilhelm/Baynes. *The I Ching*. (The Richard Wilhelm Translation. Rendered into English by Cary F. Baynes.) New York: Bollingen Foundation Inc., 1950.

Woodman, Marion. *Addiction to Perfection*. Toronto: Inner City Books, 1982.

Zukav, Gary. *The Dancing Wu Li Masters*. New York: William Morrow & Co, 1979.

# Index